THE NON-LAWYERS DIVORCE KIT

2nd Edition

*Special Book Edition
With Removeable Forms*

By Kermit Burton

Alpha Publications Of America, Inc.
P.O. Box 12488 • Tucson, AZ 85732-2488
1-800-528-3494

Copyright 1992, Alpha Publications of America, Inc.
Revised 1993

Published by:
ALPHA PUBLICATIONS OF AMERICA, INC.
P.O. Box 12488
Tucson, Arizona 85732-2488

ISBN 0-937434-108

All rights reserved. No part of this publication may be reproduced or utilized in any form or by any means, electronic or mechanical, including photocopying, recording, or by information storage and retrieval systems, without permission in writing from the publisher, except that the removeable forms included in this publication may be photocopied prior to preparation by the original purchaser of this book, only if the intended use is for the purpose of making preliminary drafted worksheets. The copyright laws do not extend copyright protection to fully prepared forms, which may be reproduced or photocopied at will.

Check List Of
CALIFORNIA DISSOLUTION FORMS

(Some of the Forms are printed on one side while others are printed on both sides. Some of the Forms are also on white, green and pink paper. The colored papers are required in San Diego County.)

Petition For Dissolution of Marriage   (2 sides)
Property Declaration, Separate Property, Attachment 4   (2 sides)(1 each White/Green)
Property Declaration, Community Property, Attachment 5   (2 sides)(1 each White/Green)
Declaration Under Uniform Child Custody Jurisdiction Act   (2 sides)
Summons   (2 sides)
Proof of Service   (1 side)
Response To Petition For Dissolution of Marriage   (2 sides)
Notice and Acknowledgment of Receipt   (1 side)
Appearance, Stipulation and Waiver   (1 side)
Application For Expedited Child Support Order/Proof Of Service   (2 sides)
Response To Application For Expedited Child Support Order/Proof Of Service   (2 sides)
Expedited Child Support Order   (1 side)
Confidential Counseling Statement   (1 side)
Income and Expense Declaration, Page One   (1 side)(1 each White/Green)
Income Information, Page 2   (1 side)(1 each White/Green)
Expense Information, Page Three   (1 side)(1 each White/Green)
Child Support Information, Page Four   (1 side)(1 each White/Green)
Stipulation To Establish or Modify Child or Family Support and Order   (2 sides)
Application And Order For Health Insurance Coverage/Declaration of Employer   (2 sides)
Employer's Health Insurance Return   (1 side)
Request To Enter Default   (2 sides)
Declaration For Default or Uncontested Dissolution   (2 sides)
Judgment   (1 side) (1 each White/Pink)
Blank Continuation of Judgment, without Judge's Signature Line   (1 side) (1 each White/Pink)
Blank Continuation of Judgment, with Judge's Signature Line   (1 side) (1 each White/Pink)
Wage and Earnings Assignment Order   (2 sides) (1 each White/Pink)
Notice of Entry of Judgment   (1 side)
Information Sheet on Waiver of Court Fees and Cost   (1 side)
Application For Waiver of Court Fees and Cost   (2 sides)
Order on Application For Waiver of Court Fees and Cost/Clerk's Certification of Mailing   (2 sides)
Notice of Waiver of Court Fees and Cost   (1 side)
Blank Continuation Page   (1 side)
Blank Property Continuation Page   (2 sides)(1 each White/Green)

The Forms described above, together with the included text material, constitute the whole of this Non-Lawyers Divorce Kit. Therefore, all of the text material is directed toward purchaser's knowledgeable use of both the text material and the forms. However, neither the author nor the publisher intends to offer the information herein contained as legal advice, which can only be offered by an Attorney licensed to practice law in your state. And while all of the herein information is believed and thought to be accurate, neither the author nor the publisher assumes any liability in connection with the use of this information and the application of the forms.

The Non-Lawyer Legal Kit perfect bound book editions...

published by Alpha Publications of America, Inc.

The Alpha Non-Lawyer Legal Kits:

- available as **Perfect Bound Books**.
- have been **Number One** in sales and satisfaction **since 1976**.
- include a **TOLL-FREE 800 NUMBER** for any questions regarding the Kit.
- valid in all **50 States**.
- includes **all of the Forms** required to accomplish the desired action.
- includes easy to understand **Step-By-Step Instructions** with fully completed examples of each Form.
- **do not require** that assistance be sought from other sources before the action can be completed.

Distributed by:

ALPHA PUBLICATIONS OF AMERICA, INC.
P.O. Box 12488 • Tucson, AZ 85732-2488
(602) 795-7100   1-800-528-3494   Fax (602) 795-0469

KIT	RETAIL
A-B TRUST	$18.95
ISBN 0937434-469	
BANKRUPTCY	27.95
ISBN 0937434-299	
CHAPTER 13	27.95
ISBN 0937434-302	
CORPORATION	26.95
ISBN 0937434-310	
DIVORCE (Some States)	21.95
ISBN 0937434-108	
HOME SALES	14.95
ISBN 0937434-329	
LIVING TRUST	14.95
ISBN 0937434-337	
LIVING WILL	12.95
ISBN 0937434-345	
NON-PROFIT CORPORATION	29.95
ISBN 0937434-353	
PARTNERSHIP	19.95
ISBN 0937434-361	
PRE-MARRIAGE	14.95
ISBN 0937434-37X	
WILL	14.95
ISBN 0937434-388	

TABLE OF CONTENTS

CHAPTER	TITLE	PAGE
INTRODUCTION		1-2
CHAPTER 1	**THE LEGAL REQUIREMENTS FOR A DIVORCE**	3-4
	a. Residency Requirement	3
	b. Legal Grounds Requirement	3
	c. Fee Requirements	3
	d. Jurisdictional Requirements (Service of Process)	3-4
	e. Statutory Waiting Period	4
	Overview	4
CHAPTER 2	**GENERAL FACTS ABOUT DIVORCE**	5-6
	1. Agreement of the Spouses	5
	2. Commencement Date of Child Support	5
	3. Contested or Uncontested	5
	4. Handwritten or Typed Forms	5
	5. Waiting Period for Final Divorce	5
	6. Income Tax Treatment of Child Support	5
	a. Child Support	5
	b. Spousal Support	6
	7. Insurance Conversion	6
	8. Mandatory Wage Assignments	6
	9. Court Hearing Required??	6
	10. Non-Paternity of Parent	6
	Overview	6
CHAPTER 3	**SUMMARY DISSOLUTIONS**	
	THE REQUIREMENTS, ADVANTAGES AND DISADVANTAGES	7-8
	A. Requirements	7
	B. Advantages	7
	C. Disadvantages	7-8
	Overview	8
CHAPTER 4	**CHILD CUSTODY, VISITATION AND SUPPORT**	9-15
	Child Custody	9
	1. Sole Physical Custody	9
	2. Joint Physical Custody	9
	3. Sole Legal Custody	9
	4. Joint Legal Custody	9
	Visitation	10
	Child Support	10-11
	A. Gross Income	11-12
	B. Allowable Deductions	12
	C. Child Support Formula	12-15
	Overview	15
CHAPTER 5	**SPOUSAL SUPPORT**	17-18
	Waiver of Spousal Support	17-18
	Health Insurance	18
CHAPTER 6	**COMMUNITY PROPERTY, RETIREMENT BENEFITS AND DEBTS**	19-22
	Community Property	19-20
	Retirement Benefits	20-21

- i -

TABLE OF CONTENTS

CHAPTER	TITLE	PAGE
	Community Debts	21
	Summary	21-22
CHAPTER 7	**THE DESCRIPTION OF THE FORMS**	**23-28**
	1. Petition For Dissolution of Marriage	23
	2. Property Declaration, Separate Property, Attachment 4	23
	3. Property Declaration, Community Property, Attachment 5	23
	4. Declaration Under Uniform Child Custody Jurisdiction Act	23
	5. Summons	23
	6. Proof of Service	24
	7. Response To Petition For Dissolution of Marriage	24
	8. Notice and Acknowledgment of Receipt (In California)	24
	9. Appearance, Stipulation and Waivers	24
	10. Application For Expedited Child Support Order/Proof of Service	24-25
	11. Response To Application For Expedited Child Support Order/Proof of Service	24
	12. Expedited Child Support Order	25
	13. Confidential Counceling Statement	25
	14. Income and Expense Declaration, Page One	25
	15. Income Information, Page Two	25
	16. Expense Information, Page Three	25
	17. Child Support Information, Page Four	25
	18. Stipulation To Establish or Modify Child or Family Support and Order	25
	19. Application and Order For Health Insurance Coverage Declaration of Employer	25-26
	20. Employer's Health Insurance Return	26
	21. Request To Enter Default	26
	22. Declaration For Default or Uncontested Dissolution	26
	23. Judgment	26
	24. Blank Continuation of Judgment	26
	25. Blank Continuation of Judgment	26
	26. Wage and Earnings Assignment Order	26
	27. Notice of Entry of Judgment	27
	28. Information Sheet on Waiver of Court Fees and cost	26-27
	29. Application For Waiver of Court Fees and Cost	27
	30. Order on Application For Waiver of Court Fees and Cost	27
	31. Notice of Waiver of Court Fees and Cost	27
	32. Blank Continuation Page	27
	33. Blank Property Continuation Page	27
	Conclusion	27
	Forms Not Included In Kit	27-28
	1. Form Set 100. Marital Settlement Agreement with children, property and debts	27-28
	2. Form Set 100. Marital Settlement Agreement without children; with property and debts	28
	3. Form Set 200. Parenting Plan Joint Custody	28
	4. Form Set 300. Non- paternity of a Parent	28
	5. Form Set 400. Service by Publication	28
	Overview	28
CHAPTER 8	**THE SELECTION AND PREPARATION OF THE FORMS; AND FILING PROCEDURES**	**29-37**
	Step One. Selecting The Forms	**30-35**
	A. Without Children, Property or Debts; no spousal support	30
	B. Without Children, Property or Debts; with spousal support	30
	C. Without Children, With Property and Debts; no spousal support	31-32

TABLE OF CONTENTS

CHAPTER	TITLE	PAGE
	D. Without children, with property, debts and spousal support	32
	E. With children, with property, debts and spousal support	33
	F. With children, without property, debts and no spousal support	33-34
	G. Waiver of filing fees	34
	Overview	34
	Step Two. Preparation Of The Forms	35
	Green and Pink Forms	35
	Handwritten or Typed	35
	Blue Manuscript Covers	35
	Two Hole Punched	35
	Copies	36
	Confidential Counseling Statement	36
	Declaration Under Uniform Child Custody Jurisdiction Act	36
	Summons	36
	Response To Petition For Dissolution of Marriage	36
	Waiver of Court Fees	36-37
	Step Three. Filing The Forms	37-38
CHAPTER 9	**SERVICE OF PROCESS OR APPEARANCE**	39-41
	a. Personal Service	39
	b. Service By Mail (Inside California)	39
	c. Service By Mail (Outside-of-California)	40
	d. Service outside-of-California (by other than mailing)	40
	e. Service By Publication	40
	f. General Appearance By Respondent	41
	Overview	41
CHAPTER 10	**MAKING THE ACTION FINAL**	43-50
	1. Marital Settlement Agreement	43
	2. Application For Expedited Child Support Order	43
	Default or Uncontested	44
	a. Default Periods	45
	b. Request To Enter Default	45
	c. Declaration For Default Or Uncontested Dissolution	46-47
	d. Judgment	47-49
	e Notice Of Entry Of Judgment	49
	The Court Hearing	49-50
APPENDIX A (California Superior Courts, Counties and Addresses)		51
California Superior Courts		53-54
APPENDIX B (Illustrated Specimen Forms)		55-116
Index To Illustrated Specimen Forms		56
Illustrated Specimen Forms		57-116
APPENDIX C (Removeable Dissolution Forms)		117
Check List of Removeable Dissolution Forms		118

- iii -

Introduction

This Non-Lawyers Divorce Kit provides an efficient and effective way of obtaining a legally valid Divorce under the Laws of the State of California.

Under California Laws, there are procedures for two types of Divorce actions, namely, a Regular Divorce and a Summary Divorce. This Kit provides both the step-by-step procedures and Forms required to obtain a Regular Divorce under California Laws, but it does not include any forms for the Summary Divorce since those Forms are available at all County Clerk offices.

This book does, however, provide needed information if a Summary Dissolution is appropriate in your case. See Chapter 3, Summary Divorce, Advantages and Disadvantages. Also, outline the requirements which must be met before the Summary Divorce procedure can be utilized.

Before you proceed further, you might want to thoroughly review the CHECK LIST OF DISSOLUTION FORMS in front of the Table of Contents in order to observe the scope of Forms included in this Kit. Keeping in mind, however, that it would indeed be a rare case which required the use of all of the Forms so included.

In fact, unless your situation is a complex case involving a great mixture of property, debts and children, this Kit is a low cost alternative to the high cost of legal services.

It does require that you expend some efforts in both reading the included material and preparing the Forms, but the dollar savings is substantial.

The availability of the Toll-Free Help Line (no charge ever) is your assurance that we stand behind your decision to do-it-yourself with our Non-Lawyer Divorce Kit.

The text material that follows will briefly outline the divorce requirements, child custody and support, community property and debts, retirement plans, health insurance, a description of all of the included Forms and the steps required to file and complete the Divorce action.

Each of these factors plays an important role in the drafting of the Divorce petition and the Court's subsequent consideration in granting the divorce.

While the word divorce is widely used both in this text and in the real world, generally, the court description of a divorce action is "Dissolution of Marriage".

Therefore, in this text, as elsewhere, the usage of the words "Divorce" and "Dissolution" are one and the same.

Since this text material is written in such a way that each point is directly discussed and resolved, it is important that you take a few moments to review this material before commencing the preparation of the Forms.

It will be mentioned here that even though the Forms included in this Book appear to cover every conceivable aspect of a divorce action, this must be qualified by pointing out that all of the Forms included here are those Forms adopted by the Judicial Council of California for mandatory use in all Dissolution, Separation or Annulment actions.

There may however be a procedural Form required by certain counties under their Local Rules which are not included in this Kit.

These types of procedural Forms are provided by those County Clerks in each such instance, and should, of course, be requested when the Petition For Dissolution of Marriage and other papers are initially filed.

There are other Forms provided by the publisher which are available upon request. This would include: (a) Form Set 100a, Marital Settlement Agreement with Children, property and debts; (b) Form Set 100b, Maritial settlement agreement without children, with property and for debts; (c) Joint Custody Parenting Plan (included with Form Set 100a, if requested) (d) Form Set 300, For child(ern) born during the marriage, but not fathered by husband, and (e) Form Set 400, Publication of Summons Supplement.

The usage of these forms will be discussed later in the text under their applicable subjects. At any rate, we do wish to extend our thanks to you for allowing us to assist you in pursuing this important event. If you have questions or comments, please feel free to call or write.

Best regards,
the author and staff

Chapter 1
THE LEGAL REQUIREMENTS FOR A DIVORCE

Under California Laws, a Divorce (Dissolution) action is a civil action that must be filed and heard in the Superior Court.

Since there are two parties to the action, the person filing is called the petitioner and the other party is called the respondent. But since California Laws provide for two types of Dissolution actions, namely a Regular Dissolution and Summary Dissolution, in a Regular Dissolution action, the person bringing the action is the petitioner and the spouse is called the respondent, while in a Summary action, the parties are co-petitioners.

There are some basic legal requirements that must be met under either action before the action can be heard and decided by the Superior Court. Each of these requirements will be described below:

a. Residency Requirement

In order to bring a Dissolution action under California Laws, the petitioner must have resided in the State for at least six (6) months prior to filing the action, and at least three (3) months in the County where the action will be filed.

b. Legal Grounds Requirement

The legal grounds for a Dissolution action under California Laws is either (1) irreconcilable differences or (2) incurable insanity. For the purposes of this Kit, the grounds which must be alleged in an action brought with this Kit is, of course, ground Number One "irreconcilable differences".

The legal definition of "irreconcilable differences" is simply that the parties have marital difficulties which cannot be reconciled, and have led to the irremediable breakdown of the marriage.

It is sufficient to state in the petition that the grounds for the dissolution of marriage is "irreconcilable differences" that cannot be reconciled.

c. Fee Requirements

It is required by law that before the clerk can accept papers for filing an action, the required filing fees must be paid or waived by court order. The fee may vary among the different counties, but the average is around $180.00.

d. Jurisdictional Requirement (Service of Process)

Before the Court can hear and decide a Dissolution action, it must have jurisdiction over the parties in the action; Otherwise, the action cannot go forward to final Judgment.

What this means is that the Court must have legal authority to make and enforce its orders against either or both parties. To have this authority, the party against whom the action is brought must be served lawful notice of the pending action and given the opportunity to respond or appear.

In this case, lawful notice is service upon respondent of the Summons, Petition and other required papers, or respondent making a general appearance by signing the Appearance, Stipulation and Waiver Form; and paying the appearance fee of $180.00 (some counties).

e. Statutory Waiting Period

There is a waiting period fixed by law that designates the date the Dissolution action becomes final and the parties are free to remarry. This waiting period is six months and one day from the date service is completed upon respondent, (if Service is made out of State by Certified Mail, service is not complete until 10 days after mailing.) In the case of a Summary Dissolution, six months and one day from the date the joint petition is filed with the court.

And since the entry of the judgment will occur within this six-month period, but after service of Summons or an appearance of respondent and possibly a Court hearing, if deemed necessary by the court, the date of the expiration of this six-month and one day period is entered in the judgment.

OVERVIEW

Since all of these legal requirements must be met before a divorce (dissolution) can be granted by the Court. It then is apparent that a good understanding of what the petitioner must do to accomplish a legal divorce is necessary.

This, of course, will be carefully outlined in the next succeeding chapters.

Chapter 2
GENERAL FACTS ABOUT DIVORCE

The intent of this Chapter is to provide answers to some informative and common questions regarding Divorce actions, that is, some of the influencing elements.

1. AGREEMENT OF THE SPOUSES.
The spouses do not have to agree to a divorce action, since the action is an adversarial action like any other civil action. It does, however, greatly simplify the procedures when the spouses do agree and cooperate in bringing the action.

2. COMMENCEMENT DATE OF CHILD SUPPORT.
The commencement date of child support is normally fixed at a date when it is anticipated that the the judgment dissolving the marriage will be signed by the Court, even though the parties will not legally be divorced for yet another six months. If the Entry of Judgment is delayed for some reason, e.g., a hearing is set or respondent opposes the action or some of the dollar amounts; then, an application expediting the payment of child support can be filed, which, when granted, will start the child support before the entry of judgment or on the anticipated date.

3. CONTESTED OR UNCONTESTED.
A divorce action can only become a contested action when the non-filing spouse files a response to the action, which opposes the action, otherwise it is an uncontested action.

4. HANDWRITTEN OR TYPED FORMS.
Some counties permit the filing of handwritten forms, whereas, other counties require the forms to be typed. To be sure, call the County Clerk where you plan to file the action and ask.

5. WAITING PERIOD FOR FINAL DIVORCE.
A divorce cannot be made final before six months and one day after the date Service of the Petition for Disolution of Marriage was completed upon respondent.

6. INCOME TAX TREATMENT OF CHILD SUPPORT.
a. Child Support.
Child support cannot be deducted from the gross income of the paying party for tax purposes. The party having physical custody of the child(ren) usually can claim the dependency deduction, unless the judgment orders otherwise.

The Internal Revenue Service considers the custodial parent to be the proper parent to claim the child(ren), a dependency deduction, unless the contrary is indicated in the judgment.

b. Spousal Support.

Spousal support is fully deductible from the gross income of the paying party and chargeable as income to the receiving party. This should be indicated in the judgment to settle any potential I.R.S. scrutiny.

7. INSURANCE CONVERSION.

Under California Laws, health, dental and vision insurance for the children must be included in the support order, if such coverage is available at a reasonable cost.

The divorce spouse has 90 days in which to notify the Insurance Plan administrator of his or her desire to continue coverage at his or her own expense.

8. MANDATORY WAGE ASSIGNMENTS.

Under Laws adopted in 1990, every support order must provide for an assignment of the payor's wages. The payor can get around this by putting a bond or cash deposit equal to 3 months support, or the parties agree on other acceptable means of payment.

9. COURT HEARING REQUIRED??

A court hearing is not required in every case if the petitioner takes the steps necessary to complete an action by mail (discussed in a later chapter).

Even if such steps are taken, the court can still set the matter down for a hearing if there are unresolved questions regarding certain facts included in the papers submitted.

And, of course, a Summary Divorce does not require a court hearing by virtue of its restrictive requirements.

10. NON-PATERNITY OF PARENT.

If the parties have been separated for an extended period of time and there are children (or a child) born during this period who was not fathered by husband, then you will need to contact the publisher and obtain the papers necessary to terminate the parental right of the non-paternal parent (Form Set 300).

OVERVIEW

Now that you have had a chance to review some of the more common questions regarding divorce actions, the legal requirements for a divorce will follow.

Chapter 3

**SUMMARY DISSOLUTION
THE REQUIREMENTS, ADVANTAGES AND DISADVANTAGES**

Since it has been mentioned on several occasions that a Summary Dissolution of Marriage is possible as an alternative to a Regular Dissolution action, the requirements, advantages and disadvantages will be outlined here.

A. REQUIREMENTS. There are several requirements which must be met before a Summary Dissolution can even be considered, namely:

1. The marriage must be less than five (5) years duration.

2. You must first obtain from the County Clerk's office the free booklet of Forms and Instructions on Summary Dissolution and read the same with understanding.

3. You must meet the residency requirements of six months in California prior to the filing of the action, and at least three of the six months in the County where the action will be filed.

4. The wife is not pregnant and there are no minor children of the marriage.

5. Neither spouse has any interest in any real property anywhere.

6. The total community debts, less any automobile loans, are less than $5,000.

7. The value of all community property, less automobiles, is less than $25,000.

8. The total value of all property separately owned by either spouse is less than $25,000.

B. ADVANTAGES. The advantage that a Summary Dissolution holds over a Regular Dissolution is its simplicity of preparation, which is really based on the restrictive requirements, as set forth above under A.

By way of simplicity, it is not required that the Summons be issued, or the entry of the default be made.

It may, however, be required that a Marital Settlement Agreement be prepared and filed with the final judgment.

The single most important advantage of the Summary Dissolution is that it requires the spouses to cooperate and work together, thus minimizing many of the animosities inherent in the breakup of a marriage.

C. DISADVANTAGES. The one clear and glaring disadvantage of a Summary Dissolution is that either spouse can have a change of mind during the six-month waiting period and revoke the action. Whereas, under a Regular Dissolution, after the default is entered, this change of mind cannot result in the revocation of the action.

Another glaring disadvantage is the less-than-five-year-period of marriage. This appears to be unnecessarily restrictive since it could cause a rush into the action if the five-year period was fast approaching, minimizing concerted efforts to either work things out or to better prepare for the action.

OVERVIEW

It is not intended that these are all of the advantages and disadvantages inherent in a Summary Dissolution action, there may be others of equal or greater importance, but for starters, these are the most significant in the eyes of this writer.

Chapter 4

CHILD CUSTODY, VISITATION AND SUPPORT

CHILD CUSTODY

This section will outline the four (4) different types of child custody recognized under State Laws, namely: Joint Physical Custody, Joint Legal Custody, Sole Physical Custody and Sole Legal Custody.

The definition of each is as follows:

1. SOLE PHYSICAL CUSTODY.
Sole Physical Custody means the child (or children) shall reside with and under the supervision of one parent, subject to the power of the court to order visitation.

2. JOINT PHYSICAL CUSTODY.
Joint physical custody means that each of the parents shall have significant periods of physical custody. Joint physical custody shall be shared by the parents in such a way so as to assure a child of frequent and continuing contact with both parents.

3. SOLE LEGAL CUSTODY.
Sole legal custody means that one parent shall have the right and the responsibility to make the decisions relating to the health, education and welfare of the child(ren).

4. JOINT LEGAL CUSTODY.
Joint Legal Custody means that both parents shall share the right and the responsibility to make the decisions relating to the health, education and welfare of the child(ren).

Also, when the court grants joint legal custody, it shall specify the circumstances under which the consent of both parents is required to be obtained in order to exercise legal control of the child(ren) and the consequences of the failure to obtain mutual consent.

Since the modern trend in child custody is joint custody, it is recognized by law that the presumption that joint custody is in the best interest of the minor child(ren) when the parents have agreed to joint custody and submitted a workable "Parenting Plan".

There is no denying that joint custody is not for everyone, since it requires the parents to cooperate and lay aside all animosities for the benefit and interest of the children.

Recognizing that this may be difficult since the breakup of most marriages is a traumatic event, which distorts the common reasoning of many parents.

This then explains why sole custody continues to be the leading type of custody for most children when there is a marital breakup.

VISITATION

In recent years, the law makers have come to recognize that visitation is not something that can be easily codified into Law.

The problem lies in what is reasonable in one circumstance is not necessarily reasonable in another; therefore, a latitude of discretion is left with the parents to implement standards of visitation that are reasonable under their circumstances.

This does not, however, mean that each parent can selfishly make the rules to the detriment of the other parent or the child(ren). If this is the case, the aggrieved parent can ask the court to define and order more specific visitation.

It has also been drafted in law that any person having an interest in the welfare of the child(ren) is entitled to reasonable visitation when so ordered by the court. This would include grandparents and others.

In preparing the Dissolution papers, it is required that visitation be designated either as reasonable or supervised.

CHILD SUPPORT

Child support is a must in all actions where an award of custody of minor children is ordered.

Under California Laws, recently adopted Statewide Uniform Guidelines for Determining Child Support are now mandatory in all Counties. The courts can depart from these guidelines in only exceptional circumstances. However, the parties may still agree by stipulation to an amount less than or greater than the guideline amounts, provided, the following conditions are met:

1. The parties acknowledge that they are fully informed of their rights pursuant to this title and that the award is being agreed to without coercion or duress;

2. The parties declare that the agreement is in the best interest of the children involved and the children's needs will be adequately met by the stipulated amount;

3. The right to support has not been assigned to the county pursuant to Section 11477 of the Welfare and Institutions Code, and no public assistance application is pending.

What all of this means is that the Statewide Guidelines provide the basis from which the court will determine the correctness of any child support award.

The Guidelines do, however, provide for add-on amounts above the basic calculated amounts; for example:

a. child care cost.
b. health care and health care insurance cost.
c. cost of special educational or other needs of a child.

d. child care cost related to necessary education training for employment skills directed to parties' increased net income.
e. travel-related expenses for visitation.

It will be shown later how to calculate the child support amounts under the Statewide Guidelines, but first, it will be mentioned that all child support must be paid by an assignment of the payor's wages or other periodic earnings.

Any order for child support must include an order for the assignment of wages.

Health insurance and health plans must also be made a part of all child support orders, except that there are provisions which recognize that the cost of such plans must be reasonable.

Since health insurance is expensive, what constitutes reasonable may vary considerably. They do state that the presumption will exist that any group health insurance provided by an employer is reasonable, unless the contrary is shown.

Keep in mind that child support can be modified up or down by the court when circumstances change, since the court continues to have jurisdiction over child support and custody matters until each child reaches age 18.

Normally, child support ends when a child reaches the age of 18, or age 19 if still in high school. It can, however, be extended to cover college or other training through age 25, if the parents so agree in writing.

To calculate the child support amount, you must use the formula provided under the Statewide Uniform Guidelines for determining child support awards (See Pages 12 and 13).

This formula became effective on July 1, 1992, therefore an easy reference table is not available, but you may either calculate the amount yourself with the formula provided on the next page, or you may contact one of the many Attorneys who practice Family Law and pay them to calculate the amount for you on their computer, or you can call us with your numbers and we will calculate the amount for you.

Keep in mind that the child support calculations take into account the net disposable income that remains after all lawfully recognized deductions are made; therefore, the text that follows include definitions of Gross Income and Allowable Deductions.

A. GROSS INCOME

1. Income such as commissions, salaries, royalties, wages, bonuses, rents, dividends, pensions, interest, trust income, annuities, worker's compensation benefits, unemployment insurance benefits, disability benefits and spousal support received from a person not a party to the action.

2. Income from the proprietorship of a business, such as gross receipts from the business, less the expenditures required for operating the business.

3. Employer benefits or self-employment benefits that either benefit the employee, reduce living expenses, or other measurable benefits.

4. The court may take into consideration the earning capacity of a parent instead of the present rate of wages. (Example, a teacher working as a dishwasher).

5. Gross income does not include child support payments actually received, or any public assistance based on need.

B. ALLOWABLE DEDUCTIONS

Itemized below are those deductions which are lawfully allowed against gross income, namely:

1. State and Federal Income Taxes that bear an accurate relationship to the tax status of the parties.

2. Contributions to Social Security (F.I.C.A.), or an amount not to exceed the allowed F.I.C.A. if the party is not subject to F.I.C.A. withholdings.

3. Deductions for mandatory union dues and retirement benefits, if required as a condition of employment.

4. Deductions for health insurance premiums and State disability insurance premiums.

5. Child or spousal support actually being paid under a support order, or, if not under a court order, the allowable amount established under those guidelines.

6. Job-related expenses, that are deemed necessary.

C. CHILD SUPPORT FORMULA

Every attempt will be made here to simplify the child support formula, but, you must know that some basic math skills will be required. For example, when there are numbers both inside and outside of a bracket, plus numbers in brackets, like 25[2000 - (.38)(670)], you must first multiply the numbers in the inter most brackets, then preform the indicated addition or subtraction. Then multiply this result by the number outside of the bracket. With this in mind, the child support amount can be easily computed by using the Child Support Formula below.

The child support formula is: **CS** = **K**[**HN** - (**H%**)(**TN**)], plus **K** = 1 + H% × (**MWF**) or **K** = 2 - H% × (**MWF**), depending on whether H% is less than 50% or more than 50%. See **K Calculation**, next page.

The definition of each component of the formula is as follows:

CS is the calculated child support amount.

K is the monthly wage adjustment variable

HN is the higher earner's net monthly income

H% is the percentage of time the higher earner will have primary physical responsibility for the child(ren).

TN is the total net combined income of both parties (spouses).

MWF is the monthly wage fraction.

Each component of the Child Support Formula requiring calculation will be outlined below:

H% Calculation

H% must be calculated before the value of **K** can be determined. Therefore, to calculate the value of **H%**, first determine the total number of days each year the higher earner will have physical custody or primary physical responsibility for the child(ren) and divide that number by 365. For example, 55 days a year divided by 365 equal 15% (or H% is .15).

If, however, no percentage is given and the action is a Default Proceeding with **HN** being the non-custodial parent, then **H%** is **0**. If **HN** is the custodial parent, then **H%** is **100.**

K Calculation

K is a 2 part formula which must be combined when each half is separately calculated:

K = 1 + H% × (MWF) (When **H%** is 50% of less).
K = 2 - H% × (MWF) (When **H%** is more than 50%).

MWF Calculation

The monthly wage fraction (MWF) is calculated from the schedule below:

Net Monthly Wages	MW FRACTION
$0 to $800	.20 + TN divided by 16,000
$801 to $7,000	.25
$7,001 to $10,000	.20 + 350 divided by TN
$10,000 to $20,000	.16 + 400 divided by TN
over $20,000	.12 + 800 divided by TN

When there is more than one child of the marriage, then the child support amount calculated with the formula must be multiplied by the applicable multiplier for 2 or more children as indicated below:

Multiplier For 2 or More Children

2 Children by 1.6	7 Children by 2.75
3 Children by 2.0	8 Children by 2.813
4 Children by 2.3	9 Children by 2.844
5 Children by 2.5	10 Children by 2.86
6 Children by 2.625	

In order to assist your understanding of this child Support Formula, the next two pages will present working examples using this child support formula.

Working Examples

The examples that follow are called "Working Examples" because they have been written to identify with real life marital situations. But, more importantly, they are presented here to assist both your understanding of the Child Support Formula and how to calculate your own child support:

Example No. 1. Husband's net income $2,000; Wife's net income $1,500; H% is 38%; and 2 children.

The formula: **CS** = **K[HN - (H%)(TN)]**.
And since H% is less than 50%, **K** = **1** + **H%** × (**MWF**).

First, calculate the value of **K**:
K = **1** + .38(H%) × .25(MWF)
K = 1.38 × .25, or **K** = .345

Now, to restate the formula with the "Example" numerical values:
CS = .345(K)[2000(HN) - .38(H%) × 3500(TN)]
CS = .345(2000 - 1330), or .345 × 670
CS = $231.15 (times the 2 children multiplier of 1.6).

The Child Support amount **CS** is $369.84

Example No. 2. Husband's net income $3,000; Wife's net income $2,200; H% is 18%; and 1 child.

The formula: **CS** = **K[HN - (H%)(TN)]**.
And since H% is less than 50%, **K** = **1** + **H%** × (**MWF**).

First, calculate the value of **K**:
K = **1** + .18(H%) × .25(MWF)
K = 1.18 × .25, or **K** = .295

Now, to restate the formula with the "Example" numerical values:
CS = .295(K)[3000(HN) - .18(H%) × 5200(TN)]
CS = .295(3000 - 936), or .295 × 2064
CS = $608.88

The Child Support amount **CS** is $608.88

Example No. 3. Husband's net income $7,500; Wife's net income $-0-; H% is 62%; and 3 children.

The formula: **CS** = **K[HN - (H%)(TN)]**.
And since H% is more than 50%, **K** = **2** - **H%** × (**MWF**).

First, calculate the value of **K**:
K = **2** - .62(H%) × (.20 + 350 divided by 7500)(MWF)
K = 1.38 × .20 + .0466 (rounded to .047)

K = 1.38 × .247 or **K** = .341

Now, to restate the foumula with the "Example" numerical values:
CS = .341(K)[7500(HN) - .62(H%) × 7500(TN)]
CS = .341(7500 - 4650), or .341 × 2850
CS = $971.85 (times the 3 children multiplier of 2.0).

The Child Support amount **CS** is $1,943.70

Example No. 4. Husband's net income $1,200; Wife's net income $2,700; H% is 74%; and 4 children.

The formula: **CS** = **K**[**HN** - (**H%**)(**TN**)].
And since H% is more than 50%, **K** = **2 - H%** × (**MWF**).

First, calculate the value of **K**:
K = 2 - .74(H%) × .25(MWF)
K = 2 - 1.26 × .25, or K = .315

Now, to restate the formula with the "Example" numerical values:
CS = .315(K)[2700(HN) - .74(H%) × 3900(TN)]
CS = .315(2700 - 2886), or .315 × (-186)
CS = -$58.59 (times the 4 children multiplier of 2.3) = -$134.75.

The Child Support amount **CS** is -$134.75; but, since this is a negative amount, the lower earner pays this amount to the higher earner. And in this case, the husband pays the child support amount to the wife even though she makes more than twice his income.

If, under these same set of facts, the husband decides to keep the children for a longer period, which works out to be, for example, 49%, then we can re-calculate the child support with the wife having primary custody only 51% of the time.

To restate the example: Husband's net income $1,200; Wife's net income $2,700; H% is 51%; and 4 children.

The formula: **CS** = **K**[**HN** - (**H%**)(**TN**)].
And since H% is more than 50%, **K** = **2 - H%** × (**MWF**).

First, calculate the value of **K**:
K = 2 - .51(H%) × .25(MWF)
K = 1.49 × .25, or **K** = .373

Now, to restate the formula with the "Example" numerical values:
CS = .373(K)[2700(HN) - .51(H%) × 3900(TN)]
CS = .373(2700 - 1989), or .373 × 711
CS = -$265.20 (times the 4 children multiplier of 2.3) = $609.97.

The Child Support amount **CS** is $609.97, which is the amount the wife will pay to the husband.

OVERVIEW

The Court can change or modify a child support order any time, therefore, you might want to review the Guideline amounts and then consider what is actually needed to adequately support the children. Remember, the support amounts can be raised above the Guideline amounts.

Also, the child support must be paid by a mandatory wage assignment, however, the court can stay the wage assignment order if the paying spouse posts a bond equal to 3 monthly payments, or if the spouses agree in writing as to some other acceptable method of payment, for example, from a trust account, annuity account, insurance annuity, etc.

Chapter 5
SPOUSAL SUPPORT

Spousal support, as it is now commonly called, has in the past been known as alimony.

The Laws are such now that spousal support is not at all considered when the marriage is of a short duration, there are no minor children and both spouses are gainfully employed.

This does not mean that the parties cannot agree on spousal support, which the court is, more or less, bound to accept. But, what it does mean is that the circumstances must be such that a hardship will result if the payee spouse did not receive spousal support, for at least a period of time.

Under California Laws, like the Laws of most States, the deciding factor regarding spousal support is the need to maintain the spouse at the customary standard of living.

In other words, the law recognizes that a wife (or husband) should not be forced to live at a level below that enjoyed during the marriage.

Another factor to be considered is whether the supported spouse has marketable skills or can be trained under the circumstances.

Other considerations involve the responsibilities and demands of being a housekeepeer, the contributions to the other spouse's career, the duration of the marriage, etc.

Each of these factors play an important role in considering the amount and duration of spousal support.

Also, since there is no firm figure as to what is appropriate under the circumstances, the amount payable can be up to 40% of the paying spouse's net income after deducting child support, less 50% of the amount of the supported spouse's net income not directed to her(his) share of actual child care.

Since this is a complicated issue, it is best that the spouses work this out between themselves and enter the agreed upon amount in the dissolution papers. This would be an appropriate item to list in the Marital Settlement Agreement.

Also, if spousal support is ordered, it will also be made by an assignment of wages, the same as child support, unless other written agreements are made.

WAIVER OF SPOUSAL SUPPORT

Spousal support can be waived by the recipient spouse, but it should be in writing signed by the spouse so effected.

If the husband is the petitioner, it is generally not enough to simply allege in the petition that the respondent wife waives spousal support, without requiring the respondent to acknowledge such waiver in writing.

If the wife is the petitioner, then this is no problem since the waiver can be included in the petition, and subsequently entered in the judgment.

Spousal support can run for an unlimited period, subject to the death or remarriage of the recipient spouse, or it can be fixed to terminate on a certain date.

When the court retains jurisdiction over spousal support, the amounts can be either raised or lowered at a later date, therefore, in many cases, a minimal amount of $1.00 per year is ordered, which keeps the jurisdiction of the court intact, and thus allows for the possibility of raising the amount at a later date.

The bottom line is simply that the parties should agree on not only spousal support, but also the conditions of payment, duration of payments and the termination date of the court's jurisdiction.

HEALTH INSURANCE

Unless it is agreed and included in a Marital Settlement Agreement, the health insurance on the spouse does not have to be paid by the other spouse upon the dissolution of the marriage. However, the laws are such that the divorced spouse is given the right to continue the insurance coverage at her(his) own expense up to 3 years at the same or similar rates.

In order to exercise this right, the spouse must notify the Insurance Plan Administrator in writing within 90 days after entry of the judgment of the election to continue the coverage.

This does not, however, mean that the rate will be the same as that paid by the spouse, since the spouse's payment is based on the employer paying a portion of the total group premium.

If the payments appear to be exorbitant, it would be wise to shop around for similar coverage.

Chapter 6

COMMUNITY PROPERTY, RETIREMENT BENEFITS AND DEBTS

This chapter will outline the extent of community property under California Laws in divorce actions.

COMMUNITY PROPERTY

Since California is a community property State, all property acquired during the term of the marriage is community property, unless such property was either: (1) acquired with funds or assets of one spouse that are clearly traceable as belonging to one spouse prior to the marriage, or (2) the property passed from an estate to one spouse, or (3) one spouse disclaimed an interest in the property in writing.

In an action under Family Law, the concerns in a dissolution of marriage action is the equitable division of the community property or the quasi-community property held in another State. If there is no community property, then there is no issue for the court to decide in regards to community property.

The character of property is fixed at the time of its acquisition, that is, if the property is purchased with community funds and one spouse did not disclaim an interest, then its character is community property.

On the other hand, if the property was bequeathed under a will, and passed to one spouse from a probate distribution, then such property is lawfully the separate property of the spouse receiving title to such property.

This, however, does not end the issue of separate or community property since it is what happens afterward that may have a significant effect on the character of the property. For example, if the bequeathed property is real property with a structure or structures, and improvements are later made with funds or assets of the community, then it is safe to conclude that the community now has an interest in the property, at least to the extent of its appreciated value.

In such a situation, this property would be subject to division in the divorce action, and therefore must be made a part of the action.

Now, if the property in question was not ever commingled with other community property, or subjected to any improvements, or whatever, with community funds, then it is safe to say that the property is the separate property of the receiving spouse.

If it is questionable as to whether or not the property can be lawfully construed as separate property, then it is best that the property be included in the dissolution action for distribution to the receiving spouse. At the least, this will clear the title of any questionable claims by the other spouse.

While the character of Personal Property is less complicated than is real property, it nevertheless is subject to the same set of rules of Law. The only significant difference is that ownership of property may or may not be evidenced by written title, thus, leaving in question real legal ownership.

The exception, of course, is large items like automobiles, mobile homes, machinery equipment, etc., or financial items like stocks, bonds, bank accounts, etc.

In many cases, the spouses agree to divide the community property before commencing the dissolution action. If that be the case, then it is apparent that the action can be filed without declaring any property.

It would be wise, however, to list all of the property so divided in order to make a legal record of the division, plus it may eliminate a later controversy regarding the ownership of certain property.

If the family home becomes an issue when one spouse opts to sell the home, while the other spouse is opposed to the sale, it is usually decided that the spouse who opposes the sale can continue to live in the home until certain conditions are met, like, for example, the children finish high school, etc., then the house may be sold with the proceeds being divided as previously agreed upon.

This type of transaction should most certainly be made a part of a Marital Settlement Agreement and/or the Judgment.

Keep in mind that upon the court's entry of the judgment, the legal transfer of the property is complete, even though it may be conditional.

RETIREMENT BENEFITS

The Law is well settled that accrued or vested Retirement Benefits are community property, thus subject to division in a dissolution action.

The Retirement Benefits which are subject to this community property application include military pensions, veterans educational benefits, ERISA funds, etc.

There are, however, certain pensions that are not subject to the community property application; they include: Railroad Retirement Benefits, Social Security payments, Compensation for Military injuries and worker's compensation disability awards.

Even though certain benefits may be deemed not to be community property, they can be considered in light of the total community assets, and thus, made a part of any trade offs whose purpose is to provide an equality of division.

Therefore, even though the pension may be separate property under law, its value may be considered when the court exercises its discretionary authority to divide the community property.

In all dissolution actions, no matter the length of the marriage, the issue of retirement benefits should be settled one way or the other, for example, the Petition, Marital Settlement Agreement and Judgment should all provide either for the spouse's waiver of retirement benefits or the division of any such benefits.

COMMUNITY DEBTS

Like community property, all debts contracted during the term of the marriage are community debts, and thus, each spouse is severably liable for such debts.

What this means in plain terms is that any debt contracted or incurred by either spouse during the marriage obligates the other spouse to the extent that the creditor, in the event of default, can bring an action to recover against either or both spouses.

In an action dissolving the marriage, even though the court's judgment awards certain of the debts to each spouse, if the spouse who is awarded the debt fails to discharge the debt as agreed, the creditor can still bring an action against the other spouse, notwithstanding the judgment awarding the debt to the other spouse.

The offended spouse is not, however, without remedies, for instance, a civil action can be brought against the ex-spouse for recovery of all amounts expended to pay the debt awarded to said ex-spouse, or the offended spouse can bring a "contempt of court" action under the judgment awarding the debt to the ex-spouse, before the court that granted the original judgment.

You must consider that debts, unlike property, cannot be easily transferred or divided to the extent that one spouse is fully released from the obligation since the interest of the creditor is as compelling as the debtors.

SUMMARY

The most important fact to remember when dividing the community property and debts is that the division must appear fair and equitable to the court.

The court does not pick and choose which property or which debt each party is awarded; this determination is made in either or both the Petition or Respondent's Response to the action, then ultimately entered in the judgment.

What the court looks at is the fairness of the division, and if the division appears to be patently unfair to one or both parties, the Judge will not sign the judgment, but will advise the parties to rework the division and reappear at a later date for reconsideration.

This means in substance that it is better to amicably resolve the division of property and debts in such a way that any reasonable person can readily observe the fairness.

Chapter 7
THE DESCRIPTION OF THE FORMS

This chapter will describe the application and purpose of each Form included in this text, plus those Forms available from the publisher without cost.

The Forms described here are all of the Forms listed in the Check List of Dissolution Forms in the front of this Book, as follows:

1. Petition For Dissolution of Marriage

This 2-sided Form is the formal application to the Court, requesting a dissolution of the marriage.

It includes all pertinent facts regarding the marriage, that is, whether there are children, any separate property, any community property, child custody, child support, spousal support, restoration of wife's former name, etc.

2. Property Declaration, Separate Property, Attachment 4

This is a 2-sided form which must be used if more than a miminal amount of separate property is to be confirmed by the court

3. Property Declaration, Community Property, Attachment 5

This is a 2-sided form which must be used if more than a minimal amount of Community or Quasi-Community Property is to be divided by the court.

4. Declaration Under Uniform Child Custody Jurisdiction Act

This 2-sided Form is only required if there is some action or controversy either by a another party or in another jurisdiction (State or County), which involves one or more of the minor child(ren) of petitioner and respondent in this present dissolution action. Otherwise, it is sufficient to simply check Box 3(c)(1) in the Petition For Dissolution of Marriage, indicating which parent the child(ren) presently reside with, and the County of residence.

5. Summons

This 2-sided Form is the Court's Notice to the party against whom the action is being brought (the respondent) that a Response to the action must be filed in 30 days.

It also includes a Restraining Order on the backside that prohibits and restrains certain conduct and actions.

6. Proof of Service

This Form is prepared and filed by the person serving the required papers on the respondent. It can be anyone at least 18 years of age, not a party to the action or related.

7. Response To Petition For Dissolution of Marriage

This 2-sided Form is the Respondent's Response To the Petition For Dissolution of Marriage.

It is not required that a response be filed by respondent, but it shorten the actual dissolution dates effectually, plus it allows respondent to show that he or she agrees with the action, thus making it likely the case will proceed without a Court Hearing.

8. Notice and Acknowledgment of Receipt (In California)

This Form is resondent's acknowledgment that he(she) received a copy of the required papers, as shown on the Form, through the United States Postal Service.

This Form must be sent to respondent, together with the other required papers, when service is made by mail inside California.

9. Appearance, Stipulation and Waiver

This Form is respondent's general appearance; waiver of rights if in the military; stipulation and consent to judgment; and waive the issuance of Summons.

It is not required that respondent file this Form unless either: Respondent is in the military, previously filed a response and the opposition has been settled, or the parties are in complete agreement and desire to end the marriage as quickly as possible. Some Courts charge a Response Fee ($180) when this form is filed, but it does eliminate the Summons, response, etc.

10. Application For Expedited Child Support Order/Proof of Service

This 2-sided Form is petitioner's (or respondent's) formal request for child support prior to the entry of judgment in the case. Since a divorce cannot be made final for six months, this application, if granted, allows the payment of child support prior to the entry of the judgment.

The backside of the Form is the Proof of Service which is completed by the person making service upon respondent.

11. Response to Application for Expedited Child Support Order/ Proof of Service

This 2-sided Form is respondent's response to the application seeking expedited child support. It is not required that respondent respond to the application, but the response Form must be served with the application.

The backside is respondent's proof of service upon petitioner of a copy of the response.

12. Expedited Child Support Order

This Form is the Court's Order granting the Expedited Child Support Request. It is signed by the Judge when the application is heard and granted.

13. Confidential Counseling Statement

This Form must be prepared and filed with the petition in those Counties which have Conciliation Courts.

14. Income and Expense Declaration, Page One

This Form, together with the next three forms are only required if the petitioner request either Child Support or Spousal Support. The information requested is both personal and financial.

15. Income Information, Page Two

This Form is Page Two of the Income and Expense Declaration, which requires information relevant to petitioner's income.

16. Expense Information, Page Three

This Form is Page Three of the Income and Expense Declaration, which request information relevant to all living expenses.

17. Child Support Information, Page Four

This Form is Page Four of the Income and Expense Declaration, and it is only required if child support is an issue.

18. Stipulation To Establish or Modify Child or Family Support and Order

This 2-sided Form is an agreement by both spouses as to the amount of child support which shall be paid. It is required when the child support amounts are less than the guideline amounts, epecially in Joint Custody cases, or it may be required in all cases when a Marital Settlement Agreement is filed.

19. Application and Order For Health Insurance Covereage/ Declaration of Employer

This 2-sided Form is applicant's request that spouse's employer be ordered to enroll or maintain health insurance coverage on the minor children.

The backside is the Employer's Declaration that no health insurance is available.

20. Employer's Health Insurance Return

This Form is the employer's response to the status of spouse's health insurance.

21. Request To Enter Default

This 2-sided Form is the petitioner's request to the clerk to enter the default of respondent when no response is filed by respondent in the required 30-day period.

22. Declaration For Default or Uncontested Dissolution

This 2-sided Form must be used if the Dissolution action will be finalized by mail. In other words, the petitioner does not appear in court, unless the Court questions something in the submitted papers and sets the case down for a hearing; Otherwise, the matter is handled entirely by mail.

23. Judgment

This Form is either one page or it will have other or additional pages attached, which constitute the formal judgment of the court granting the Dissolution of the Marriage, and other relief requested in the petition.

24. Blank Continuation of Judgment

This Form will be Page 2 of a 3 or more page Judgment, which allows additional requested items or provisions to be added in the Judgment. Since this form does not include the Judge's signature line, it cannot be used as the last page of the Judgment (See No. 25 below).

25. Blank Continuation of Judgment

This Form is the last page of the Judgment when the judgment consist of 2 or more pages. It includes provisions for both the Judge's signature and approval of content and form by petitioner and respondent.

26. Wage and Earnings Assignment Order

This 2-sided Form is the court's order directed to the employer of the spouse ordered to pay child support.

27. Notice of Entry of Judgment

This Form is required when the Declaration For Default or Uncontested Dissolution is used. It must accompany the Declaration with 2 prestamped envelopes, one addressed to petitioner and the other to respondent.

When the judgment is signed by the Court, this Form will be mailed to both petitioner and respondent informing them of the entry date of the judgment.

28. Information Sheet on Waiver Of Court Fees and Cost.

This information sheet merely provides information as to the possibility and requirements for filing a Court action without having to pay the Court Fees.

29. Application For Waiver of Court Fees and Cost

This 2-sided Form must be used when petitioner desires to waive the court fees. On the back is a detailed financial questionnaire.

30. Order on Application For Waiver of Court Fees and Costs.

This 2-sided Form is the court's order granting the application to waive filing fees.

The backside is the Clerk's Certification of Mailing.

31. Notice of Waiver of Court Fees and Cost

This Form is the Clerk's Notice to all concerned that the court has waived payment of the filing fees.

32. Blank Continuation Page

This blank page can be used when any of the Forms require an additional attached page.

33. Blank Property Continuation Page

This Form must be used when space is needed to list additional items of property under either of the property declarations.

CONCLUSION

This concludes the description of the Forms included in this Non-Lawyers Divorce Kit. The next section will describe those Forms not included in this Kit, but are available from the publisher at a modest cost.

FORMS NOT INCLUDED IN THE KIT

1. **Form Set 100a**   **Marital Settlement Agreement With Children, Property and Debts**

This Form Set includes the Marital Settlement Agreement for a Dissolution action that includes child custody, sole or joint custody, child support, visitation, spousal support, division of community, quasi-community and separate property, community debts, retirement Benefits, insurance coverage on the minor children and tax refunds and obligations.

2. Form Set 100b Marital Settlement Agreement Without Children; with Property and Debts.

This Form Set includes a Marital Settlement Agreement for a dissolution action without minor children; with or without community, quasi-community or separate property, community debts, spousal support, insurance, retirement benefit plans, etc.

3. Form Set 200 Joint Custody Parenting Plan

This Parenting Plan allows the parents to enter into a detailed joint custody arrangement that includes: custody periods with each parent, schooling, educational, recreational, medical, religious and financial concerns regarding the children. This Form Set is included with Form Set 100a, if requested.

4. Form Set 300 Non-Paternity of a Parent

If a child (or children) was born during the term of the marriage, but not fathered by husband, then this Form Set is required since it provides for the termination of all parental rights and obligations that exist between husband and said child (or children).

5. Form Set 400 Service By Publication

This Service by publication form set is requred if you do not know the whereabouts of your spouse (Respondent). The set includes: (1) Application For Order For Publication of Summons, (2) Order For Publication Of Summons, (3) Proof Of Service and (4) Declaration Of Mailing.

OVERVIEW

All of the Forms described in both sections of this Chapter provide an efficient and effective way of doing-your-own Dissolution of Marriage with the same expertise as a Lawyer.

If you need any of the Form Sets included in this last section, simply send $4.00 cash, check or money order to the publisher, at the address on the back of inside cover of this text, or you may call Toll-Free at 1-800-528-3494 and place your order with any major Credit Card.

Since some of the Counties require different methods of filing the Marital Settlement Agreement and Parenting Plan, you will need to inform us as to which County the action will be filed.

Chapter 8

THE SELECTION AND PREPARATION OF THE FORMS; AND FILING PROCEDURES

This Chapter will guide the selection, preparation and filing procedures for a Regular Divorce under California Laws.

If you have thoroughly reviewed all of the previous text material, and concluded that your case complies with the Summary Dissolution requirements, then you should stop here, and go to one of the courts listed in Appendix A (yellow pages) and pick up the **Summary Dissolution Packet**, which includes most of the Forms needed for the Summary Dissolution and an instruction guide that directs their use.

To quickly review the requirements of a Summary Dissolution, they are:

1. Petitioner has resided in this State for at least six months, and 3 months in the County where the action will be filed.

2. There are no minor children.

3. Wife is not pregnant.

4. Neither spouse has any interest in any real estate anywhere.

5. Community debts are less than $5,000, not including vehicle loans.

6. The value of all community property is less than $25,000, not including vehicles.

7. The value of any separate property owned by either spouse does not exceed $25,000, not including vehicles.

8. The term of marriage must be less than 5 years.

OVERVIEW

If you meet these requirements and decide to pursue the Summary Dissolution, keep in mind that the main disadvantage of the Summary Dissolution is the right of either party to revoke the action anytime up to the date it becomes final, that is, six months from the date of filing the papers.

If the Summary action is revoked, the Regular Dissolution action can still be pursued, and it does not provide for a six-month revocation period.

If, however, your situation either does not qualify you for the Summary Dissolution, or you don't want to take the chance that spouse might revoke the action several months down the road, then you must begin with the text that starts on the next page.

Step One Selecting The Forms.

Before selecting any of the forms, you must first consider the scope of your divorce situation, that is, whether your action includes: (1) child custody and support, (2) community debts, (3) community and/or separate property, (4) spousal support, etc.

Remember, you can simplify your situation by transferring or dividing property before filing your papers with the Court. If there are children, child suppport, property and debts, you should consider using a Marital Settlement Agreement (See Page 27).

There are six (6) possible divorce situations which are indicated under their respective alphabetical designations of "A" to "F". Once you have determined your divorce situation, find its appropriate designation under "A" to "F" (beginning on the next page) and select the forms so indicated.

There are, however, some forms which are common to each marital situation that are either optional or required under certain circumstances. For example, each of the A to F situations include the *Appearance, Stipulation and Waiver Form* (Number 9), even though its use may be limited or simply not desired.

This form is, however, required if respondent is in Military Service (Block Numbered 3 must be checked), however, no response fee is required to file the form.

This form can also be used to somewhat simplify the dissolution action, that is, if respondent will agree to pay the appearance fee of ($180.00), since its use will eliminate: the Summons, Proof Of Service, Response To Petition, Notice and Acknowledgment of Receipt and a Court Hearing.

In other words, if respondent is not in Military Service, but agrees to sign this form and pay the response fee, then it will not be necessary to select or prepare either the Summons, Proof of Service, Response, or Notice and Acknowledgement of Receipt.

Also, under alphabetical designations, E and F (with children) there is an optional Form entitled, *Stipulation To Establish or Modify Child or Family Support*; some Counties, however, charge an Appearance Fee of $180.00 when this Form is filed, therefore, you may want to consider using a Marital Settlement Agreement.

Unable To Pay The Court Fees?

If you are unable to pay the required Court Fees, and you qualify based on the maximum allowable income listed on Page 36 and on the Form entitled "Information Sheet On Waiver Of Court Fees And Cost," then you will need to select, in addition to the forms designated under your divorce situation, those forms listed on Page 34 under "Waiver of Filing Fees."

In selecting the appropriate forms under the designations that follow on the next page, you will notice that some of the forms are green and pink. This is so because, in San Diego County, it is required that all Financial Forms be *green* and the Judgment Forms be *pink*; therefore, this text includes white, green and pink forms; therefore, unless your action is being filed in San Diego County, you will only need to select and use the WHITE FORMS.

A. Without children, property or debts; no spousal support.

Select:
1. Petition For Dissolution of Marriage
2. Summons
3. Proof of Service
4. Response To Petition For Dissolution of Marriage
5. Notice and Acknowledgment of Receipt
6. Appearance, Stipulation and Waiver (optional)
7. Confidential Counseling Statement (some Counties)
8. Declaration For Default
9. Request To Enter Default
10. Judgment (Pink, San Diego County)
11. Notice of Entry of Judgment

B. Without children, property or debts; with spousal support.

Select:
1. Petition For Dissolution of Marriage
2. Summons
3. Proof of Service
4. Response To Petition For Dissolution of Marriage
5. Notice and Acknowledgment of Receipt
6. Appearance, Stipulation and Waiver (optional)
7. Confidential Counseling Statement (some Counties)
8. Income and Expense Declaration, Page 1 (Green, San Diego County)
9. Income Information, Page 2 (Green, San Diego County)
10. Expense Information, Page 3 (Green, San Diego County)
11. Declaration For Default
12. Request To Enter Default
13. Judgment (Pink, San Diego County)
14. Continuation of Judgment (optional)(Pink, San Diego County)
15. Continuation of Judgment (optional)(Pink, San Diego County)
16. Wage and Earnings Assignment Order (optional)(Pink, San Diego County)
17. Notice of Entry of Judgment

C. Without children; with property and debts; no spousal support

Select:
1. Petition For Dissolution of Marriage
2. Property Declaration, Separate Property, Attachment 4 (optional)(Green, San Diego County)
3. Property Declaration, Community Property, Attachment 5 (optional)(Green, San Diego County)
4. Summons
5. Proof of Service

(List continues to next page)

(List continued from previous page)

6. Response To Petition For Dissolution of Marriage
7. Notice and Acknowledgment of Receipt
8. Appearance, Stipulation and Waiver (optional)
9. Confidential Counseling Statement (some Counties)
10. Request To Enter Default
11. Declaration For Default
12. Judgment (Pink, San Diego County)
13. Continuation of Judgment (optional)(Pink, San Diego County)
14. Continuation of Judgment (optional)(Pink, San Diego County)
15. Notice of Entry of Judgment
16. Blank Additional Page (optional)
17. Continuation of Property Declaration (optional)(Green, San Diego County)

D. Without children; with property, debts and spousal support

Select:
1. Petition For Dissolution of Marriage
2. Property Declaration, Separate Property, Attachment 4 (optional)(Green, San Diego County)
3. Property Declaration, Community Property, Attachment 5 (optional)(Green, San Diego County)
4. Summons
5. Proof of Service
6. Response To Petition For Dissolution of Marriage
7. Notice and Acknowledgment of Receipt
8. Appearance, Stipulation and Waiver (optional)
9. Confidential Counseling Statement (some Counties)
10. Income and Expense Declaration, Page 1 (Green, San Diego County)
11. Income Information, Page 2 (Green, San Diego County)
12. Expense Information, Page 3 (Green, San Diego County)
13. Request To Enter Default
14. Declaration For Default
15. Judgment (Pink, San Diego County)
16. Continuation of Judgment (optional)(Pink, San Diego County)
17. Continuation of Judgment (optional)(Pink, San Diego County)
18. Wage and Earnings Assignment Order (optional)(Pink, San Diego County)
19. Notice of Entry of Judgment
20. Blank Additional Page (optional)
21. Continuation of Property Declaration (optional)(Green, San Diego County)

(Situation E on next page)

E. With children; with property, debts and spousal support

Select:
1. Petition For Dissolution of Marriage
2. Property Declaration, Separate Property, Attachment 4 (optional)(Green, San Diego County)
3. Property Declaration, Community Property, Attachment 5 (optional)(Green, San Diego County)
4. Declaration Under Uniform Child Custody Jurisdiction Act (Optional, see page 23)
5. Summons
6. Proof of Service
7. Response To Petition For Dissolution of Marriage
8. Notice and Acknowledgment of Receipt
9. Appearance, Stipulation and Waiver (optional)
10. Application For Expedited Child Support Order (optional)
11. Response To Application For Expedited Child Support Order (optional)
12. Expedited Child Support Order (optional)
13. Confidential Counseling Statement (some Counties)
14. Income and Expense Declaration, Page 1 (Green, San Diego County)
15. Income Information, Page 2 (Green, San Diego County)
16. Expense Information, Page 3 (Green, San Diego County)
17. Child Support Information, Page 4 (Green, San Diego County)
18. Stipulation To Establish or Modify Child Support and Order (optional)
19. Application and Order For Health Insurance Coverage
20. Employer's Health Insurance Return
21. Request To Enter Default
22. Declaration For Default
23. Judgment (Pink, San Diego County)
24. Continuation of Judgment (optional)(Pink, San Diego County)
25. Continuation of Judgment (optional)(Pink, San Diego County)
26. Wage and Earnings Assignment Order (optional)(Pink, San Diego County)
27. Notice of Entry of Judgment
28. Blank Additional Page (optional)
29. Continuation of Property Declaration (optional)(Green, San Diego County)

F. With children; without property, debts and no spousal support

Select:
1. Petition For Dissolution of Marriage
2. Declaration Under Uniform Child Custody Jurisdiction Act (optional, see page 23)
3. Summons

(Situation F continues to next page)

(List continued from previous page)

4. Proof of Service
5. Response To Petition For Dissolution of Marriage
6. Notice and Acknowledgment of Receipt
7. Appearance, Stipulation and Waiver (optional)
8. Application For Expedited Child Supoport Order (optional)
9. Response To Application For Expedited Child Support Order (optional)
10. Expedited Child Support Order (optional)
11. Confidential Counseling Statement (some Counties)
12. Income and Expense Declaration, Page 1 (Green, San Diego County)
13. Income Information, Page 2 (Green, San Diego County)
14. Expense Information, Page 3 (Green, San Diego County)
15. Child Support Information, Page 4 (Green, San Diego County)
16. Stipulation To Establish or Modify Child Support and Order (optional)
17. Application and Order For Health Insurance Coverage
18. Employer's Health Insurance Return
19. Request To Enter Default
20. Declaration For Default
21. Judgment (Pink, San Diego County)
22. Continuation of Judgment (optional)(Pink, San Diego County)
23. Continuation of Judgment (optional)(Pink, San Diego County)
24. Wage and Earnings Assignment Order (optional)(Pink, San Diego County)
25. Notice of Entry of Judgment
26. Blank Additional Page (optional)

Waiver of Filing Fees

If you plan to waive (not pay) the Court Filing Fees, you will need to select the following forms:

1. Information Sheet On Waiver of Court Fees and Costs
2. Application For Waiver of Court Fees and Cost
3. Order on Application For Waiver of Court Fees and Cost
4. Notice of Waiver of Court Fees and Cost.

OVERVIEW

If you have completed the selection of the forms applicable to your marital situation, you are now ready to commence the preparation of the forms; but, before going further, keep in mind that there may be some additional forms required and supplied by the local courts, for example, if you plan to file your action in a Branch Court, they will provide you with an Assignment Form to complete.

Step Two   Preparation Of The Forms.

The preparation of the Forms has been greatly simplified by including in this text, in Appendix B (Blue Pages), fully illustrated (typed) examples of each form, with differing circumstances, for example, there are three (3) separate examples of a completed Petition For Dissolution of Marriage, namely: (1) Without minor children and two vehicles to be confirmed as separate property, (2) With minor children and no separate property, and (3) Without minor children and separate property to be confirmed as listed in Attachment 4.

Each of these examples are accurately displayed to illustrate real-life situations.

It has been our experience over the past 15 years that completed examples offer much more assistance than does written text, thus, this is the unique characteristic of the Non-Lawyer Legal Kits.

Green and Pink Forms

It has been previously mentioned that the Green and Pink Forms are required in San Diego County; therefore, unless your action will be filed in San Diego County, disregard the Green and Pink Forms.

Handwritten Or Typed

Now, there are some Counties which allow the Forms to be handwritten, but usually they must be typed with a typewriter with type size no smaller than pica type. If, however, you don't have a typewriter, you should call the Court where you plan to file the papers and ask if they accept handwritten forms.

Blue Manuscript Covers

There is an antiquated condition imposed in Los Angeles and Riverside Counties, that is, you must place a Blue Manuscript Cover on the back of each original paper filed (not the copies).

If there are Forms which include two or more pages, for example, the Income And Expense Declaration, then you must include the complete set (pages 1 through 4, etc.) under the same blue cover.

You can purchase this paper at most Stationery and Office Supply Stores. When shopping for the paper, ask for "Blue Manuscript Covers." And before you staple the cover over the top of the forms, you must type the Form name at the bottom of the blue cover sheet near right side.

Two-Hole Punched

Some Counties require that the Forms be puched with two holes at the top of each page. The clerk generally will not punch these holes for you, but they will supply the "Two-Hole Punch."

Copies

Upon completion of all of the Forms, except the Confidential Counseling Statement, three additional copies of each Form should be made in order to insure that the local requirements are met.

Some counties require that an additional copy of each Form be filed if the original filing is in one of the branch offices, therefore, to be safe, make 4 copies of each Form instead of 3.

Confidential Counseling Statement

It is required that this Form be completed by the petitioner and a blank copy of the Form served upon the respondent, together with the Petition, Summons and other required papers, therefore, make a blank copy before completing the Form.

Declaration Under Uniform Child Custody Jurisdiction Act

This Form is only required if the minor children are involved in an action or controversy in another jurisdiction (State or County), which may or may not include the respondent in the present dissolution action.

If the dissolution is without any controversy regarding the minor children, then it is sufficient to check Box 3(c)(1) in the Petition, provide the information requested and disregard this Form.

Summons

The Summons should be prepared in every case, since a verbal agreement made by respondent to sign the *Appearance, Stipulation and Waiver* may be rescinded after the action is filed; thus, requiring a second trip to the Court to get the Summons issued.

Response to Petition

It is required by the Court Rules that a blank copy of the Response be served upon respondent with the other required papers. You should, however, prepare the top section of the Response, i.e., name and address, court name and address, designation of the action, etc. There is no fee required when this form is filed with the Court

Waiver of Court Fees

If you selected the forms required to waive the Court Fees and Cost, you should be aware that there are some severe restrictions as to the amount of monthly income you can have, for example, the table below indicates the maximum family income with the designated number of children.

Number in Family	Family Income	Number in Family	Family Income
1	$ 709.38	5	$1,701.05
2	957.30	6	1,948.96
3	1,205.21	7	2,196.88
4	1,453.13	8	2,444.80

If it appears from the schedule on the previous page that a person must be close to destitute in order to waive the filing fees, your observation is somewhat correct; but, it is not the whole picture since on the back of the application for waiving the filing fees, there is a detailed financial questionnaire that allows you to show that even though your income exceeds the amounts on the schedule, your financial plight is not good.

There is, of course, a chance that the Judge may be convinced you are sincere and grant your application waiving the fee. Keep in mind, however, that you can be ordered to pay the waived filing fees up to a period of three (3) years after the divorce is final.

Step Three   Filing The Forms

After you have completed the preparation of each Form, you are now ready to file them with the Court to start the action.

The addresses of all of the Superior Courts are listed in Appendix A (Yellow Pages), therefore, you must file in the county where you presently reside.

The following Forms should be initially filed with the Clerk of the Court (some of which, may not be applicable to your divorce situation or required in your County):

1. Petition For Dissolution of Marriage
2. Property Declaration, Attachment 4, if separate property
3. Property Declaration, Attachment 5, if community property
4. Declaration Under Uniform Child Custody Jurisdiction Act (only if you checked Box 3(c)(2) in the Petition)
5. Summons (not filed, only signed by Clerk)
6. Confidential Counseling Statement
7. Income and Expense Declaration, Pages 1 through 3, if no minor children, but spousal support will be paid, or Pages 1 through 4, if there are minor children.
8. Expense Information, Page Three and Four of Four Pages

After you have filed your papers with the Court Clerk, you must now either serve the required papers upon respondent, or have respondent sign the Appearance, Stipulation and Waiver Form (which may require the payment of an appearance fee of $180.00), if applicable.

The next chapter will fully outline all of the lawful methods of serving process upon the respondent.

Chapter 9

SERVICE OF PROCESS OR APPEARANCE

In Chapter 1, pages 3 and 4, it was stated that..."Before the Court can hear and decide a Dissolution Action, it must have jurisdiction over the parties in the action, otherwise the action cannot go forward to final judgment." And what this means in simple terms is that, the respondent must either be legally served a copy of the Petition, blank Response, other required papers and the Summons, or the respondent can waive service of the Summons and make a general appearance by signing the Appearance, Stipulation and Waiver Form, and pay the appearance fee of $180.00 (some Counties).

Each method of service will be fully described under its respective subtitle below; but, keep in mind that service of the papers or the signing of any forms by respondent cannot take place until after the initial papers are filed with the Court.

a. Personal Service.

First off, the petitioner in the action cannot make legal service upon the respondent. Service must be made either by any person over the age of 18, a Private Process Server, a Constable, a Deputy Sheriff, or any other person authorized by law to serve legal papers.

So, the reference here to "Personal Service" means the respondent will be served personally, not by mail.

Personal Service can; therefore, be made by anyone over the age of 18, who must complete and file the Proof Of Service after service is completed upon respondent.

The papers that must be delivered to the person who will make such service include: (1) Petition For Dissolution of Marriage, (2) Summons (Original plus 1 copy), (3) Blank Response, (4) Blank Confidential Counseling Statement, (4) and, if required under the circumstances, Property Declarations, Income and Expense Declarations, Declaration under Uniform Child Custody, etc.

Private Process Server, Constable or Deputy Sheriff

If service is made by a Private Process Server, Constable, or Deputy Sheriff, you may or may not need the Proof of Service, since these individuals usually have their own Proof Of Service Form; however, you must ask if the Proof of Service is required, and if so, complete the top section, i.e., name of parties and case number.

b. Service By Mail (Inside California)

Service of the papers upon respondent by mail can be accomplished in California, provided, however, respondent signs and returns the Notice and Acknowledgement of Receipt.

The papers must **not** be mailed by petitioner; but, by someone over the age of 18, who shall include in the mailing, an envelope addressed to petitioner with postage affixed.

The sender must, of course, prepare the Proof of Service, attach both the Mailing Receipt and the Notice and Acknowledgment of Receipt signed by respondent, and either file the same with the Court of deliver to petitioner for filing.

c. Service By Mail (Outside-of-California)

If respondent resides outside of the State of California, service of the papers can be made by Certified Mail with a Return Receipt, which must be signed by respondent acknowledging actual receipt of the mailing.

Again, the papers must be mailed by someone other than petitioner. And, it is not required that the Notice and Acknowledgment of Receipt be included in this mailing since this Form is only required when service is made inside California.

The person sending the papers must prepare the Proof of Service, attach both the Mailing Receipt and Return Receipt signed by respondent and either file the same with the Court or deliver the same to petitioner for filling.

Service of Process is not complete until 10 days after the mailing is sent to respondent.

d. Service Outside-of-California (by other than mailing)

If you know respondent's out-of-state address, but respondent will not sign for the Certified Mailing, or otherwise cooperate in receiving service of the papers by mail, then you will need to obtain the services of either a Private Process Server or a Deputy Sheriff in the County of the State where respondent is residing

You will need to send to the person serving process, all of the required papers, including 2 copies of the Summons (original and 1 copy). When service is completed by such person, the proof of service must be entered on the back of the Summons or with a separate affidavit provided by the Process Server.

Service is complete the date it is made by the Process Server.

e. Service by Publication

If the whereabouts of respondent is not known, then legal service can be made by publishing the Summons in a general circulation newspaper in the County where the action is filed.

However, before the Summons can be published, an application must be made to the Court for an order authorizing the publication of the Summons.

The forms and instructions necessary to request an order from the Court to publish the Summons is not included in this text, but is available from the publisher, see Page 28.

You must make diligent efforts to locate respondent before you can make a request to the Court for an order to publish the Summons. Diligent efforts include: sending a Certified Letter to the last known address of respondent, contacting relatives and friends, if known, and any other method that will show the Court that you (petitioner) has tried to locate respondent.

f. General Appearance By Respondent

As indicated at the beginning of this chapter, the respondent can make a general apearance by signing the Appearance, Stipulation and Waiver Form, and pay the required appearance fee of $180.00 (some Counties), which effectively eliminates the issuance of the Summons when Box Numbered 10 is checked.

When Boxes Numbered 1, 4 and 6 are checked on this Form, the action will proceed as an uncontested matter before a Commissioner sitting as Judge.

If a Marital Settlement Agreement is filed in the action, then Box Number 7 must also be checked.

Overview

After you have completed one of the methods of service outlined in this Chapter, or Respondent has agreed to make a general appearance, then your next step is to make the action final, that is, present the Judgment to the Court for the Judge's Signature.

The next Chapter will outline and describe the procedures necessary to complete the dissolution action.

Chapter 10

MAKING THE ACTION FINAL

To make the action final means you will submit your Judgment (and any other applicable forms) to the Court for the Judge's Signature. The conditional factors being: (1) The time period for submission of the Judgment and (2) whether or not a Court Hearing will be required.

Each of these conditional factors will be thoroughly defined in this Chapter; but, before you proceed with making the dissolution action final, you may want to consider the importance of both the: *Marital Settlement Agreement* and *Application For Expedited Child Support Order*.

A brief outline of the advantages of each is stated below:

1. **Marital Settlement Agreement.**
On Pages 27 and 28 of this text, descriptions of two Marital Settlement Agreements were presented, that is, (1) Form Set 100a, Marital Settlement Agreement with children, property and debts, and (2) Form Set 100b, Marital Settlement Agreement without children, with property and debts; both of which, are available from the publisher, if you should decide their applicability in your case.

If the dissolution action includes children, property and/or debts, then a Marital Settlement Agreement is important to the extent that it simplifies the presentation of your case to the court.

As an example, it effectively eliminates the Property Declarations that may be otherwise required to provide for the Court's disposition of community and/or quasi-community property and debts.

A review of the *Request To Enter Default* will show that paragraph 3 and sub-paragraph 2, provide for the elimination of the Property Declaration when the disposition is made by written agreement (This, of course, would be a written Marital Settlememt Agreement).

Also, a further review of the *Declaration For Default or Uncontested Dissolution* shows that paragraphs 4(b) and 5(a), provide for the inclusion of a Marital Settlement Agreement in the action.

The thrust of what this means is that, if there is more than a minimal amount of property and debts, and/or children, then a Marital Settlement Agreement is a must, if a Court Hearing is to be avoided.

In other words, if the action will be finalized by mail (without a hearing) and the Court is being asked to order the disposition of community or quasi-community property and debts and/or child custody, visition, support, etc., then it is imperative that a Marital

Settlement Agreement be utilized.

This, of course, assumes that attitutes of the parties are civil to the extent that they can agree to a fair and equitable division of the community property and debts, and other conditions or provisions, since it is not possible for the petitioner to prepare a Marital Settlement Agreement without the cooperation of respondent.

2. **Application For Expedited Child Support Order.**

This kit includes the three (3) Forms required to initiate and complete an action to expedite child support payments. In other words, if the dissolution action includes minor children and child support will be ordered by the Court; then, rather than wait an uncertain period of time for the Court to order the commencement of child support, an action brought under this application for expedited child support can effectively start the child support immediately upon the Judge's signing of the Order.

This procedure is especially important if respondent will not cooperate in paying for the support of the minor children while the dissolution action is awaiting finality.

If your dissolution action is such that one or both of these procedures have a measure of importance in your action, then now is the time to prepare the forms for filing with the court.

The Marital Settlement Agreement can be filed with the Judgment, while the Application For Expedited Child Support Order can be filed at any time, that is, immediately after filing the initial papers with the Clerk or any time prior to filing the Judgment

Default or Uncontested

In order for the dissolution action to proceed to final judgment and result in the dissolution of the marriage, it is necessary that the case be heard either as a default case or as an uncontested case. Both can proceed without an open court hearing.

Keeping in mind, however, that whether or not an open court hearing will be held is left to the discretion of the Judge or Commissioner assigned to the case, who, after looking over the submitted papers, will either sign the Judgment dissolving the marriage or set the matter down for an open court hearing.

In other words, if the submitted papers are correctly prepared and presented, and no issues remain that have to be decided at an open court hearing, then both a default case and an uncontested case can be handled entirely by mail after the initial papers are filed and the applicable time periods have expired, assuming respondent was served process or made an appearance.

Since the final judgment must be based on the default of respondent or an uncontested entry of judgment, the text that follows will defined the: (a) Default Periods, (b) Request To Enter Default, (c) Declaration For Default Or Uncontested Dissolution, (d) Judgment, and (e) Notice Of Entry Of Judgment.

a. Default Periods.

Since the default periods are based on how respondent was lawfully served process (the required papers), the default period for each of the four (4) lawful methods of service are as follows:

1. 31 days when personal service is made inside California

2. 41 days when personal service is made outside California by Certified Mail.

3. 31 days when personal service is made outside California by a Process Server or Deputy Sheriff, and

4. 37 days after publication when service is made by publication of the Summons in a local newspaper.

b. Request To Enter Default.

At the expiration of the default periods indicated above, a *Request To Enter Default* must be filed with the Court, unless respondent either filed a Response or signed and filed the *Appearance, Stipulation and Waiver Form*, stipulating to the uncontested disposition of the case.

If respondent is in military service, then he or she must sign the *Appearance, Stipulation and Waiver Form* since on the backside of the *Request To Enter Default Form* is a Declaration of Nonmilitary Status.

If this Declaration of Nonmilitary Status is not sworn to (signed), then the *Request To Enter Default* must be accompanied by respondent's signed *Appearance, Stipulation and Waiver Form* with box number 3 checked.

There is no appearance fee required when this Appearance Form is filed with only box number 3 checked; but, there may be an appearance fee required when other boxes in addition to box number 3 are checked.

Keeping in mind that the *Request To Enter Default* must not be filed before the expiration of the time period dictated by the method of service; therefore, the default of respondent occurs when either of the following events become a fact, namely:

1. Personal Service made inside California was completed upon respondent more than 31 days ago, or, if by mail, 31 days have expired since respondent signed the *Notice And Acknowledgment of Receipt*.

2. Personal Service made outside California by Certified Mail was completed upon respondent more than 41 days ago.

3. Personal Service made outside California by a Process Server or Deputy Sheriff was completed upon respondent more than 31 days ago.

4. Service made by publication, when the whereabouts of

respondent is unknown, and more than 37 days have expired since the last date of publication

When the *Request To Enter Default* is filed, and depending on the factual circumstances alleged or requested in the Petition For Dissolution Of Marriage, the action will either be set down for a Default Hearing before the Court, or the action will be handled entirely by mail (when filed together with the *Declaration For Default or Uncontested Dissolution*).

c. Declaration For Default Or Uncontested Dissolution.

The *Declaration For Default Or Uncontested Dissolution* provides an alternative to an open court hearing; therefore, this DECLARATION may be used to avoid an open court hearing if respondent performed any one of the following acts in the case:

1. Respondent has not filed a response that contest the dissolution action within the applicable default period

2. Respondent has filed a response that: (a) does not contest the action, (b) agrees with the facts set out in the PETITION and other applicable forms, and (3) request dissolution of the marriage based on irreconcilable differences.

3. Respondent signed the *Appearance, Stipulation and Waiver Form*, making a general appearance and stipulating that the cause may be tried as an uncontested matter, and paid the appearance fee, if required.

The text that follows this paragraph illustrates the sworn facts stated in the Declaration, and the preparation requirements necessary to show other pertinent facts in the case:

1. That the truth of the facts stated would be testified to in open court if called;

2. Petitioner's stipulation that proof will be by the DECLARATION; but, he or she will appear in court if called;

3. That the information in the Petition and Response is true;

4. If the action will be finalized on the default of respondent, then box 4(a) must be checked; however, if the action will be finalized by either respondent's signing of the Appearance, Stipulation and Waiver Form or the preparation and filing of a Marital Settlement Agreement, then box 4(b) must be checked;

5. If a Marital Settlement Agreement is filed in the case, then box 5(a) must be checked; however, if there is no marital settlement agreement, or there is no property and/or debts to divide, or the division of the community property and debts listed on the Property Declaration Forms (Attachments 4 or 5)

then box 5(b)(3) must be checked;

6. That spousal support is either waived or the court has the right to make an award at a later date [paragraph 6(a)(1-2-3)];

7. Child support, child custody and visitation, if applicable, must be indicated by checking the appropriate boxes under paragraph 6(b), 9 and 10.

8. That petitioner has been a resident of California for 6 months and a resident of the County for 3 months (paragraph 13);

9. That the Declaration may be reviewed by a Commissioner sitting as a Temporary Judge (paragraph 11);

10. That irreconcilable differences have lead to the irremediable breakdown of the marriage with no possibility of saving the marriage through counseling or other means (paragraph 14);

11. That wife request restoration of fomer name (paragraph 16);

12. That petitioner or respondent is or is not receiving public assistance, or intend to apply for such public assistance (paragraphs 7 and 8).

In other words, the *Declaration For Default Or Uncontested Dissolution* is a complete sworn presentation of petitioner's entire case. And if all of the provisions are correctly completed, even if filed without a Marital Settlement Agreement, the Court will usually sign the Judgment dissolving the marriage without requiring a Court Hearing.

Remember, however, that the decision as to whether or not a Court Hearing shall be held rest solely with the Judge or Commissioner assigned to the case.

While it may be rare for a Court Hearing to be held in most Counties of the State, it is not inconceivable, therefore, that some of the less populus Counties, not suffering from crowded Court Calenders, may require an open court hearing regardless of the accuracy of the submitted papers.

This should not, however, be cause for alarm since the DECLARATION is the a sworn statement as to the true facts of the case, which can be verbally recited in open court, if need be.

When the DECLARATION is completed, three (3) additional copies should be made of the original.

The DECLARATION can be filed with the *Request To Enter Default*, and any other papers that further the completion of the action, including the Judgment.

d. The Judgment.
The Judgment is the Court's Order dissolving the marriage,

confirming separate property, dividing the community and/or quasi-community property and debts, and ordering the other relief requested in the Petition.

The Judgment can either be a single page Judgment, if the case is a simple one without children, property and debts, or it can be a multi-page Judgment consisting of two or more continuation pages.

If the Judgment consist of two or more pages, the signature of the Judge must appear on the last page, meaning, the Continuation of Judgment Page with the Judge's Signature line must be the last page of the Judgment.

You will find that completion of the Judgment is a fairly simple matter (See example in Appendix B); therefore, a brief review of what is required in the Judgment is as follows:

Judgment Paragraphs:

Paragraph 1. You will need to check the box indicating whether the Court held a default or uncontested hearing or the judgment was granted by declaration under Civil Code Section 4511.

Remember, in every case, you hope to avoid an open court hearing; therefore, you will always proceed by declaration. When the Judgment is submitted, you will not know for sure that the Judgment will be granted on the Declaration without a hearing; therefore, it may be wise to leave Box Number 1 blank.

If your case is a simple one with only the single page judgment, that is, without children, property or debts, then you can check the Declaration box with good confidence that the matter will be heard without a court appearance.

You will, of course, leave blank the remainder of number 1, that is, subsections a through e, unless there is a hearing held, in which case, you must check box c.

Paragraph 2. The date the Court acquired jurisdiction over the respondent is the date service of proces was completed upon respondent or respondent appeared by signing the *Appearance, Stipulation and Waiver Form*, check the applicable box.

Paragraph 3. Box 3(a) would, of course, be checked since the action is a dissolution action. Box number 1 under 3(a) requires the entry of the marital terminattion date, which is six months and one day from the date either service of process was completed upon respondent, or respondent made an appearance.

If wife will be restored her former name, then check box 3(b), and enter the former name in the space provided.

If the case is a simple one, nothing more is required in the Judgment, except the page number in the lower right section below the Judge's signature line.

If the Judgment is only one page, then enter number 1, which indicates "page 1 of 1 page," if there are continuation pages, then the total number of pages would be entered on the right line, for example, "page 1 of 5 pages."

Paragraph 4. Under this paragraph, the total number of additional pages must be indicated in the space provided.

If a Marital Settlement Agreement will be filed in the action, then box 3(g) must be checked, and the acceptance and approval of the Marital Settlement Agreement by the Court must be added.

The Marital Settlement Agreements Sets, which we provide, include a Judgment with the Court's acceptance and approval as required in some counties.

Some Counties (Los Angles County, in particular), also require that the Marital Settlement Agreement be filed in the case as Exhibit 1, and all of the agreement provisions fully set out in the Judgment; therefore, when we provide a Marital Settlement Agreement for filing in Los Angeles County (or any other County who may require the Exhibit 1 notation), page 1 of the Marital Settlement Agreement includes the Exhibit 1 notation in the lower left corner, plus, the Judgment continuation pages list all of the Marital Settlement Agreement provisions.

e. Notice of Entry of Judgment.

This Notice of Entry of Judgment must be furnished to the Court when the Declaration For Default Or Uncontested Dissolution and Judgment Forms are filed with the Court, together with **two (2) pre-stamped envelopes**, one address to petitioner and the other to respondent.

The real purpose of the Notice of Entry of Judgment is simply to notify petitioner and respondent that Judgment has been entered (signed) by the Court.

If you desire a copy of the original Judgment, you will have to contact the Court Clerk and obtain a copy. If your dissolution action includes the division of real property, you will need to record a Certified Copy of the Judgment in the County Records, that is, Hall of Records, County Recorder, etc.

If the Judge does not sign your Judgment, for whatever reason, and set the matter down for a hearing, you might want to review the next section (The Court Hearing) before you appear in Court.

The Court Hearing

The court hearing can be either formal or informal. What this means is that at an informal hearing, the Judge may question you about certain facts stated in the papers, whereas, at a formal hearing, you must present your case from the beginning.

Unless you are the first person called, you can get a very good idea of what needs to be said by listening to others that come before you.

If you have observed an attorney examining his client with the facts of the case, then this is in effect what you will be doing, except you will not have an attorney asking all of the right questions.

So what happens is, you have to give an oral presentation of your case, for example, when you are sworn in, you will say:

1. **My name is. .** (your name) . . . . ,then add **"I am the Petitioner in this case;**

2. **"All of the facts stated in the Petition** (and other described papers, if applicable) **are true;**

3. **"I have been a resident of California for more than six months, and a resident of this County for more than 3 months, prior to the filing of my Petition;**

4. **"During the term of my marriage, there arose irreconcilable differences which led to the irremediable breakdown of my marriage.**

   "There is no chance for reconciliation; therefore, I request that the marriage be dissolved."

5. Then state each and every fact alleged in the petition, for example, **"There are no children of the marriage, I do not want spousal support."**

6. **"There is no community property or debts for the court to divide or any separate property for the Court to confirm,"** etc.

If you have filed a Marital Settlement Agreement in your case, you can effectively recite the facts of your case from the agreement

At the conclusion of your court hearing, the Judge will either sign the Judgment or indicate on the record what needs to be changed, modified or corrected.

It is not fatal if the Judge does not sign your Judgment, you will simply need to make the changes and re-submit it for signature.

If the Judge does sign the Judgment, that means your case is over except for the marital status termination date, which is six months and one day starting from the date service of process was completed upon respondent, or six months and one day starting from the date respondent signed the Appearance, Stipulation and Waiver Form (see page 45, Default Periods). This date must be entered on the Judgment under Line 3(a)(1).

When the Judge signs the Judgment, you will then complete, and give to the clerk, the original and 3 copies of the Notice of Entry of Judgment, together with two pre-stamped envelopes, one addressed to you and one to respondent.

APPENDIX A

CALIFORNIA SUPERIOR COURTS

County And Court Addresses

CALIFORNIA SUPERIOR COURTS
COUNTY AND COURT ADDRESSES

Alameda County
County Courthouse
1225 Fallon Street
Oakland, CA 94612

Alpine County
County Courthouse
PO Box 158
Markleeville, CA 96120

Amador County
County Courthouse
108 Court Street
Jackson, CA 95642

Butte County
PO Drawer 269
Oroville, CA 95965

Calaveras County
Government Center
San Andreas, CA 95249

Colusa County
County Courthouse
546 Jay Street
Colusa, CA 95932

Contra Costa County
Courthouse
PO Box 911
Martinez, CA 94553

Del Norte County
County Courthouse
Crescent City, CA 95531

El Dorado County
County Courthouse
495 Main Street
Placerville, CA 95667

Fresno County
County Courthouse
PO Box 1628
Fresno, CA 93717

Glenn County
County Courthouse
Willows, CA 95988

Humboldt County
County Courthouse
825 5th Street
Eureka, CA 95501

Imperial County
County Courthouse
El Centro, CA 92243

Inyo County
County Courthouse
PO Drawer F
Independence, CA 93526

Kern County
Kern County Civic Center
1415 Truxtun Avenue
Bakersfield, CA 93301

Kings County
Courthouse
1400 W. Lacey Blvd.
Hanford, CA 93230

Lake County
County Courthouse
255 N. Forbes
Lakeport, CA 95453

Lassen County
County Courthouse
Susanville, CA 96130

Los Angeles County
Main Court
    111 N. Hill Street
    Los Angeles, CA 90012

Branch Courts
    300 E. Olive Street
    Burbank, CA 91502

    200 W. Compton Blvd.
    Compton, CA 90220

    600 E. Broadway
    Glendale, CA 91205

    600 E. Broadway
    Glendale, CA 91205

    1040 W. Avenue J
    Lancaster, CA 93534

    415 W. Ocean Blvd.
    Long Beach, CA 90802

    12520 Norwalk Blvd.
    Norwalk, CA 90650

    300 E. Walnut Street
    Pasadena, CA 91101

    400 Civic Center Plaza
    Pomona, CA 91766

    1725 Main Street
    Santa Monica, CA 90401

    825 Maple Avenue
    Torrance, CA 90503

    6230 Sylmar Avenue
    Van Nuys, CA 91401

Madera County
Madera County Government Center
209 W. Yosemite Avenue
Madera, CA 93637

Marin County
Hall of Justice, Civic Center
San Rafael, CA 94903

Mariposa County
County Courthouse
PO Box 247
Mariposa, CA 95338

Mendocino County
County Courthouse
PO Box 148
Ukiah, CA 95482

Merced County
County Courts Blvd.
2222 M Street
Merced, CA 95340

Modoc County
County Courthouse
Alturas, CA 96101

Mono County
County Courthouse
PO Box 537
Bridgeport, CA 93517

Monterey County
Main Court
    County Courthouse
    240 Church Street
    Salinas, CA 93901

Branch Court
    1200 Aguajito
    Monterey, CA 93940

Napa County
County Courthouse
PO Box 880
Napa, CA 94558

Nevada County
Courthouse Annex
201 Church Street
Nevada City, CA 95959

Orange County
700 Civic Center Drive West
Santa Ana, CA 92701

Placer County
County Courthouse
Room 34
Auburn, CA 95603

Plumas County
Courthouse
PO Box 201
Quincy, CA 95971

Riverside County
Main Court
    County Courthouse
    PO Box 431
    Riverside, CA 92502

Branch Court
    46-209 Oasis Street
    PO Box 1745
    Indio, CA 92201

Sacramento County
720 9th Street
Sacramento, CA 95814

CALIFORNIA SUPERIOR COURTS
COUNTY AND COURT ADDRESSES, CONTINUED

San Benito County
County Courthouse
Room 206
Hollister, CA 95023

San Bernardino County
Main Court
  Courthouse Addition
  San Bernardino, CA 92415

Branch Courts
  14455 Civic Drive
  Victorville, CA 92392

  1540 N. Mountain Avenue
  Ontario, CA 91762

San Diego County
Main Court
  County Courthouse
  220 W. Broadway
  San Diego, CA 92101

Branch Court
  325 S. Melrose Drive
  Vista, CA 92083

San Francisco County
480 City Hall
San Francisco, CA 94102

San Joaquin County
County Courthouse
222 E. Weber Avenue
Stockton, CA 95202

San Luis Obispo County
Courthouse Annex
San Obispo, CA 93408

San Mateo County
Hall of Justice
Redwood City, CA 94063

Santa Barbara County
Main Court
  County Courthouse
  Santa Barbara, CA 93101

Branch Court
  312 E. Cook Street
  Santa Maria, CA 93454

Santa Clara County
Main Court
  County Courthouse
  191 N. 1st Street
  San Jose, CA 95113

Branch Court
  270 Grant Avenue
  Palo Alto, CA 94303

Santa Cruz County
701 Ocean Street
PO Box 644
Santa Cruz, CA 95060

Shasta County
County Courthouse
PO Box 880
Redding, CA 96001

Sierra County
County Courthouse
Box 95
Downieville, CA 95936

Siskiyou County
County Courthouse
Yreka, CA 96097

Solano County
Hall of Justice
Fairfield, CA 94533

Sonoma County
Hall of Justice
2555 Mendocino Avenue
Santa Rosa, CA 95401

Stanislaus County
County Courthouse
PO Box 1098
Modesto, CA 95353

Sutter County
County Couthouse
463 - 2nd Street
Yuba City, CA 95991

Tehama County
County Courthouse
PO Box 250
Red Bluff, CA 96080

Trinity County
County Courthouse
PO Drawer AK
Weaverville, CA 96093

Tulare County
County Courthouse
Visalia, CA 93277

Tuolumne County
County Courthouse
2 South Green Street
Sonora, CA 95370

Ventura County
800 S. Victoria Avenue
Ventura, CA 93001

Yolo County
County Courthouse
725 Court Street
Woodland, CA 95695

Yuba County
County Courthouse
215 - 5th Street
Marysville, CA 95901

APPENDIX B

SPECIMEN FORMS

This Appendix B includes fully prepared illustrated Specimens of each of the CALIFORNIA DISSOLUTION FORMS Forms included in this book.

INDEX TO APPENDIX B

DESCRIPTION	PAGE NO.
Petition for Dissolution of Marriage (Front) without children and no separate property	57
Petition for Dissolution of Marriage (Front) without children with separate property listed in Attachment 4	58
Petition for Dissolution of Marriage (Front) with children and separate property listed under Section 4	59
Petition for Dissolution of Marriage (Front) with minor children, with separate property listed in Attachment 4	60
Petition for Dissolution of Marriage (Back) without children, no community property and no spousal support	61
Petition for Dissolution of Marriage (Back) with children, community property, debts and spousal support	62
Petition for Dissolution of Marriage (Back) with children, community property and joint custody requested	63
Property Declaration, (Front) Separate Property, Attachment 4	64
Property Declaration, (Back) Separate Property, Attachment 4	65
Property Declaration, (Front) Community Property, Attachment 5	66
Property Declaration, (Back) Community Property, Attachment 5	67
Declaration Under Uniform Child Custody Jurisdiction Act (Front)	68
Declaration Under Uniform Child Custody Jurisdiction Act (Back)	69
Summons (English and Spanish), (Front)	70
Summons (English and Spanish), (Back)	71
Proof of Service of Summons by personal delivery	72
Proof of Service of Summons by mail	73
Response to Petition For Dissolution of Marriage (Front) without children, property or debts	74
Response to Petition For Dissolution of Marriage (Front) with children and separate property	75
Response to Petition For Dissolution of Marriage (Back) without children, property or debts	76
Response to Petition For Dissolution of Marriage (Back) with children, property and debts	77
Notice and Acknowledgment of Receipt of Summons (When mailed inside California)	78
Appearance, Stipulation and Waiver, respondent's appearance, consent and Marital Settlement Agreement	79
Appearance, Stipulation and Waiver when respondent is in military	80
Application for Expedited Child Support Order (Front)	81
Proof of Service (Back of Application for Expedited Child Support Order)	82
Response to Application for Expedited Child Support (Front)	83
Proof of Service (back of the Response to Application for Expedited Child Support)	84
Expedited Child Support Order	85
Confidential Counseling Statement (Required in some Counties)	86
Income and Expense Declaration (With children, page 1 of 4 pages) (Without children, page 1 of 3 pages)	87
Income Information (With children, page 2 of 4 pages) (Without children, page 2 of 3 pages)	88
Expense Information (With children, page 1 of 4 pages) (Without children, page 1 of 3 pages)	89
Child Support Information (With children, Page 4)	90
Stipulation to Establish or Modify Child or Family Support and Order (Front)	91
Stipulation to Establish or Modify Child or Family Support and Order (Back)	92
Application and Order for Health Insurance Coverage (Front)	93
Application and Order for Health Insurance Coverage (Back) (Declaration of no Insurance)	94
Employer's Health Insurance Return (Employer's response)	95
Request to Enter Default (Front) (No children, property or debts)	96
Request to Enter Default (Front) (With Income, Expenses and Property Declarations attached)	97
Request to Enter Default (Front) (With Marital Settlement Agreement attached)	98
Request to Enter Default (Back) (When respondent not in military service)	99
Request to Enter Default (Back) (When respondent is in military service)	100
Declaration for Default (Front) (Default entered; with property, debts and spousal support)	101
Declaration for Default (Front) (Respondent signed Appearance Form and a Marital Settlement Agreement is filed)	102
Declaration for Default (Back) (With children and reason for unavailability to attend hearing given)	103
Judgment, (When Page 1 of 1) By Declaration; Respondent appeared; no children, property, debts, spousal support or retirement benefit claims; wife restored former name	104
Judgment, (When Page 1 of 1) By Declaration; Respondent appeared; Marital Settlement Agreement approved, etc.	105
Judgment, (When Page 1 of 4) By Default; Respondent Served Process; 2 Continuation of Judgment pages attached for children, property and debts	106
Continuation of Judgment, (When Page 2 of 4) with child custody, support, visitation, health insurance, etc.	107
Continuation of Judgment, (When Page 3 of 4) with spousal support, confirmation of separate property, etc.	108
Continuation of Judgment, (When Page 4 of 4) with division of community property and debts, etc.	109
Wage and Earnings Assignment Order (Front)	110
Wage and Earnings Assignment Order (Back)	111
Notice and Entry of Judgment	112
Application for Waiver of Court Fees and Costs (Front)	113
Application for Waiver of Court Fees and Costs (Back)	114
Order on Application for Waiver of Court Fees and Costs	115
Notice of Waiver of Court Fees and Costs	116

PETITION FOR DISSOLUTION OF MARRIAGE
Page One (Front) of the Petition
An example when without minor children and no separate property.

ATTORNEY OR PARTY WITHOUT ATTORNEY *(Name and Mailing Address)*:
JANE J. DOE
123 ANY STREET
LOS ANGELES, CA 92000

TELEPHONE NO.: 213-000-0000

FOR COURT USE ONLY

ATTORNEY FOR *(Name)*: In propria persona

SUPERIOR COURT OF CALIFORNIA, COUNTY OF LOS ANGELES
STREET ADDRESS: 111 N. HILL STREET
MAILING ADDRESS:
CITY AND ZIP CODE: LOS ANGELES, CA 90012
BRANCH NAME:

MARRIAGE OF
PETITIONER: JANE JUANITA DOE

RESPONDENT: JOHN JAMES DOE

PETITION FOR
[X] Dissolution of Marriage
[ ] Legal Separation
[ ] Nullity of Marriage
[ ] And Declaration Under Uniform Child Custody Jurisdiction Act

CASE NUMBER: TO BE SUPPLIED BY COURT

1. RESIDENCE (Dissolution only) [X] Petitioner [ ] Respondent has been a resident of this state for at least six months and of this county for at least three months immediately preceding the filing of this Petition for Dissolution of Marriage.

2. STATISTICAL FACTS
   a. Date of marriage: MAY 1, 1985
   b. Date of separation: JUNE 1, 1991
   c. Period between marriage and separation
      Years: 6   Months: 1
   d. Petitioner's Social Security No.: 431-00-0000
   f. Respondent's Social Security No.: 529-00-0000

3. DECLARATION REGARDING MINOR CHILDREN OF THIS MARRIAGE
   a. [X] There are no minor children.
   b. [ ] The minor children are:

   Child's name   Birthdate   Age   Sex

   c. IF THERE ARE MINOR CHILDREN, COMPLETE EITHER (1) OR (2)
   (1) [ ] Each child named in 3b is presently living with [ ] petitioner [ ] respondent
       in the following county *(specify)*:
       During the last five years each child has lived in no state other than California and with no person other than petitioner or respondent or both. Petitioner has not participated in any capacity in any litigation or proceeding in any state concerning custody of any minor child of this marriage. Petitioner has no information of any pending custody proceeding or of any person not a party to this proceeding who has physical custody or claims to have custody or visitation rights concerning any minor child of this marriage.
   (2) [ ] A completed Declaration Under Uniform Child Custody Jurisdiction Act is attached.

4. [ ] **Petitioner requests** confirmation as separate assets and obligations the items listed
   [ ] in Attachment 4   [ ] below:
   Item   Confirm to

   NONE

(Continued on reverse)

Form Adopted by Rule 1281
Judicial Council of California
1281 (Rev. January 1, 1993)

PETITION
(Family Law)

Civil Code, §§ 4503, 5158
Cal. Rules of Court, rule 1215

- 57 -

PETITION FOR DISSOLUTION OF MARRIAGE
Page One (Front) of the Petition
An example when without minor children and separate property listed in Attachment 4.

ATTORNEY OR PARTY WITHOUT ATTORNEY (Name and Mailing Address): **JANE J. DOE**
123 ANY STREET
LOS ANGELES, CA 92000
TELEPHONE NO.: 213-000-0000

ATTORNEY FOR (Name): In propria persona

SUPERIOR COURT OF CALIFORNIA, COUNTY OF LOS ANGELES
STREET ADDRESS: 111 N. HILL STREET
MAILING ADDRESS:
CITY AND ZIP CODE: LOS ANGELES, CA 90012
BRANCH NAME:

MARRIAGE OF
PETITIONER: JANE JUANITA DOE
RESPONDENT: JOHN JAMES DOE

FOR COURT USE ONLY

CASE NUMBER: TO BE SUPPLIED BY COURT

PETITION FOR
[X] Dissolution of Marriage
[ ] Legal Separation
[ ] Nullity of Marriage
[ ] And Declaration Under Uniform Child Custody Jurisdiction Act

---

1. RESIDENCE (Dissolution only) [X] Petitioner [ ] Respondent has been a resident of this state for at least six months and of this county for at least three months immediately preceding the filing of this Petition for Dissolution of Marriage.

2. STATISTICAL FACTS
   a. Date of marriage: **MAY 1, 1985**
   b. Date of separation: **JUNE 1, 1991**
   c. Period between marriage and separation
      Years: **6** Months: **1**
   d. Petitioner's Social Security No.: **431-00-0000**
   f. Respondent's Social Security No.: **529-00-0000**

3. DECLARATION REGARDING MINOR CHILDREN OF THIS MARRIAGE
   a. [X] There are no minor children.
   b. [ ] The minor children are:

   Child's name   Birthdate   Age   Sex

   c. IF THERE ARE MINOR CHILDREN, COMPLETE EITHER (1) OR (2)
   (1) [ ] Each child named in 3b is presently living with [ ] petitioner [ ] respondent in the following county (specify):
   During the last five years each child has lived in no state other than California and with no person other than petitioner or respondent or both. Petitioner has not participated in any capacity in any litigation or proceeding in any state concerning custody of any minor child of this marriage. Petitioner has no information of any pending custody proceeding or of any person not a party to this proceeding who has physical custody or claims to have custody or visitation rights concerning any minor child of this marriage.
   (2) [ ] A completed Declaration Under Uniform Child Custody Jurisdiction Act is attached.

4. [X] Petitioner requests confirmation as separate assets and obligations the items listed
   [X] in Attachment 4 [ ] below:
   Item   Confirm to

   (ATTACHMENT 4 IS THE SEPARATE PROPERTY DECLARATION.
   SEPARATE PROPERTY MUST NOT BE ON THE SAME FORM WITH
   COMMUNITY PROPERTY.)

(Continued on reverse)

Form Adopted by Rule 1281
Judicial Council of California
1281 (Rev. January 1, 1993)

PETITION
(Family Law)

Civil Code, §§ 4503, 5158
Cal. Rules of Court, rule 1215

PETITION FOR DISSOLUTION OF MARRIAGE
Page One (Front) of the Petition

An example when with minor children, the Declaration Regarding Minor Children Box 3(c)(1) is checked and separate property is listed under Section 4.

ATTORNEY OR PARTY WITHOUT ATTORNEY (Name and Mailing Address):
JANE J. DOE
123 ANY STREET
LOS ANGELES, CA 92000

TELEPHONE NO.: 213-000-0000

FOR COURT USE ONLY

ATTORNEY FOR (Name): In propria persona

SUPERIOR COURT OF CALIFORNIA, COUNTY OF LOS ANGELES
STREET ADDRESS: 111 N. HILL STREET
MAILING ADDRESS:
CITY AND ZIP CODE: LOS ANGELES, CA 90012
BRANCH NAME:

MARRIAGE OF
PETITIONER: JANE JUANITA DOE
RESPONDENT: JOHN JAMES DOE

PETITION FOR
[X] Dissolution of Marriage   [X] And Declaration Under Uniform Child Custody Jurisdiction Act
[ ] Legal Separation
[ ] Nullity of Marriage

CASE NUMBER: TO BE SUPPLIED BY COURT

---

1. **RESIDENCE** (Dissolution only) [X] Petitioner [ ] Respondent has been a resident of this state for at least six months and of this county for at least three months immediately preceding the filing of this Petition for Dissolution of Marriage.

2. **STATISTICAL FACTS**
   a. Date of marriage: **MAY 1, 1986**
   b. Date of separation: **MAY 15, 1991**
   c. Period between marriage and separation
      Years: **5**   Months: **6**
   d. Petitioner's Social Security No.: **431-00-0000**
   f. Respondent's Social Security No.: **529-00-0000**

3. **DECLARATION REGARDING MINOR CHILDREN OF THIS MARRIAGE**
   a. [ ] There are no minor children.
   b. [X] The minor children are:

Child's name	Birthdate	Age	Sex
ROBERT J. DOE	7-25-87	5 YRS. 7 MOS.	M
JUANITA J. DOE	3-1-89	3 YRS. 11 MOS.	F

   c. IF THERE ARE MINOR CHILDREN, COMPLETE EITHER (1) OR (2)
   (1) [X] Each child named in 3b is presently living with [X] petitioner [ ] respondent in the following county (specify): **LOS ANGELES COUNTY**
   During the last five years each child has lived in no state other than California and with no person other than petitioner or respondent or both. Petitioner has not participated in any capacity in any litigation or proceeding in any state concerning custody of any minor child of this marriage. Petitioner has no information of any pending custody proceeding or of any person not a party to this proceeding who has physical custody or claims to have custody or visitation rights concerning any minor child of this marriage.
   (2) [ ] A completed Declaration Under Uniform Child Custody Jurisdiction Act is attached.

4. [X] **Petitioner requests** confirmation as separate assets and obligations the items listed
   [ ] in Attachment 4   [X] below:

Item		Confirm to
a.	1984 CHEVROLET BLAZER, VIN AF73802943	PETITIONER
b.	1985 FORD BRONCO, VIN 4BV0396407	RESPONDENT

   (Continued on reverse)

Form Adopted by Rule 1281
Judicial Council of California
1281 (Rev. January 1, 1993)

PETITION
(Family Law)

Civil Code, §§ 4503, 5158
Cal. Rules of Court, rule 1215

PETITION FOR DISSOLUTION OF MARRIAGE
Page One (Front) of the Petition

An example when with minor children, the Declaration Under Uniform Child Custody Jurisdiction Act is attached and separate property is listed in Attachment 4.

ATTORNEY OR PARTY WITHOUT ATTORNEY (Name and Mailing Address): **TELEPHONE NO.:** 213-000-0000

JANE J. DOE
123 ANY STREET
LOS ANGELES, CA 92000

ATTORNEY FOR (Name): In propria persona

SUPERIOR COURT OF CALIFORNIA, COUNTY OF LOS ANGELES
STREET ADDRESS: 111 N. HILL STRET
MAILING ADDRESS:
CITY AND ZIP CODE: LOS ANGELES, CA 90012
BRANCH NAME:

MARRIAGE OF
PETITIONER: JANE JUANITA DOE
RESPONDENT: JOHN JAMES DOE

PETITION FOR
[X] Dissolution of Marriage [ ] And Declaration Under Uniform
[ ] Legal Separation   Child Custody Jurisdiction Act
[ ] Nullity of Marriage

CASE NUMBER: (TO BE SUPPLIED BY COURT)

---

1. **RESIDENCE** (Dissolution only) [X] Petitioner [ ] Respondent has been a resident of this state for at least six months and of this county for at least three months immediately preceding the filing of this Petition for Dissolution of Marriage.

2. **STATISTICAL FACTS**
   a. Date of marriage: MAY 1, 1985   b. Date of separation: JUNE 1, 1991
   c. Period between marriage and separation   d. Petitioner's Social Security No.: 431-00-0000
      Years: 6 Months: 1   f. Respondent's Social Security No.: 529-00-0000

3. **DECLARATION REGARDING MINOR CHILDREN OF THIS MARRIAGE**
   a. [ ] There are no minor children.   b. [X] The minor children are:

Child's name	Birthdate	Age	Sex
ROBERT J. DOE	7-25-87	5 YRS. 7 MOS.	M
JUANITA J. DOE	3-1-89	3 YRS 11 MOS.	F

   c. IF THERE ARE MINOR CHILDREN, COMPLETE EITHER (1) OR (2)
   (1) [ ] Each child named in 3b is presently living with [X] petitioner [ ] respondent in the following county (specify): During the last five years each child has lived in no state other than California and with no person other than petitioner or respondent or both. Petitioner has not participated in any capacity in any litigation or proceeding in any state concerning custody of any minor child of this marriage. Petitioner has no information of any pending custody proceeding or of any person not a party to this proceeding who has physical custody or claims to have custody or visitation rights concerning any minor child of this marriage.
   (2) [X] A completed Declaration Under Uniform Child Custody Jurisdiction Act is attached.

4. [X] **Petitioner requests** confirmation as separate assets and obligations the items listed
   [X] in Attachment 4 [ ] below:

Item	Confirm to

   ATTACHMENT 4 IS THE SEPARATE PROPERTY DECLARATION.
   NOTE: SEPARATE PROPERTY CANNOT BE LISTED ON THE SAME DECLARATION AS COMMUNITY PROPERTY.

(Continued on reverse)

Form Adopted by Rule 1281
Judicial Council of California
1281 [Rev. January 1, 1993]

PETITION
(Family Law)

Civil Code, §§ 4503, 5158
Cal. Rules of Court, rule 1215

PETITION FOR DISSOLUTION OF MARRIAGE
Page Two (Back) of the Petition
An example when without children, no community property and no spousal support.

MARRIAGE OF *(last name, first name of parties)*: DOE, JANE AND JOHN	**CASE NUMBER:** (SUPPLIED BY COURT)

5. DECLARATION REGARDING COMMUNITY AND QUASI-COMMUNITY ASSETS AND OBLIGATIONS AS PRESENTLY KNOWN
   a. [X] There are no such assets or obligations subject to disposition by the court in this proceeding.
   b. [ ] All such assets and obligations have been disposed of by written agreement.
   c. [ ] All such assets and obligations are listed [ ] in Attachment 5 [ ] below *(specify)*:

6. Petitioner requests
   a. [X] Dissolution of the marriage based on
      (1) [X] irreconcilable differences. CC 4506(1)
      (2) [ ] incurable insanity. CC 4506(2)
   b. [ ] Legal separation of the parties based on
      (1) [ ] irreconcilable differences. CC 4506(1)
      (2) [ ] incurable insanity. CC 4506(2)
   c. [ ] Nullity of void marriage based on
      (1) [ ] incestuous marriage. CC 4400
      (2) [ ] bigamous marriage. CC 4401
   d. [ ] Nullity of voidable marriage based on
      (1) [ ] petitioner's age at time of marriage. CC 4425(a)
      (2) [ ] prior existing marriage. CC 4425(b)
      (3) [ ] unsound mind. CC 4425(c)
      (4) [ ] fraud. CC 4425(d)
      (5) [ ] force. CC 4425(e)
      (6) [ ] physical incapacity. CC 4425(f)

7. Petitioner requests the court grant the above relief and make injunctive (including restraining) and other orders as follows:

	Petitioner	Respondent	Joint	Other
a. Legal custody of children to	[ ]	[ ]	[ ]	[ ]
b. Physical custody of children to	[ ]	[ ]	[ ]	[ ]
c. Child visitation be granted to	[ ]	[ ]	[ ]	[ ]
[ ] supervised as to *(specify)*:				
d. Spousal support payable by (wage assignment will be issued)	[ ]	[ ]		
e. Attorney fees and costs payable by	[ ]	[ ]		

   f. [ ] Terminate the court's jurisdiction (ability) to award spousal support to respondent.
   g. [ ] Property rights be determined.
   h. [X] Wife's former name be restored *(specify)*: JANE JUANITA ROE
   i. [X] Other *(specify)*: AWARD NO SPOUSAL MAINTENANCE TO EITHER PARTY IN THIS ACTION.

8. If there are minor children of this marriage, the court will make orders for the support of the children without further notice to either party. A wage assignment will be issued.

9. I have read the restraining orders on the back of the Summons, and I understand that they apply to me when this petition is filed.

I declare under penalty of perjury under the laws of the State of California that the foregoing is true and correct.

Date: FEBRUARY 1, 1993

▶ *[signature]*
(SIGNATURE OF PETITIONER)

........In pro per..........
(TYPE OR PRINT NAME OF ATTORNEY)

▶
(SIGNATURE OF ATTORNEY FOR PETITIONER)

NOTICE: Please review your will, insurance policies, retirement benefit plans, credit cards, other credit accounts and credit reports, and other matters you may want to change in view of the dissolution or annulment of your marriage, or your legal separation. However, some changes may require the agreement of your spouse or a court order (see section 412.21 of the Code of Civil Procedure).

1281 [Rev. January 1, 1993] **PETITION** (Family Law) Page two

PETITION FOR DISSOLUTION OF MARRIAGE
Page Two (Back) of the Petition
An example when with children, community property and debts, and spousal support.

MARRIAGE OF (last name, first name of parties): DOE, JANE AND JOHN	CASE NUMBER: (SUPPLIED BY COURT)

5. DECLARATION REGARDING COMMUNITY AND QUASI-COMMUNITY ASSETS AND OBLIGATIONS AS PRESENTLY KNOWN
   a. [ ] There are no such assets or obligations subject to disposition by the court in this proceeding.
   b. [ ] All such assets and obligations have been disposed of by written agreement.
   c. [X] All such assets and obligations are listed [X] in Attachment 5 [ ] below (specify):

   (ATTACHMENT 5 IS THE COUMMUNITY PROPERTY DECLARATION)

6. Petitioner requests
   a. [X] Dissolution of the marriage based on
      (1) [X] irreconcilable differences. CC 4506(1)
      (2) [ ] incurable insanity. CC 4506(2)
   b. [ ] Legal separation of the parties based on
      (1) [ ] irreconcilable differences. CC 4506(1)
      (2) [ ] incurable insanity. CC 4506(2)
   c. [ ] Nullity of void marriage based on
      (1) [ ] incestuous marriage. CC 4400
      (2) [ ] bigamous marriage. CC 4401
   d. [ ] Nullity of voidable marriage based on
      (1) [ ] petitioner's age at time of marriage. CC 4425(a)
      (2) [ ] prior existing marriage. CC 4425(b)
      (3) [ ] unsound mind. CC 4425(c)
      (4) [ ] fraud. CC 4425(d)
      (5) [ ] force. CC 4425(e)
      (6) [ ] physical incapacity. CC 4425(f)

7. Petitioner requests the court grant the above relief and make injunctive (including restraining) and other orders as follows:

	Petitioner	Respondent	Joint	Other
a. Legal custody of children to	X			
b. Physical custody of children to	X			
c. Child visitation be granted to		X		
[ ] supervised as to (specify):				
d. Spousal support payable by (wage assignment will be issued)		X		
e. Attorney fees and costs payable by				

   f. [ ] Terminate the court's jurisdiction (ability) to award spousal support to respondent.
   g. [X] Property rights be determined.
   h. [ ] Wife's former name be restored (specify):
   i. [ ] Other (specify):

8. If there are minor children of this marriage, the court will make orders for the support of the children without further notice to either party. A wage assignment will be issued.

9. I have read the restraining orders on the back of the Summons, and I understand that they apply to me when this petition is filed.

I declare under penalty of perjury under the laws of the State of California that the foregoing is true and correct.

Date: FEBRUARY 1, 1993

▶ _(signature)_
(SIGNATURE OF PETITIONER)

in pro per
(TYPE OR PRINT NAME OF ATTORNEY)

▶
(SIGNATURE OF ATTORNEY FOR PETITIONER)

NOTICE: Please review your will, insurance policies, retirement benefit plans, credit cards, other credit accounts and credit reports, and other matters you may want to change in view of the dissolution or annulment of your marriage, or your legal separation. However, some changes may require the agreement of your spouse or a court order (see section 412.21 of the Code of Civil Procedure).

1281 (Rev. January 1, 1993)

PETITION
(Family Law)

Page two

PETITION FOR DISSOLUTION OF MARRIAGE
Page Two (Back) of the Petition
An example when with children, community property and debts, and joint custody requested.

MARRIAGE OF *(last name, first name of parties):* DOE, JANE AND JOHN	CASE NUMBER: (SUPPLIED BY COURT)

5. DECLARATION REGARDING COMMUNITY AND QUASI-COMMUNITY ASSETS AND OBLIGATIONS AS PRESENTLY KNOWN
   a. [ ] There are no such assets or obligations subject to disposition by the court in this proceeding.
   b. [ ] All such assets and obligations have been disposed of by written agreement.
   c. [X] All such assets and obligations are listed [ ] in Attachment 5 [X] below *(specify):*

   a. ALL HOUSEHOLD FURNISHINGS AND EFFECTS IN THE PETITIONER'S RESIDENCE AT 123 ANY STREET, LOS ANGELES, CALIFORNIA

   b. ALL HOUSEHOLD FURNISHINGS AND EFFECTS IN RESPONDENT'S RESIDENCE AT 321 ANY STREET, SAN DIEGO, CALIFORNIA

6. Petitioner requests
   a. [X] Dissolution of the marriage based on
      (1) [X] irreconcilable differences. CC 4506(1)
      (2) [ ] incurable insanity. CC 4506(2)
   b. [ ] Legal separation of the parties based on
      (1) [ ] irreconcilable differences. CC 4506(1)
      (2) [ ] incurable insanity. CC 4506(2)
   c. [ ] Nullity of void marriage based on
      (1) [ ] incestuous marriage. CC 4400
      (2) [ ] bigamous marriage. CC 4401
   d. [ ] Nullity of voidable marriage based on
      (1) [ ] petitioner's age at time of marriage. CC 4425(a)
      (2) [ ] prior existing marriage. CC 4425(b)
      (3) [ ] unsound mind. CC 4425(c)
      (4) [ ] fraud. CC 4425(d)
      (5) [ ] force. CC 4425(e)
      (6) [ ] physical incapacity. CC 4425(f)

7. Petitioner requests the court grant the above relief and make injunctive (including restraining) and other orders as follows:

	Petitioner	Respondent	Joint	Other
a. Legal custody of children to	[ ]	[ ]	[X]	[ ]
b. Physical custody of children to	[ ]	[ ]	[X]	[ ]
c. Child visitation be granted to	[ ]	[ ]	[X]	[ ]
[ ] supervised as to *(specify):*				
d. Spousal support payable by (wage assignment will be issued)	[ ]	[ ]		
e. Attorney fees and costs payable by	[ ]	[ ]		

   f. [ ] Terminate the court's jurisdiction (ability) to award spousal support to respondent.
   g. [X] Property rights be determined.
   h. [ ] Wife's former name be restored *(specify):*
   i. [ ] Other *(specify):*

8. If there are minor children of this marriage, the court will make orders for the support of the children without further notice to either party. A wage assignment will be issued.

9. I have read the restraining orders on the back of the Summons, and I understand that they apply to me when this petition is filed.

I declare under penalty of perjury under the laws of the State of California that the foregoing is true and correct.

Date: FEBRUARY 1, 1993

▶ *Jane J. Doe* (signature)
(SIGNATURE OF PETITIONER)

in pro per
(TYPE OR PRINT NAME OF ATTORNEY)

▶
(SIGNATURE OF ATTORNEY FOR PETITIONER)

NOTICE: Please review your will, insurance policies, retirement benefit plans, credit cards, other credit accounts and credit reports, and other matters you may want to change in view of the dissolution or annulment of your marriage, or your legal separation. However, some changes may require the agreement of your spouse or a court order (see section 412.21 of the Code of Civil Procedure).

1281 (Rev. January 1, 1993)
PETITION (Family Law)
Page two

PROPERTY DECLARATION, ATTACHMENT 4
Page One (Front) of the Separate Property Declaration
An example when separate property is listed

ATTORNEY OR PARTY WITHOUT ATTORNEY (NAME AND ADDRESS): JANE J. DOE, 123 ANY STREET, LOS ANGELES, CA 92000	TELEPHONE NO 213-000-0000	FOR COURT USE ONLY

ATTORNEY FOR (NAME): In propria persona

SUPERIOR COURT OF CALIFORNIA, COUNTY OF LOS ANGELES
STREET ADDRESS: 111 N. HILL STREET
MAILING ADDRESS:
CITY AND ZIP CODE: LOS ANGELES, CA 90012
BRANCH NAME:

MARRIAGE OF
PETITIONER: JANE JUANITA DOE
RESPONDENT: JOHN JAMES DOE

[ ] PETITIONER'S [X] RESPONDENT'S (ATTACHMENT 4)
[ ] COMMUNITY & QUASI-COMMUNITY PROPERTY DECLARATION
[X] SEPARATE PROPERTY DECLARATION

CASE NUMBER (SUPPLIED BY COURT)

INSTRUCTIONS
When this form is attached to Petition or Response, values and your proposal regarding division need not be completed. Do not list community, including quasi-community, property with separate property on the same form. Quasi-community property must be so identified. For additional space, use the form "Continuation of Property Declaration."

ITEM NO	BRIEF DESCRIPTION	GROSS FAIR MARKET VALUE	AMOUNT OF DEBT	NET FAIR MARKET VALUE	PROPOSAL FOR DIVISION AWARD TO PETITIONER	RESPONDENT
		$	$	$	$	$
1.	REAL ESTATE					
2.	HOUSEHOLD FURNITURE, FURNISHINGS, APPLIANCES					
3.	JEWELRY, ANTIQUES, ART, COIN COLLECTIONS, etc					
4.	VEHICLES, BOATS, TRAILERS	2,000.00	0.00	2,000.00		2,000.00
5.	SAVINGS, CHECKING, CREDIT UNION, CASH	500.00	0.00	500.00		500.00

(Continued on reverse)

The declaration under penalty of perjury must be signed in California or in a state that authorizes use of a declaration in place of an affidavit, otherwise an affidavit is required.

Form Adopted by Rule 1285.55
Judicial Council of California
Effective January 1, 1980

**PROPERTY DECLARATION
(FAMILY LAW)**

PROPERTY DECLARATION, ATTACHMENT 4
Page One (Back) of the Separate Property Declaration
An example when separate property is listed

ITEM NO	BRIEF DESCRIPTION	GROSS FAIR MARKET VALUE	AMOUNT OF DEBT	NET FAIR MARKET VALUE	PROPOSAL FOR DIVISION AWARD TO PETITIONER	RESPONDENT
		$	$	$	$	$
6.	LIFE INSURANCE (CASH VALUE)					
7.	EQUIPMENT, MACHINERY, LIVESTOCK					
8.	STOCKS, BONDS, SECURED NOTES					
9.	RETIREMENT, PENSION, PROFIT-SHARING, ANNUITIES					
10.	ACCOUNTS RECEIVABLE, UNSECURED NOTES, TAX REFUNDS					
11.	PARTNERSHIPS, OTHER BUSINESS INTERESTS					
12.	OTHER ASSETS AND DEBTS **VISA ACCOUNT WITH SECOND FED. BANK** ACCT. NO. 3047986823		4,000.00			4,000.00
13.	TOTAL FROM CONTINUATION SHEET					
14.	TOTALS	2500.00	4,000.00	2,500.00	2,500.00	4,000.00

15. ☐ A Continuation of Property Declaration is attached and incorporated by reference.

_____   _____
(Type or print name of attorney)   (Signature of attorney)

I declare under penalty of perjury that, to the best of my knowledge, the foregoing is a true and correct listing of assets and obligations and that the amounts shown are correct; and that this declaration was executed on (date): FEBRUAARY 1, 1993 at (place): LOS ANGELES ...., California.

JANE JUANITA DOE, IN PRO PER   *(signed) Jane J. Doe*
(Type or print name)   (Signature)

PROPERTY DECLARATION, ATTACHMENT 5
Page One (Front) of the Community Property Declaration
An example when Community property is listed

ATTORNEY OR PARTY WITHOUT ATTORNEY (NAME AND ADDRESS): JANE JUANITA DOE, 123 ANY STREET, LOS ANGELES, CA 90012	TELEPHONE NO. 213-000-0000	FOR COURT USE ONLY
ATTORNEY FOR (NAME): In propria persona		

SUPERIOR COURT OF CALIFORNIA, COUNTY OF LOS ANGELES
STREET ADDRESS: 111 N. HILL STREET
MAILING ADDRESS:
CITY AND ZIP CODE: LOS ANGELES, CA 90012
BRANCH NAME:

MARRIAGE OF
PETITIONER: JANE JUANITA DOE
RESPONDENT: JOHN JAMES DOE

[X] PETITIONER'S [ ] RESPONDENT'S   (ATTACHMENT 5)
[X] COMMUNITY & QUASI-COMMUNITY PROPERTY DECLARATION
[ ] SEPARATE PROPERTY DECLARATION

CASE NUMBER:
(SUPPLIED BY COURT)

INSTRUCTIONS

When this form is attached to Petition or Response, values and your proposal regarding division need not be completed. Do not list community, including quasi-community, property with separate property on the same form. Quasi-community property must be so identified. For additional space, use the form "Continuation of Property Declaration."

ITEM NO	BRIEF DESCRIPTION	GROSS FAIR MARKET VALUE	AMOUNT OF DEBT	NET FAIR MARKET VALUE	PROPOSAL FOR DIVISION AWARD TO PETITIONER	RESPONDENT
1.	REAL ESTATE 3 BEDROOM RESIDENCE LEGALLY DESCRIBED AS: LOT 1020, VALLEY SUB-DIVISION, LOS ANGELES COUNTY, CALIFORNIA	35,000.00	20,000.00	15,000.00	15,000.00	
2.	HOUSEHOLD FURNITURE, FURNISHINGS, APPLIANCES	5,000.00	1,500.00	3,500.00	3,500.00	
3.	JEWELRY, ANTIQUES, ART, COIN COLLECTIONS, etc	1,000.00	0.00	1,000.00	1,000.00	
4.	VEHICLES, BOATS, TRAILERS	12,000.00	0.00	12,000.00		12,000.00
5.	SAVINGS, CHECKING, CREDIT UNION, CASH	2,000.00 1,500.00		2,000.00 1,500.00	1,500.00	2,000.00

(Continued on reverse)

The declaration under penalty of perjury must be signed in California or in a state that authorizes use of a declaration in place of an affidavit, otherwise an affidavit is required

Form Adopted by Rule 1285.55
Judicial Council of California
Effective January 1, 1980

PROPERTY DECLARATION (FAMILY LAW)

PROPERTY DECLARATION, ATTACHMENT 5
Page One (Back) of the Community Property Declaration
An example when Community property is listed

ITEM NO	BRIEF DESCRIPTION	GROSS FAIR MARKET VALUE	AMOUNT OF DEBT	NET FAIR MARKET VALUE	PROPOSAL FOR DIVISION AWARD TO PETITIONER	RESPONDENT
		$	$	$	$	$
6.	LIFE INSURANCE (CASH VALUE)	5,000.00	0.00	5,000.00		5,000.00
7.	EQUIPMENT, MACHINERY, LIVESTOCK	3,000.00		3,000.00		2,000.00
8.	STOCKS, BONDS, SECURED NOTES					
9.	RETIREMENT, PENSION, PROFIT-SHARING, ANNUITIES					
10.	ACCOUNTS RECEIVABLE, UNSECURED NOTES, TAX REFUNDS					
11.	PARTNERSHIPS, OTHER BUSINESS INTERESTS					
12.	~~OTHER ASSETS~~ AND DEBTS ROYAL FINANCE CO. BANK OF AMERICA CITI-BANK VISA SEARS TIME PAY ACCT. BROADWAY STORES ALLIED DEPT. STORES		2,700.00 4,500.00 2,200.00 1,500.00 1,200.00 800.00		1,500.00 1,200.00 800.00	2,700.00 4,500.00 2,200.00
13.	TOTAL FROM CONTINUATION SHEET					
14.	TOTALS	64,500.00	14,400.00	43,000.00	24,500.00	30,400.00

15. ☐ A Continuation of Property Declaration is attached and incorporated by reference

JANE J. DOE, In pro per
(Type or print name of attorney)   (Signature of ~~XXXXXXX~~ Petitioner)

I declare under penalty of perjury that, to the best of my knowledge, the foregoing is a true and correct listing of assets and obligations and that the amounts shown are correct; and that this declaration was executed on (date): FEBRUARY 1, 1993 at (place): LOS ANGELES ...., California.

JANE JUANITA DOE, In pro per
(Type or print name)   (Signature)

DECLARATION UNDER UNIFORM CHILD CUSTODY JURISDICTION ACT

Page One (Front) of the Declaration

An example of the Declaration when with two minor children and both are parties to an action in another jurisdiction

---

ATTORNEY OR PARTY WITHOUT ATTORNEY *(Name and Address)*:
JANE JUANITA DOE
123 ANY STREET
LOS ANGELES, CA 92000

TELEPHONE NO.: 213-000-0000

FOR COURT USE ONLY

ATTORNEY FOR *(Name)*: IN PROPRIA PERSONA

SUPERIOR COURT OF CALIFORNIA, COUNTY OF LOS ANGELES
STREET ADDRESS: 111 N. HILL STREET
MAILING ADDRESS:
CITY AND ZIP CODE: LOS ANGELES, CA 90012
BRANCH NAME:

CASE NAME: MARRIAGE OF JANE JUANITA DOE, PETITIONER
JOHN JAMES DOE, RESPONDENT

DECLARATION UNDER UNIFORM CHILD CUSTODY JURISDICTION ACT (UCCJA)

CASE NUMBER: (SUPPLIED BY COURT)

---

1. I am a party to this proceeding to determine custody of a child.
2. *(Number)*: **2** minor children are subject to this proceeding as follows:
   (Insert the information requested below. The residence information must be given for the last FIVE years.)

a. Child's name: ROBERT JAMES DOE
- **Place of birth:** LOS ANGELES, CALIF.
- **Date of birth:** 7-25-87
- **Sex:** M

Period of residence	Address	Person child lived with (name and present address)	Relationship
MAY 1991 to present	123 ANY STREET, LOS ANGELES, CA 92000	JANE J. DOE, 123 ANY STREET, LOS ANGELES, CA 92000	MOTHER
JULY 1987 to MAY 1991	3333 BUSY STREET, LOS ANGELES, CA 92000	JANE J. DOE/JOHN J. DOE, 3333 BUSY STREET, LOS ANGELES, CA 92000	MOTHER/FATHER
to			
to			
to			

b. Child's name: JUANITA JANE DOE
- **Place of birth:** LOS ANGELES, CALIF.
- **Date of birth:** 3-1-89
- **Sex:** F

[X] Residence information is the same as given above for child a. *(If NOT the same, provide the information below.)*

Period of residence	Address	Person child lived with (name and present address)	Relationship
to present			
to			
to			
to			
to			

c. [ ] Additional children are listed on Attachment 2c. *(Provide requested information for additional children on an attachment.)*

(Continued on reverse)

Form Approved by the Judicial Council of California
MC 150 [Rev. January 1, 1987] [Cor. 1/2/87]

DECLARATION UNDER UNIFORM CHILD CUSTODY JURISDICTION ACT (UCCJA)

Civil Code, § 5158
Probate Code, §§ 1510(f), 1512

DECLARATION UNDER UNIFORM CHILD CUSTODY JURISDICTION ACT
Page Two (Back) of the Declaration
An example of the Declaration when a custody and visitation action is pending in another jurisdiction

SHORT TITLE: DOE, JANE AND JOHN	CASE NUMBER: (SUPPLIED BY COURT)

3. Have you participated as a party or a witness or in some other capacity in another litigation or custody proceeding, in California or elsewhere, concerning custody of a child subject to this proceeding?
   [ ] No [X] Yes *(If yes, provide the following information:)*

   a. Name of each child: ROBERT JAMES DOE

   b. Capacity of declarant: [X] party [ ] witness [ ] other *(specify)*:
   c. Court *(specify name, state, location)*: SUPERIOR COURT OF CALIFORNIA, COUNTY OF SAN DIEGO, 220 W. BROADWAY, SAN DIEGO, CALIFORNIA
   d. Court order or judgment *(date)*: DECEMBER 5, 1992

4. Do you have information about a custody proceeding pending in a California court or any other court concerning a child subject to this proceeding, other than that stated in item 3?
   [X] No [ ] Yes *(If yes, provide the following information:)*

   a. Name of each child:

   b. Nature of proceeding: [ ] dissolution or divorce [ ] guardianship [ ] adoption [ ] other *(specify)*:

   c. Court *(specify name, state, location)*:

   d. Status of proceeding:

5. Do you know of any person who is not a party to this proceeding who has physical custody or claims to have custody of or visitation rights with any child subject to this proceeding?
   [ ] No [X] Yes *(If yes, provide the following information:)*

a. Name and address of person	b. Name and address of person	c. Name and address of person
WALTER J. DOE 555 STATE STREET SAN DIEGO, CA 92100	EMMA E. DOE 777 COUNTY STREET SAN DIEGO, CA 92200	
[ ] Has physical custody [ ] Claims custody rights [X] Claims visitation rights	[ ] Has physical custody [ ] Claims custody rights [X] Claims visitation rights	[ ] Has physical custody [ ] Claims custody rights [ ] Claims visitation rights
Name of each child ROBERT J. DOE JUANITA J. DOE	Name of each child JUANITY J. DOE ROBERT J. DOE	Name of each child

I declare under penalty of perjury under the laws of the State of California that the foregoing is true and correct.

Date: FEBRUARY 1, 1993

JANE JUANITA DOE, IN PRO PER
(TYPE OR PRINT NAME)   (SIGNATURE OF DECLARANT)

6. [ ] Number of pages attached after this page:

NOTICE TO DECLARANT: You have a continuing duty to inform this court if you obtain any information about a custody proceeding in a California court or any other court concerning a child subject to this proceeding.

MC-150 (Rev. January 1, 1987)
(Cor. 1/2/87)

DECLARATION UNDER UNIFORM CHILD CUSTODY JURISDICTION ACT (UCCJA)

Page two

SUMMONS
(English and Spanish)
Frontside

SUMMONS—FAMILY LAW   *CITACION JUDICIAL—DERECHO DE FAMILIA*

NOTICE TO RESPONDENT *(Name)*:   JOHN JAMES DOE
AVISO AL DEMANDADO (Nombre):

FOR COURT USE ONLY
(SOLO PARA USO DE LA CORTE)

| You are being sued. *A usted le estan demandando.* |

PETITIONER'S NAME IS: JANE JUANITA DOE
EL NOMBRE DEL DEMANDANTE ES:

CASE NUMBER: *(Número del Caso)*
(SUPPLIED BY COURT)

You have **30 CALENDAR DAYS** after this Summons and Petition are served on you to file a Response (form 1282) at the court and serve a copy on the petitioner. A letter or phone call will not protect you.	*Usted tiene **30 DIAS CALENDARIOS** después de recibir oficialmente esta citación judicial y petición, para completar y presentar su formulario de Respuesta (Response form 1282) ante la corte. Una carta o una llamada telefónica no le ofrecerá protección.*
If you do not file your Response on time, the court may make orders affecting your marriage, your property, and custody of your children. You may be ordered to pay support and attorney fees and costs. If you cannot pay the filing fee, ask the clerk for a fee waiver form.	*Si usted no presenta su Respuesta a tiempo, la corte puede expedir órdenes que afecten su matrimonio, su propiedad y que ordenen que usted pague mantención, honorarios de abogado y las costas. Si no puede pagar las costas por la presentación de la demanda, pida al actuario de la corte que le dé un formulario de exoneración de las mismas (Waiver of Court Fees and Costs).*
If you want legal advice, contact a lawyer immediately.	*Si desea obtener consejo legal, comuníquese de inmediato con un abogado.*

NOTICE *The restraining orders on the back are effective against both husband and wife until the petition is dismissed, a judgment is entered, or the court makes further orders. These orders are enforceable anywhere in California by any law enforcement officer who has received or seen a copy of them.*

AVISO Las prohibiciones judiciales que aparecen al reverso de esta citación son efectivas para ambos cónyuges, tanto el esposo como la esposa, hasta que la petición sea rechazada, se dicte una decisión final o la corte expida instrucciones adicionales. Dichas prohibiciones pueden hacerse cumplir en cualquier parte de California por cualquier agente del orden público que las haya recibido o que haya visto una copia de ellas.

1. The name and address of the court is: *(El nombre y dirección de la corte es)*

    SUPERIOR COURT OF LOS ANGELES COUNTY
    111 N. HILL STREET
    LOS ANGELES, CA 90012

2. The name, address, and telephone number of petitioner's attorney, or petitioner without an attorney, is:
    (El nombre, la dirección y el número de teléfono del abogado del demandante, o del demandante que no tiene abogado, es)

    JANE JUANITA DOE
    123 ANY STREET
    LOS ANGELES, CA 92000

    213-000-0000

[SEAL]   Date *(Fecha)*:   Clerk *(Actuario)*, by _____, Deputy

NOTICE TO THE PERSON SERVED: You are served
a. [X] as an individual.
b. [ ] on behalf of respondent
    under: [ ] CCP 416.60 (minor)   [ ] CCP 416.90 (individual)
            [ ] CCP 416.70 (ward or conservatee)   [ ] other:
c. [ ] by personal delivery on *(date)*:

(Read the reverse for important information)
(Lea el reverso para obtener información de importancia)

Form Adopted by Rule 1283   **SUMMONS**   Code of Civil Procedure, § 412.21
Judicial Council of California   (Family Law)   California Rules of Court, rule 1216
1283 [Rev January 1, 1991]

SUMMONS
(English and Spanish)
Backside

PROHIBICIONES JUDICIALES ESTANDARES—DERECHO DE FAMILIA

STANDARD FAMILY LAW RESTRAINING ORDERS
Starting immediately, you and your spouse are restrained from
1. removing the minor child or children of the parties, if any, from the state without the prior written consent of the other party or an order of the court;
2. cashing, borrowing against, canceling, transferring, disposing of, or changing the beneficiaries of any insurance or other coverage including life, health, automobile, and disability held for the benefit of the parties and their minor child or children; and
3. transferring, encumbering, hypothecating, concealing, or in any way disposing of any property, real or personal, whether community, quasi-community, or separate, without the written consent of the other party or an order of the court, except in the usual course of business or for the necessities of life.

   You must notify each other of any proposed extraordinary expenditures at least five business days prior to incurring these extraordinary expenditures and account to the court for all extraordinary expenditures made after these restraining orders are effective. However, nothing in the restraining orders shall preclude you from using community property to pay reasonable attorney fees in order to retain legal counsel in the action.

PROHIBICIONES JUDICIALES ESTANDARES—DERECHO DE FAMILIA
A usted y a su cónyuge se les prohibe
1. *que saquen del estado al hijo o hijos menores de las partes, si los hay, sin el consentimiento previo por escrito de la otra parte o sin una orden de la corte; y*
2. *que cobren en efectivo, usen como colateral para préstamos, cancelen, transfieran, descontinúen o cambien los beneficiarios de, cualquier póliza de seguro u otras coberturas de seguro, inclusive los de vida, salud, automóvil e incapacidad mantenido para el beneficio de las partes y su hijo o hijos menores; y*
3. *que transfieran, graven, hipotequen, escondan o de cualquier otra manera enajenen cualquier propiedad mueble o inmueble, ya sean bienes de la sociedad conyugal, quasi conyugales o bienes propios de los cónyuges, sin el consentimiento por escrito de la otra parte o sin una orden de la corte, excepto en el curso normal de los negocios o para atender a las necesidades de la vida.*

   Ustedes deben notificarse entre sí sobre cualquier gasto extraordinario propuesto, por lo menos con cinco días de antelación a la fecha en que se van a incurrir dichos gastos extraordinarios y responder ante la corte por todo gasto extraordinario hecho después de que estas prohibiciones judiciales entren en vigor. Sin embargo, nada de lo contenido en las prohibiciones judiciales le impedirá que use bienes de la sociedad conyugal para pagar honorarios razonables de abogados con el fin de obtener representación legal durante el proceso.

Proof of Service *(optional)*:

1283 (Rev. January 1, 1991)   **STANDARD RESTRAINING ORDERS**   Page two
SUMMONS
(Family Law)

PROOF OF SERVICE OF SUMMONS

An example when service was made by personal delivery

MARRIAGE OF (last name, first name of parties): DOE, JANE AND JOHN	CASE NUMBER: (SUPPLIED BY COURT)

Serve a copy of the documents on the person to be served. Complete the proof of service. Attach it to the original documents. File them with the court.

PROOF OF SERVICE OF SUMMONS (Family Law)

1. I served the Summons with Standard Restraining Orders (Family Law), **blank Response**, and Petition (Family Law) on respondent (name):
   a. with (1) [X] blank Confidential Counseling Statement (4) [X] completed and blank Income and
      (2) [ ] Order to Show Cause and Application   Expense Declarations
      (3) [X] blank Responsive Declaration   (5) [X] completed and blank Property Declarations
                                                         (6) [ ] Other (specify):

   b. [ ] By leaving copies with (name and title or relationship to person served):

   c. [X] By delivery at [X] home [ ] business
      (1) Date of: FEBRUARY 15, 1993   (3) Address: 321 ANY STREET
      (2) Time of: 2:00 PM   SAN DIEGO, CA 92000

   d. [ ] By mailing (1) Date of: (2) Place of:

2. Manner of service: (Check proper box)
   a. [X] **Personal service.** By personally delivering copies to the person served. (CCP 415.10)
   b. [ ] **Substituted service on natural person, minor, incompetent.** By leaving copies at the dwelling house, usual place of abode, or usual place of business of the person served in the presence of a competent member of the household or a person apparently in charge of the office or place of business, at least 18 years of age, who was informed of the general nature of the papers, and thereafter mailing (by first-class mail, postage prepaid) copies to the person served at the place where the copies were left. (CCP 415.20(b)) **(Attach separate declaration stating acts relied on to establish reasonable diligence in first attempting personal service.)**
   c. [ ] **Mail and acknowledge service.** By mailing (by first-class mail or airmail) copies to the person served, together with two copies of the form of notice and acknowledgment and a return envelope, postage prepaid, addressed to the sender. (CCP 415.30) **(Attach completed acknowledgment of receipt.)**
   d. [ ] **Certified or registered mail service.** By mailing to address outside California (by registered or certified airmail with return receipt requested) copies to the person served. (CCP 415.40) **(Attach signed return receipt or other evidence of actual delivery to the person served.)**
   e. [ ] Other (specify code section):
         [ ] Additional page is attached.

3. The NOTICE TO THE PERSON SERVED on the summons was completed as follows (CCP 412.30, 415.10, and 474):
   a. [X] as an individual
   b. [ ] on behalf of Respondent
      under [ ] CCP 416.90 (Individual) [ ] CCP 416.70 (Ward or Conservatee) [ ] CCP 416.60 (Minor)
            [ ] Other (specify):
   c. [X] by personal delivery on (date): FEBRUARY 16, 1993

4. At the time of service I was at least 18 years of age and not a party to this action.
5. Fee for service: $
6. Person serving:
   a. [X] Not a registered California process server.   e. [ ] California sheriff, marshal, or constable.
   b. [ ] Registered California process server.   f. Name, address, and telephone number and, if
   c. [ ] Employee or independent contractor of a   applicable, county of registration and number:
         registered California process server.
   d. [ ] Exempt from registration under Bus. & Prof.   WILLIAM P. RIZT
         Code section 22350(b).   789 WHY STREET
                                                                PASADENA, CA 92000
                                                                213-000-0000

I declare under penalty of perjury under the laws of the State   (For California sheriff, marshal, or constable use only)
of California that the foregoing is true and correct.   I certify that the foregoing is true and correct.
Date: Date:

▶ *William P Rizt*
       (SIGNATURE)   (SIGNATURE)

Form Adopted by Rule 1283.5
Judicial Council of California
1283.5 (New January 1, 1991)

PROOF OF SERVICE OF SUMMONS
(Family Law)

PROOF OF SERVICE OF SUMMONS

An example when service was made by mail

MARRIAGE OF (last name, first name of parties):	CASE NUMBER:
DOE, JANE JUANITA and JOHN JAMES	Supplied by Court

Serve a copy of the documents on the person to be served. Complete the proof of service. Attach it to the original documents. File them with the court.

PROOF OF SERVICE OF SUMMONS (Family Law)

1. I served the Summons with Standard Restraining Orders (Family Law), **blank Response**, and Petition (Family Law) on respondent *(name)*: **John James Doe**
   a. with (1) [x] blank Confidential Counseling Statement
      (2) [ ] Order to Show Cause and Application
      (3) [x] blank Responsive Declaration
      (4) [ ] completed and blank Income and Expense Declarations
      (5) [ ] completed and blank Property Declarations
      (6) [ ] Other *(specify)*:

   b. [ ] By leaving copies with *(name and title or relationship to person served)*:

   c. [ ] By delivery at [ ] home [ ] business
      (1) Date of:
      (2) Time of:
      (3) Address:

   d. [x] By mailing (1) Date of: **February 15, 1993** (2) Place of: **321 Any Street, San Diego, CA 91000**

2. Manner of service: *(Check proper box)*
   a. [ ] **Personal service.** By personally delivering copies to the person served. (CCP 415.10)
   b. [ ] **Substituted service on natural person, minor, incompetent.** By leaving copies at the dwelling house, usual place of abode, or usual place of business of the person served in the presence of a competent member of the household or a person apparently in charge of the office or place of business, at least 18 years of age, who was informed of the general nature of the papers, and thereafter mailing (by first-class mail, postage prepaid) copies to the person served at the place where the copies were left. (CCP 415.20(b)) **(Attach separate declaration stating acts relied on to establish reasonable diligence in first attempting personal service.)**
   c. [x] **Mail and acknowledge service.** By mailing (by first-class mail or airmail) copies to the person served, together with two copies of the form of notice and acknowledgment and a return envelope, postage prepaid, addressed to the sender. (CCP 415.30) **(Attach completed acknowledgment of receipt.)**
   d. [ ] **Certified or registered mail service.** By mailing to address outside California (by registered or certified airmail with return receipt requested) copies to the person served. (CCP 415.40) **(Attach signed return receipt or other evidence of actual delivery to the person served.)**
   e. [ ] Other *(specify code section)*:
      [ ] Additional page is attached.

3. The NOTICE TO THE PERSON SERVED on the summons was completed as follows (CCP 412.30, 415.10, and 474):
   a. [x] as an individual
   b. [ ] on behalf of Respondent
      under [ ] CCP 416.90 (Individual) [ ] CCP 416.70 (Ward or Conservatee) [ ] CCP 416.60 (Minor)
      [ ] Other *(specify)*:
   c. [ ] by personal delivery on *(date)*:

4. At the time of service I was at least 18 years of age and not a party to this action.
5. Fee for service: $
6. Person serving:
   a. [x] Not a registered California process server.
   b. [ ] Registered California process server.
   c. [ ] Employee or independent contractor of a registered California process server.
   d. [ ] Exempt from registration under Bus. & Prof. Code section 22350(b).
   e. [ ] California sheriff, marshal, or constable.
   f. Name, address, and telephone number and, if applicable, county of registration and number:

   WILLIAM P. RIZT
   789 WHY STREET
   PASADENA, CA 92000
   213-000-1000

I declare under penalty of perjury under the laws of the State of California that the foregoing is true and correct.
Date:
▶ *William P Rizt*
(SIGNATURE)

(For California sheriff, marshal, or constable use only)
I certify that the foregoing is true and correct.
Date:
▶
(SIGNATURE)

PROOF OF SERVICE OF SUMMONS (Family Law)

Form Adopted by Rule 1283.5
Judicial Council of California
1283.5 (New January 1, 1991)

RESPONSE TO PETITION FOR DISSOLUTION OF MARRIAGE
Page One (Front) of the Response
An example when without children, property or debts

ATTORNEY OR PARTY WITHOUT ATTORNEY (Name and Mailing Address):
JANE J. DOE
123 ANY STREET
LOS ANGELES, CA 92000

TELEPHONE NO.: 213-000-0000

FOR COURT USE ONLY

ATTORNEY FOR (Name): In propria persona

SUPERIOR COURT OF CALIFORNIA, COUNTY OF LOS ANGELES
STREET ADDRESS: 111 N. HILL STREET
MAILING ADDRESS:
CITY AND ZIP CODE: LOS ANGELES, CA 90012
BRANCH NAME:

MARRIAGE OF
PETITIONER: JANE JUANITA DOE
RESPONDENT: JOHN JAMES DOE

RESPONSE [ ] **and REQUEST FOR**
[X] Dissolution of Marriage   [ ] And Declaration Under Uniform
[ ] Legal Separation   Child Custody Jurisdiction Act
[ ] Nullity of Marriage

CASE NUMBER:

1. **RESIDENCE** (Dissolution only) [X] Petitioner [ ] Respondent has been a resident of this state for at least six months and of this county for at least three months immediately preceding the filing of this Petition for Dissolution of Marriage.

2. **STATISTICAL FACTS**
   a. Date of marriage: MAY 1, 1985
   b. Date of separation: JUNE 1, 1992
   c. Period between marriage and separation
   d. Petitioner's Social Security No.: 431-00-0000
      Years: 7   Months: 1
   e. Respondent's Social Security No.: 529-00-0000

3. **DECLARATION REGARDING MINOR CHILDREN OF THIS MARRIAGE**
   a. [X] There are no minor children.   b. [ ] The minor children are:
   Child's name   Birthdate   Age   Sex

   c. IF THERE ARE MINOR CHILDREN, COMPLETE EITHER (1) OR (2)
   (1) [ ] Each child named in 3b is presently living with [ ] petitioner [ ] respondent
       in the following county (specify):
       and during the last five years has lived in no state other than California and with no person other than petitioner or respondent or both. Respondent has not participated in any capacity in any litigation or proceeding in any state concerning custody of any minor child of this marriage. Respondent has no information of any pending custody proceeding or of any person not a party to this proceeding who has physical custody or claims to have custody or visitation rights concerning any minor child of this marriage.
   (2) [ ] A completed Declaration Under Uniform Custody of Minors Act is attached.

4. [ ] **Respondent requests** confirmation as separate assets and obligations the items listed
       [ ] in Attachment 4 [ ] below:
       Item   Confirm to

(Continued on reverse)

Form Adopted by Rule 1282
Judicial Council of California
1282 [Rev. January 1, 1993]

RESPONSE
(Family Law)

Civil Code, § 4355
Cal. Rules of Court, rule 1215

RESPONSE TO PETITION FOR DISSOLUTION OF MARRIAGE
Page One (Front) of the Response
An example when with children and request the confirmation of separate property listed in petitioner's Attachment 4

ATTORNEY OR PARTY WITHOUT ATTORNEY *(Name and Mailing Address)*:
JANE J. DOE
123 ANY STREET
LOS ANGELES, CA 92000

TELEPHONE NO.: 213-000-0000

FOR COURT USE ONLY

ATTORNEY FOR *(Name)*: In propria persona

SUPERIOR COURT OF CALIFORNIA, COUNTY OF LOS ANGELES
STREET ADDRESS: 111 N. HILL STREET
MAILING ADDRESS:
CITY AND ZIP CODE: LOS ANGELES, CA 90012
BRANCH NAME:

MARRIAGE OF
PETITIONER: JANE JUANITA DOE
RESPONDENT: JOHN JAMES DOE

RESPONSE [ ] **and REQUEST FOR**
[X] Dissolution of Marriage   [ ] And Declaration Under Uniform
[ ] Legal Separation   Child Custody Jurisdiction Act
[ ] Nullity of Marriage

CASE NUMBER: (SUPPLIED BY COURT)

---

1. **RESIDENCE** (Dissolution only) [ ] Petitioner [ ] Respondent has been a resident of this state for at least six months and of this county for at least three months immediately preceding the filing of this Petition for Dissolution of Marriage.

2. **STATISTICAL FACTS**
   a. Date of marriage: MAY 1, 1985
   b. Date of separation: JUNE 1, 1992
   c. Period between marriage and separation
   d. Petitioner's Social Security No.: 431-00-0000
      Years: 7   Months: 1
   e. Respondent's Social Security No.: 529-00-0000

3. **DECLARATION REGARDING MINOR CHILDREN OF THIS MARRIAGE**
   a. [ ] There are no minor children.
   b. [X] The minor children are:

Child's name	Birthdate	Age	Sex
ROBERT J. DOE	7-25-87	5 YRS. 7 MOS.	M
JUANITA J. DOE	3-1-89	3 YRS. 11 MOS.	F

   c. IF THERE ARE MINOR CHILDREN, COMPLETE EITHER (1) OR (2)
   (1) [X] Each child named in 3b is presently living with [X] petitioner [ ] respondent in the following county *(specify)*: LOS ANGELES COUNTY and during the last five years has lived in no state other than California and with no person other than petitioner or respondent or both. Respondent has not participated in any capacity in any litigation or proceeding in any state concerning custody of any minor child of this marriage. Respondent has no information of any pending custody proceeding or of any person not a party to this proceeding who has physical custody or claims to have custody or visitation rights concerning any minor child of this marriage.
   (2) [ ] A completed Declaration Under Uniform Custody of Minors Act is attached.

4. [X] **Respondent requests** confirmation as separate assets and obligations the items listed
   [X] in Attachment 4   [ ] below:
      Item   Confirm to

(Continued on reverse)

Form Adopted by Rule 1282
Judicial Council of California
1282 [Rev. January 1, 1993]

RESPONSE
(Family Law)

Civil Code, § 4355
Cal. Rules of Court, rule 1215

RESPONSE TO PETITION FOR DISSOLUTION OF MARRIAGE
Page Two (Back) of the Response
An example when without children, property or debts

MARRIAGE OF *(last name, first name of parties)*: DOE, JANE AND JOHN

CASE NUMBER: (SUPPLIED BY COURT)

5. DECLARATION REGARDING COMMUNITY AND QUASI-COMMUNITY ASSETS AND OBLIGATIONS AS PRESENTLY KNOWN
   a. [X] There are no such assets or obligations subject to disposition by the court in this proceeding.
   b. [ ] All such assets and obligations have been disposed of by written agreement.
   c. [ ] All such assets and obligations are listed [ ] in Attachment 5 [ ] below:

6. [ ] Respondent contends there is a reasonable possibility of reconciliation.

7. [ ] Respondent denies the grounds set forth in item 6 of the petition.

8. [X] Respondent requests
   a. [X] Dissolution of the marriage based on
      (1) [X] irreconcilable differences. CC 4506(1)
      (2) [ ] incurable insanity. CC 4506(2)
   b. [ ] Legal separation of the parties based on
      (1) [ ] irreconcilable differences. CC 4506(1)
      (2) [ ] incurable insanity. CC 4506(2)
   c. [ ] Nullity of void marriage based on
      (1) [ ] incestuous marriage. CC 4400
      (2) [ ] bigamous marriage. CC 4401
   d. [ ] Nullity of voidable marriage based on
      (1) [ ] respondent's age at time of marriage CC 4425(a)
      (2) [ ] prior existing marriage. CC 4425(b)
      (3) [ ] unsound mind. CC 4425(c)
      (4) [ ] fraud. CC 4425(d)
      (5) [ ] force. CC 4425(e)
      (6) [ ] physical incapacity. CC 4425(f)

9. Respondent requests the court grant the above relief and make injunctive (including restraining) and other orders as follows:

	Petitioner	Respondent	Joint	Other
a. Legal custody of children to	[ ]	[ ]	[ ]	[ ]
b. Physical custody of children to	[ ]	[ ]	[ ]	[ ]
c. Child visitation be granted to	[ ]	[ ]	[ ]	[ ]
[ ] supervised as to *(specify)*:				
d. Spousal support payable by (wage assignment will be issued)	[ ]	[ ]		
e. Attorney fees and costs payable by	[ ]	[ ]		

   f. [X] Terminate the court's jurisdiction (ability) to award spousal support to petitioner.
   g. [ ] Property rights be determined.
   h. [ ] Wife's former name be restored *(specify)*:
   i. [ ] Other *(specify)*:

10. If there are minor children of this marriage, the court will make orders for the support of the children without further notice to either party. A wage assignment order will be issued.

I declare under penalty of perjury under the laws of the State of California that the foregoing is true and correct.

Date: MARCH 1, 1993

▶ *John J. Doe*
(SIGNATURE OF RESPONDENT)

▶ _____
(TYPE OR PRINT NAME OF ATTORNEY)   (SIGNATURE OF ATTORNEY FOR RESPONDENT)

The original response must be filed in the court with proof of service of a copy on petitioner.

1282 [Rev. January 1, 1993]

RESPONSE
(Family Law)

Page two

RESPONSE TO PETITION FOR DISSOLUTION OF MARRIAGE
Page Two (Back) of the Response
An example when with children, property and debts

MARRIAGE OF (last name, first name of parties): DOE, JAME AND JOHN	CASE NUMBER: (SUPPLIED BY COURT)

5. DECLARATION REGARDING COMMUNITY AND QUASI-COMMUNITY ASSETS AND OBLIGATIONS AS PRESENTLY KNOWN
   a. [ ] There are no such assets or obligations subject to disposition by the court in this proceeding.
   b. [ ] All such assets and obligations have been disposed of by written agreement.
   c. [X] All such assets and obligations are listed [X] in Attachment 5 [ ] below:

6. [ ] Respondent contends there is a reasonable possibility of reconciliation.

7. [ ] Respondent denies the grounds set forth in item 6 of the petition.

8. [X] Respondent requests
   a. [X] Dissolution of the marriage based on
      (1) [X] irreconcilable differences. CC 4506(1)
      (2) [ ] incurable insanity. CC 4506(2)
   b. [ ] Legal separation of the parties based on
      (1) [ ] irreconcilable differences. CC 4506(1)
      (2) [ ] incurable insanity. CC 4506(2)
   c. [ ] Nullity of void marriage based on
      (1) [ ] incestuous marriage. CC 4400
      (2) [ ] bigamous marriage. CC 4401
   d. [ ] Nullity of voidable marriage based on
      (1) [ ] respondent's age at time of marriage CC 4425(a)
      (2) [ ] prior existing marriage. CC 4425(b)
      (3) [ ] unsound mind. CC 4425(c)
      (4) [ ] fraud. CC 4425(d)
      (5) [ ] force. CC 4425(e)
      (6) [ ] physical incapacity. CC 4425(f)

9. Respondent requests the court grant the above relief and make injunctive (including restraining) and other orders as follows:

	Petitioner	Respondent	Joint	Other
a. Legal custody of children to	[ ]	[ ]	[X]	[ ]
b. Physical custody of children to	[ ]	[ ]	[X]	[ ]
c. Child visitation be granted to	[ ]	[ ]	[X]	[ ]

   [ ] supervised as to (specify):
   d. Spousal support payable by (wage assignment will be issued) [ ] [ ]
   e. Attorney fees and costs payable by [ ] [ ]
   f. [ ] Terminate the court's jurisdiction (ability) to award spousal support to petitioner.
   g. [X] Property rights be determined.
   h. [ ] Wife's former name be restored (specify):
   i. [ ] Other (specify):

10. If there are minor children of this marriage, the court will make orders for the support of the children without further notice to either party. A wage assignment order will be issued.

I declare under penalty of perjury under the laws of the State of California that the foregoing is true and correct.

Date: MARCH 1, 1993

▶ _(signature)_ (SIGNATURE OF RESPONDENT)

▶ _____
(TYPE OR PRINT NAME OF ATTORNEY)   (SIGNATURE OF ATTORNEY FOR RESPONDENT)

The original response must be filed in the court with proof of service of a copy on petitioner.

1282 (Rev. January 1, 1993) **RESPONSE** (Family Law) Page two

NOTICE AND ACKNOWLEDGMENT OF RECEIPT

An example when respondent acknowledges receipt of the Summons and other included papers

---

NAME AND ADDRESS OF **SENDER**:	TELEPHONE NO.:	For Court Use Only:
JANE J. DOE 123 ANY STREET LOS ANGELES, CA 90000 In propria persona	213-000-0000	

Insert name of court, judicial district or branch court, if any, and Post Office and Street Address:

LOS ANGELES COUNTY SUPERIOR COURT
111 N. HILL STREET
LOS ANGELES, CA 90012

PLAINTIFF:
JANE JUANITA DOE

DEFENDANT:
JOHN JAMES DOE

NOTICE AND ACKNOWLEDGMENT OF RECEIPT	Case Number: (SUPPLIED BY COURT)

TO: JOHN JAMES DOE
   (Insert name of individual being served)

This summons and other document(s) indicated below are being served pursuant to Section 415.30 of the California Code of Civil Procedure. Your failure to complete this form and return it to me within 20 days may subject you (or the party on whose behalf you are being served) to liability for the payment of any expenses incurred in serving a summons on you in any other manner permitted by law.

If you are being served on behalf of a corporation, unincorporated association (including a partnership), or other entity, this form must be signed by you in the name of such entity or by a person authorized to receive service of process on behalf of such entity. In all other cases, this form must be signed by you personally or by a person authorized by you to acknowledge receipt of summons. Section 415.30 provides that this summons and other document(s) are deemed served on the date you sign the Acknowledgment of Receipt below, if you return this form to me.

Dated: FEBRUARY 15, 1993   *William P. Right*
                                            (Signature of sender)

ACKNOWLEDGMENT OF RECEIPT

This acknowledges receipt of: (To be completed by sender before mailing)
1. ☐ A copy of the summons and of the complaint.
2. ☒ A copy of the summons and of the Petition (Marriage) and:
   - ☒ Blank Confidential Counseling Statement (Marriage)
   - ☐ Order to Show Cause (Marriage)
   - ☒ Blank Responsive Declaration
   - ☒ Blank Financial Declaration
   - ☐ Other: (Specify)

(To be completed by recipient)

Date of receipt: FEBRUARY 15, 1993   *John J. Doe*
                                                  (Signature of person acknowledging receipt, with title if
                                                  acknowledgment is made on behalf of another person)

Date this form is signed: FEBRUARY 15, 1993   JohN J. DoE
                                                  (Type or print your name and name of entity, if any,
                                                  on whose behalf this form is signed)

Form Approved by the
Judicial Council of California
Revised Effective January 1, 1975

NOTICE AND ACKNOWLEDGMENT OF RECEIPT

CCP 415.30, 417.10;
Cal. Rules of Court,
Rule 1216

APPEARANCE, STIPULATION AND WAIVER

An example when respondent appears, stipulates to an uncontested action and a Marital Settlement Agreement is filed in the action

---

ATTORNEY OR PARTY WITHOUT ATTORNEY (NAME AND ADDRESS):	TELEPHONE NO.:	FOR COURT USE ONLY
JANE J. DOE 123 ANY STREET LOS ANGELES, CA 92000	213-000-0000	
ATTORNEY FOR (NAME): In propria persona		

SUPERIOR COURT OF CALIFORNIA, COUNTY OF LOS ANGELES
STREET ADDRESS: 111 N. HILL STREET
MAILING ADDRESS:
CITY AND ZIP CODE: LOS ANGELES, CA 90012
BRANCH NAME:

MARRIAGE OF
PETITIONER: JANE JUANITA DOE

RESPONDENT: JOHN JAMES DOE

APPEARANCE, STIPULATION AND WAIVERS	CASE NUMBER: TO BE SUPPLIED BY COURT

1. [X] Respondent makes a general appearance.
2. [ ] Respondent has previously made a general appearance.
3. [ ] Respondent is a member of the military services of the United States of America and waives all rights under the Soldiers and Sailors Civil Relief Act of 1940, as amended, and does not contest this proceeding.
4. [X] The parties stipulate that this cause may be tried as an uncontested matter.
5. [ ] The parties waive their rights to notice of trial, findings of fact and conclusions of law, motion for new trial, and the right to appeal.
6. [X] This matter may be tried by a commissioner sitting as a temporary judge.
7. [X] A written settlement agreement has been entered into between the parties.
8. [ ] A stipulation for judgment will be submitted to the court at the uncontested proceeding.
9. [ ] None of these stipulations or waivers shall apply unless the court approves the written settlement agreement or stipulation for judgment.
10. [X] Respondent waives the issuance and service of summons, and further, acknowledge and stipulate to the restrictive conditions and conduct directed in the "Standard Family Law Restraining Order," as included on the back of the Summons approved 1990 by the Judicial Council of California.

11. Total number of boxes checked (specify): 5

Dated: MARCH 1, 1993   *Jane J. Doe*
                                (Signature of Petitioner)

Dated: MARCH 1, 1993   *John J. Doe*
                                (Signature of Respondent)

Dated: ....

_____   _____
(Type or print name)   (Signature of Attorney for Petitioner)

Dated: ....

_____   _____
(Type or print name)   (Signature of Attorney for Respondent)

Form Approved by Rule 1282.50
Judicial Council of California
Effective January 1, 1980

**APPEARANCE, STIPULATION AND WAIVERS
(FAMILY LAW)**

APPEARANCE, STIPULATION AND WAIVER

An example when respondent is in military service

ATTORNEY OR PARTY WITHOUT ATTORNEY (NAME AND ADDRESS): JANE J. DOE 123 ANY STREET LOS ANGELES, CA 92000	TELEPHONE NO.: 213-000-0000	FOR COURT USE ONLY
ATTORNEY FOR (NAME): In propria persona		
SUPERIOR COURT OF CALIFORNIA, COUNTY OF LOS ANGELES STREET ADDRESS: 111 N. HILL STREET MAILING ADDRESS: CITY AND ZIP CODE: LOS ANGELES, CA 90012 BRANCH NAME:		
MARRIAGE OF PETITIONER: JANE JUANITA DOE RESPONDENT: JOHN JAMES DOE		
APPEARANCE, STIPULATION AND WAIVERS		CASE NUMBER: (TO BE SUPPLIED BY COURT)

1. ☐ Respondent makes a general appearance.
2. ☐ Respondent has previously made a general appearance.
3. ☒ Respondent is a member of the military services of the United States of America and waives all rights under the Soldiers and Sailors Civil Relief Act of 1940, as amended, and does not contest this proceeding.
4. ☐ The parties stipulate that this cause may be tried as an uncontested matter.
5. ☐ The parties waive their rights to notice of trial, findings of fact and conclusions of law, motion for new trial, and the right to appeal.
6. ☐ This matter may be tried by a commissioner sitting as a temporary judge.
7. ☐ A written settlement agreement has been entered into between the parties.
8. ☐ A stipulation for judgment will be submitted to the court at the uncontested proceeding.
9. ☐ None of these stipulations or waivers shall apply unless the court approves the written settlement agreement or stipulation for judgment.
10. ☐ Respondent waives the issuance and service of summons, and further, acknowledge and stipulate to the restrictive conditions and conduct directed in the "Standard Family Law Restraining Order," as included on the back of the Summons approved 1990 by the Judicial Council of California.

11. Total number of boxes checked (specify):   **1**

Dated: MARCH 1, 1993   *(Signature of Petitioner)*

Dated: MARCH 1, 1993   *(Signature of Respondent)*

Dated: _____

_____   _____
(Type or print name)   (Signature of Attorney for Petitioner)

Dated: _____

_____   _____
(Type or print name)   (Signature of Attorney for Respondent)

Form Approved by Rule 1282.50
Judicial Council of California
Effective January 1, 1980

**APPEARANCE, STIPULATION AND WAIVERS
(FAMILY LAW)**

APPLICATION FOR EXPEDITED CHILD SUPPORT ORDER
Page One (Front) of the Application
An example of an Application requesting an immediate child support order

---

ATTORNEY OR PARTY WITHOUT ATTORNEY (Name and Address):	TELEPHONE NO.:	FOR COURT USE ONLY
JANE JUANITA DOE 123 ANY STREET LOS ANGELES, CA 92000 In propria persona	213-000-0000	

SUPERIOR COURT OF CALIFORNIA, COUNTY OF LOS ANGELES
STREET ADDRESS: 111 N. HILL STREET
MAILING ADDRESS:
CITY AND ZIP CODE: LOS ANGELES, CA 90012
BRANCH NAME:

PETITIONER/PLAINTIFF: JANE JUANITA DOE

RESPONDENT/DEFENDANT: JOHN JAMES DOE

APPLICATION FOR EXPEDITED CHILD SUPPORT ORDER [Civil Code, § 4357.5]	CASE NUMBER: (SUPPLIED BY COURT)

Notice to applicant: This form must be served before it is filed with the court.

To (name): JOHN JAMES DOE

1. I am requesting the court to order you to pay child support in the sum of: $ **508.00** per month until trial of this action. (See item 2 of the proposed EXPEDITED CHILD SUPPORT ORDER attached to this form.) Attached is a completed Income and Expense Declaration for each parent and a worksheet showing the basis for the support.

2. I [ ] am receiving [X] am not receiving [ ] intend to apply for public assistance for the child or children listed in the proposed order.

I declare under penalty of perjury under the laws of the State of California that the foregoing is true and correct.

Date: FERUARY 1, 1993

JANE JUANITA DOE .... ▶ /s/ Jane J. Doe
(TYPE OR PRINT NAME)   (SIGNATURE)

IF YOU DO NOT WANT TO PAY THE AMOUNT OF CHILD SUPPORT ASKED FOR, YOU MUST FILE A WRITTEN RESPONSE WITHIN 30 DAYS AND ASK FOR A COURT HEARING. The necessary forms (three blank copies of the Response to Application for Expedited Child Support Order and Notice of Hearing, and three blank copies of the Income and Expense Declaration) are attached. You do not have to pay any fee for filing the Response.

Contact the clerk's office by telephone or in person and ask for a date for a hearing. The hearing date must be at least 20 days and not more than 30 days after you file the Response to Application for Expedited Child Support Order. Complete and file the Response after serving a copy on the other parent. You must have someone over 18 years old, other than you, serve the forms. Have that person mail the papers to the address of the other parent or attorney for the other parent as shown on the top of the Application, or have that person personally give the papers to the other parent or attorney for the other parent. See the back of the Response for details. Have the person serving the Response complete and sign the Proof of Service on the back of the Response.

If you have this matter set for hearing, you must bring a copy of your most recent state income tax return (whether individual or joint) to the hearing. You may examine the other parent's tax return and ask questions about it. The other parent may examine your tax return and ask questions about it. If you cannot find a copy of your tax return you must ask for a copy from the State Franchise Tax Board, Data Storage, c/o R.I.D. Unit, Sacramento, CA 95867.

Tell them your name, the year of the return, your social security number, and the address to which they should mail the return. Sign the letter in the same way as you signed your tax return. Make a copy of the letter before you mail the original and bring it to the hearing.

If you have not filed a tax return for the last three years, you do not need to bring any return.

- IMPORTANT WARNING -
Unless you file a written response **within 30 calendar days** from the date this form is served on you, and ask the court for a hearing, you will be ordered to pay child support in the amount shown.

(Proof of service on reverse)

Form Adopted by Rule 1297
Judicial Council of California
1297 (New January 1, 1986)

APPLICATION FOR EXPEDITED
CHILD SUPPORT ORDER
[Civil Code, § 4357.5]
(Family Law)

PROOF OF SERVICE OF APPLICATION FOR EXPEDITED CHILD SUPPORT ORDER
Page Two (Back) of the Application
An example of the Proof of Service of the Application

PETITIONER/PLAINTIFF: JANE JUANITA DOE

RESPONDENT/DEFENDANT: JOHN JAMES DOE

CASE NUMBER:
(SUPPLIED BY COURT)

PROOF OF SERVICE — APPLICATION FOR EXPEDITED CHILD SUPPORT ORDER

1. I served the
   a. Application for Expedited Child Support Order, proposed Expedited Child Support Order, a completed Income and Expense Declaration for both parents, a worksheet setting forth the basis of the amount of support requested, three blank copies of the Income and Expense Declaration, and three blank copies of the Response to Application for Expedited Child Support Order and Notice of Hearing.

   b. on [ ] petitioner/plaintiff [X] respondent/defendant

   c. by serving [ ] petitioner/plaintiff [X] respondent/defendant
      [ ] other (name and title or relationship to person served):

   d. [X] by delivery [X] at home [ ] at business
      (1) date: FEBRUARY 10, 1993
      (2) time: 2:50 p.m.
      (3) address: 321 ANY STREET
                   SAN DIEGO, CA 91000

   e. [ ] by mailing
      (1) date:
      (2) place:

2. Manner of service (check proper box):
   a. [X] **Personal service.** By personally delivering copies. (CCP 415.10)
   b. [ ] **Substituted service on natural person.** By leaving copies at the dwelling house, usual place of abode, or usual place of business of the person served in the presence of a competent member of the household or a person apparently in charge of the office or place of business, at least 18 years of age, who was informed of the general nature of the papers, and thereafter mailing (by first-class mail, postage prepaid) copies to the person served at the place where the copies were left. (CCP 415.20(b)) *(Attach separate declaration or affidavit stating acts relied on to establish reasonable diligence in first attempting personal service.)*
   c. [ ] **Mail and acknowledgment service.** By mailing (by first-class mail or airmail, postage prepaid) copies to the person served, together with two copies of the form of notice and acknowledgment and a return envelope, postage prepaid, addressed to the sender. (CCP 415.30) *(Attach completed acknowledgment of receipt.)*
   d. [ ] **Certified or registered mail service.** By mailing to an address outside California (by first-class mail, postage prepaid, requiring a return receipt) copies to the person served. (CCP 415.40) *(Attach signed return receipt or other evidence of actual delivery to the person served.)*

3. At the time of service I was at least 18 years of age and not a party to this action.
4. Fee for service: $ 0.00
5. Person serving:
   a. [ ] California sheriff, marshal, or constable.
   b. [ ] Registered California process server.
   c. [ ] Employee or independent contractor of a registered California process server.
   d. [X] Not a registered California process server.
   e. [ ] Exempt from registration under Bus. & Prof. Code 22350(b).

   f. Name, address, and telephone number and, if applicable, county of registration and number:
      WILLIAM P. RITZ
      789 WHY STREET
      PASADENA, CA 92000
      NO PHONE

I declare under penalty of perjury under the laws of the State of California that the foregoing is true and correct.

(For California sheriff, marshal, or constable use only)
I certify that the foregoing is true and correct.

Date: FEBRUARY 10, 1993

▶ *William P. Ritz*
(SIGNATURE)

Date:

▶ _____
(SIGNATURE)

1297 [New January 1, 1986]

APPLICATION FOR EXPEDITED CHILD SUPPORT ORDER
[Civil Code, § 4357.5]
(Family Law)

Page two

RESPONSE TO APPLICATION FOR EXPEDITED CHILD SUPPORT ORDER
Page One (Front) of the Response
An example of the Response to Application For Expedited Child support Order

---

ATTORNEY OR PARTY WITHOUT ATTORNEY (Name and Address):	TELEPHONE NO.	FOR COURT USE ONLY
JANE JUANITA DOE 123 ANY STREET LOS ANGELES, CA 92000	213-000-0000	

ATTORNEY FOR (Name): In propria persona

SUPERIOR COURT OF CALIFORNIA, COUNTY OF LOS ANGELES
STREET ADDRESS: 111 N. HILL STREET
MAILING ADDRESS:
CITY AND ZIP CODE: LOS ANGELES, CA 90012
BRANCH NAME:

PETITIONER/PLAINTIFF: JANE JUANITA DOE

RESPONDENT/DEFENDANT: JOHN JAMES DOE

RESPONSE TO APPLICATION FOR EXPEDITED CHILD SUPPORT ORDER AND NOTICE OF HEARING [Civil Code, § 4357.5]	CASE NUMBER: (SUPPLIED BY COURT)

NOTE: THIS FORM NEED ONLY TO BE FILED IF RESPONDENT OPPOSES THE APPLICATION FOR EXPEDITED CHILD SUPPORT

To (name): JANE JUANITA DOE

1. I object to the proposed expedited child support order for the following reasons (check one or more):
   a. [ ] I am not the parent of the child or children involved in this action.
   b. [X] My income is incorrectly stated in the application.
   c. [ ] The other parent's income is incorrectly stated in the application.
   d. [ ] I am entitled to hardship deductions as shown in the attached Income and Expense Declaration.
   e. [ ] The other parent is not entitled to hardship deductions claimed in the application.
   f. [ ] The amount of support is incorrectly computed.
   g. [ ] other (specify):

2. I have attached a completed copy of my Income and Expense Declaration.

3. At my request, the court has set a hearing on the application as follows:
   a. date: time: in [ ] dept.:   [ ] rm.:
   b. The address of court [ ] is shown above [ ] is:

I declare under penalty of perjury under the laws of the State of California that the foregoing is true and correct.

Date: FEBRUARY 15, 1993

JOHN JAMES DOE _____ ▶ _John J. Doe_____
(TYPE OR PRINT NAME)   (SIGNATURE)

You must bring a copy of your most recent state income tax return (whether individual or joint) to the hearing or declare at the hearing that it doesn't exist or that you don't have it and have requested it from the Franchise Tax Board. Otherwise the court may grant the other party's request.

(Proof of service on reverse)

Form Adopted by Rule 1297.10
Judicial Council of California
1297.10 [New January 1, 1986]

RESPONSE TO APPLICATION FOR EXPEDITED CHILD SUPPORT
ORDER AND NOTICE OF HEARING
[Civil Code, § 4357.5]
(Family Law)

PROOF OF SERVICE OF RESPONSE TO APPLICATION FOR EXPEDITED CHILD SUPPORT ORDER
Page Two (Back) of the Response

An example of the Proof of Service of the Response to Application For Expedited Child support Order

---

PLAINTIFF/PETITIONER (name): JANE JUANITA DOE	CASE NUMBER:
DEFENDANT/RESPONDENT (name): JOHN JAMES DOE	(SUPPLIED BY COURT)

PROOF OF SERVICE BY [X] PERSONAL SERVICE [ ] MAIL

> Service of the response on the other party may be made by anyone at least 18 years of age EXCEPT you. Service is made in one of the following ways:
> (1) Personally delivering it to the attorney for the other party or, if no attorney, to the other party.
> **OR**
> (2) Mailing it, postage prepaid, to the last known address of the attorney for the other party or, if no attorney, to the other party.
> Anyone at least 18 years of age **EXCEPT ANY PARTY** may personally serve or mail the response. Be sure whoever served the response fills out and signs this proof of service. File this proof of service with the court as soon as the response is served.

1. At the time of service I was at least 18 years of age and **not a party to this legal action**.

2. I served a copy of the Response to Application for Expedited Child Support Order and Notice of Hearing as follows (check either a or b below):

   a. [X] **Personal service.** I personally delivered the response as follows:
      (1) Name of person served: JANE JUANITA DOE
      (2) Address where served: 123 ANY STREET
          LOS ANGELES, CA 92000

      (3) Date served: FEBRUARY 15, 1993
      (4) Time served: 4:10 p.m.

   b. [ ] **Mail.** I deposited the response in the United States mail, in a sealed envelope with postage fully prepaid. The envelope was addressed as follows:
      (1) Name of person served:
      (2) Address:

      (3) Date of mailing:
      (4) Place of mailing (city and state):
      (5) I am a resident of or employed in the county where the response was mailed.

   c. My residence or business address is (specify): 890 BEACON STREET
      SAN DIEGO, CA 91000

   d. My phone number is (specify): 619-555-0000

   I declare under penalty of perjury under the laws of the State of California that the foregoing is true and correct.

Date: FEBRUARY 15, 1993

ROBERT STILES   *Robert Stiles*
(TYPE OR PRINT NAME OF PERSON WHO SERVED THE RESPONSE)   (SIGNATURE OF PERSON WHO SERVED THE RESPONSE)

1297.10 (New January 1, 1986)

RESPONSE TO APPLICATION FOR EXPEDITED CHILD SUPPORT ORDER AND NOTICE OF HEARING
[Civil Code, § 4357.5]
(Family Law)

Page two

EXPEDITED CHILD SUPPORT ORDER

An example of the Order granting the Application for expedited child support

---

ATTORNEY OR PARTY WITHOUT ATTORNEY *(Name and Address)*: JANE J. DOE 123 ANY STREET LOS ANGELES, CA 92000 ATTORNEY FOR *(Name)*: In propria persona	TELEPHONE NO.: 213-000-0000	FOR COURT USE ONLY

SUPERIOR COURT OF CALIFORNIA, COUNTY OF LOS ANGELES

PETITIONER/PLAINTIFF: JANE JUANITA DOE

RESPONDENT/DEFENDANT: JOHN JAMES DOE

EXPEDITED CHILD SUPPORT ORDER [Civil Code, § 4357.5] ☐ Proposed	CASE NUMBER (SUPPLIED BY COURT)

THE COURT FINDS No Response to Application for Expedited Child Support Order has been filed and 30 days have elapsed since service of the application on the other parent on *(date)*: February 10, 1993

THE COURT ORDERS Pending trial or until further order of this court

1. Existing orders shall continue in effect, except as modified by this order.

2. Support of the minor children of the parties is fixed as follows beginning on *(date)*:

Child's name	Monthly amount	Payable by	Payable to	Payable on (dates)
ROBERT J. DOE	$254.00	JOHN J. DOE	JANE J. DOE	FIRST DAY OF MONTH
JUANITA J. DOE	$254.00	JOHN J. DOE	JANE J. DOE	FIRST DAY OF MONTH

3. ☐ The monthly deductions allowed for extreme financial hardship total: $

4. ☐ The hardship deduction is allowed for the period beginning *(date)*:   and ending *(date)*:

5. ☐ The payments for monthly child support shall change as follows beginning on *(date)*:

Child's name	Monthly amount	Payable by	Payable to	Payable on (dates)

6. Child support payments shall continue until further order of the court, or until the child marries, dies, is emancipated, reaches age 19, or reaches age 18 and is not a full-time high school student residing with a parent, whichever occurs first.

Date: [DATE SIGNED BY JUDGE]

_____
JUDGE OF THE SUPERIOR COURT

— NOTICE —

AN ASSIGNMENT OF YOUR WAGES WILL BE OBTAINED WITHOUT FURTHER NOTICE TO YOU IF YOU FAIL TO PAY ANY COURT-ORDERED CHILD SUPPORT OR IF REQUESTED BY THE DISTRICT ATTORNEY.

THIS ORDER IS ENFORCEABLE AS SOON AS IT HAS BEEN SIGNED BY A JUDGE.

Form Adopted by Rule 1297.20
Judicial Council of California
1297.20 (New January 1, 1986)

EXPEDITED CHILD SUPPORT ORDER
[Civil Code, § 4357.5]
(Family Law)

CONFIDENTIAL COUNSELING STATEMENT

An example of the Respondent's Confidential Counseling Statement

Name, Address and Telephone No. of Attorney(s)

Space Below for Use of Court Clerk Only

Attorney(s) for ....

SUPERIOR COURT OF CALIFORNIA, COUNTY OF LOS ANGELES

In re the marriage of

Petitioner: JANE JUANITA DOE

and

Respondent: JOHN JAMES DOE

CASE NUMBER
(SUPPLIED BY COURT)
[X] Petitioner's [ ] Respondent's

CONFIDENTIAL COUNSELING STATEMENT (MARRIAGE)

I understand that conciliation services are available to me through the court in this county.

[ ] I would like marriage counseling.

[ ] I would like to talk with a trained person about my present family situation.

[X] I do not desire counseling at this time.

Mailing address of requesting party:

Name: JANE JUANITA DOE

Street: 123 ANY STREET

City/State/Zip: LOS ANGELES, CA 92000

Mailing address of other party:

Name: JOHN JAMES DOE

Street: 321 ANY STREET

City/State/Zip: SAN DIEGO, CA 91000

Date: FEBRUARY 1, 1993

John J Doe
(Signature)

Form Adopted by Rule 1284 of The Judicial Council of California Effective January 1, 1975

CONFIDENTIAL COUNSELING STATEMENT (MARRIAGE)

INCOME AND EXPENSE DECLARATION
Page One of the Income and Expense Declaration
An example of Page 1 of the Income And Expense Declaration

ATTORNEY OR PARTY WITHOUT ATTORNEY *(Name and Address)*: JANE J. DOE, 123 ANY STREET, LOS ANGELES, CA 92000	TELEPHONE NO.: 213-000-0000	FOR COURT USE ONLY

ATTORNEY FOR *(Name)*: In propria persona

SUPERIOR COURT OF CALIFORNIA, COUNTY OF LOS ANGELES
STREET ADDRESS: 111 N. HILL STREET
MAILING ADDRESS:
CITY AND ZIP CODE: LOS ANGELES, CA 90012
BRANCH NAME:

PETITIONER/PLAINTIFF: JANE JUANITA DOE

RESPONDENT/DEFENDANT: JOHN JAMES DOE

INCOME AND EXPENSE DECLARATION	CASE NUMBER: (SUPPLIED BY COURT)

Step 1 Attachments to this summary
I have completed [X] Income [X] Expense [X] Child Support Information forms.
(If child support is not an issue, do not complete the Child Suport Information Form. If your only income is AFDC, do not complete the Income Information Form.)

Step 2 Answer all questions that apply to you
1. Are you receiving or have you applied for or do you intend to apply for welfare or AFDC?
   [ ] Receiving [ ] Applied for [ ] Intend to apply for [X] No
2. What is your date of birth *(month/day/year)*? 3-7-62
3. What is your occupation? SECRETARY
4. Highest year of education completed: 2 YEARS COLLEGE, ASSOCIATE DEGREE
5. Are you presently employed? [X] Yes [ ] No
   a. If yes: (1) Where do you work? *(name and address)*: BIG COMMUNICATIONS, 5555 LARGESS RD, LOS ANGELES, CA 91000
   (2) When did you start work there *(month/year)*? 6/90
   b. If no: (1) When did you last work *(month/year)*? .....
   (2) What were your gross monthly earnings? .....
6. What is your social security number: 431-00-0000
7. What is the total number of minor children you are legally obligated to support? 2

Step 3 Monthly income information
8. Net monthly disposable income *(from line 16a of Income Information)*: $1,401.95
9. Current net monthly disposable income *(if different from line 8, explain below or on Attachment 9)*: $1,401.95

Step 4 Expense information
10. Total monthly expenses from line 2e of Expense Information: ..... $ 575.00
11. Total monthly expenses from line 3m of Expense Information *(if completed)*: ..... $ 625.00
12. Amount of these expenses paid by others: ..... $ -0-

Step 5 Other party's income
13. My estimate of the other party's gross monthly income is: $2,700.00

Step 6 Date and sign this form
I declare under penalty of perjury under the laws of the State of California that the foregoing and the attached information forms are true and correct.

Date:

JANE JUANITA DOE, In pro per
(TYPE OR PRINT NAME OF DECLARANT)

▶ *Jane J Doe*
(SIGNATURE OF DECLARANT)

[X] Petitioner [ ] Respondent

Page one of 4

Form Adopted by Rule 1285.50
Judicial Council of California
1285.50 (Rev. January 1, 1993)

INCOME AND EXPENSE DECLARATION
(Family Law)

Civil Code, § 4721

INCOME INFORMATION
Page Two of the Income and Expense Declaration
An example of Page 2 of the Income And Expense Declaration with the Income information

PETITIONER/PLAINTIFF:	JANE JUANITA DOE	CASE NUMBER:
RESPONDENT/DEFENDANT:	JOHN JAMES DOE	(SUPPLIED BY COURT)
INCOME INFORMATION OF (name):	JANE JUANITA DOE	

1. Total gross salary or wages, including commissions, bonuses, and overtime paid during the last 12 months: 1. $ 20,400.00
2. All other money received during the last 12 months **except welfare, AFDC, SSI, spousal support from this marriage, or any child support.** *Specify sources below:*
   Include pensions, social security, disability, unemployment, military basic allowance for quarters (BAQ), spousal support from a different marriage, dividends, interest or royalty, trust income, and annuities.
   Include income from a business, rental properties, and reimbursement of job-related expenses.
   ▶ Prepare and attach a schedule showing gross receipts less cash expenses for each business or rental property.
   - 2a. $ -0-
   - 2b. $ -0-
   - 2c. $ -0-
   - 2d. $ -0-
3. Add lines 1 through 2d   3. $ 20,400.00
   Divide line 3 by 12 and place result on line 4a.

	Average last 12 months:	Last month:
4. Gross income	4a. $ 1,700.00	4b. $ 1,700.00
5. State income tax	5a. $ 28.00	5b. $ 28.00
6. Federal income tax	6a. $ 75.00	6b. $ 75.00
7. Social Security and Hospital Tax ("FICA" and "MEDI") or self-employment tax, or the amount used to secure retirement or disability benefits	7a. $ 130.05	7b. $ 130.05
8. Health insurance for you and any children you are required to support	8a. $ 65.00	8b. $ 65.00
9. State disability insurance	9a. $ -0-	9b. $ -0-
10. Mandatory union dues	10a. $ -0-	10b. $ -0-
11. Mandatory retirement and pension fund contributions. *Do not include any deduction claimed in item 7.*	11a. $	11b. $
12. Court-ordered child support, court-ordered spousal support, and voluntarily paid child support in an amount not more than the guideline amount, **actually being paid for a relationship *other* than that involved in this proceeding:**	12a. $ -0-	12b. $ -0-
13. Necessary job-related expenses *(attach explanation)*	13a. $ -0-	13b. $ -0-
14. Hardship deduction (Line 4d on Child Support Information Form)	14a. $	14b. $
15. Add lines 5 through 14. Total monthly deductions:	15a. $ 298.05	15b. $ 298.05
16. Subtract line 15 from line 4. Net monthly disposable income:	16a. $ 1,401.95	16b. $ 1,401.95

17. AFDC, welfare, spousal support from this marriage, and child support from other relationships received each month: 17. $ -0-
18. Cash and checking accounts: 18. $ 1,500.00
19. Savings, credit union, certificates of deposit, and money market accounts: 19. $ 2,000.00
20. Stocks, bonds, and other liquid assets: LIFE INSURANCE CASH VALUE   20. $ 5,000.00
21. All other property, real or personal *(specify below)*:   21. $ 21,000.00

▶ **Attach a copy of your three most recent pay stubs.**   Page 2 of 4

Form Adopted by Rule 1285.50a
Judicial Council of California
1285.50a (Rev. January 1, 1993)

INCOME INFORMATION
(Family Law)

Civil Code, § 4721

EXPENSE INFORMATION
Page Three of the Income and Expense Declaration
An example of Page 3 of the Income And Expense Declaration
with the Expense information

PETITIONER/PLAINTIFF:	JANE J. DOE	CASE NUMBER:
RESPONDENT/DEFENDANT:	JOHN JAMES DOE	(SUPPLIED BY COURT)
EXPENSE INFORMATION OF (name):	JANE J. DOE	

1. a. List all persons living in your home **whose expenses are included below** and their income:
   ☐ Continued on Attachment 1a.

name	age	relationship	gross monthly income
1. JANE J. DOE	30	MOTHER	$1,700.00
2. ROBERT J. DOE	5	SON	-0-
3. JUANITA J. DOE	3	DAUGHTER	-0-
4.			

   b. List all other persons living in your home and their income:
   ☐ Continued on Attachment 1b.

MONTHLY EXPENSES

2. *Required to be listed in all cases*
   a. Residence payments
      (1) [X] Rent or ☐ mortgage ......$ 300.00
      (2) Taxes ......$ 25.00
      (3) Insurance ......$ -0-
      (4) Maintenance ......$
   b. Unreimbursed medical and dental expenses ......$ 50.00
   c. Child care ......$ 200.00
   d. Children's education ......$ -0-
   e. TOTAL ITEM 2 EXPENSES ......$ 575.00

3. *Required for spousal support or special needs*
   a. Food at home and household supplies ......$ 200.00
   b. Food eating out ......$ -0-
   c. Utilities ......$ 75.00
   d. Telephone ......$ 25.00
   e. Laundry and cleaning ......$ 25.00
   f. Clothing ......$ 25.00
   g. Insurance *(life, accident, etc. Do not include auto, home, or health insurance)* ......$ -0-
   h. Education *(specify)*: ......$
   i. Entertainment ......$ 25.00
   j. Transportation and auto expenses (insurance, gas, oil, repair) ......$ 50.00
   k. Installment payments *(insert total and itemize below in item 4)* ......$ 175.00
   l. Other *(specify)*: INCIDENTALS ......$ 25.00
   m. TOTAL ITEM 3 EXPENSES ......$ 625.00

4. ITEMIZATION OF INSTALLMENT PAYMENTS OR OTHER DEBTS ☐ Continued on Attachment 4.

CREDITOR'S NAME	PAYMENT FOR	MONTHLY PAYMENT	BALANCE	DATE LAST PAYMENT MADE
SEARS TIME PAY ACCT	FURNITURE AND APPLIANCES	30.00	$1,500.00	1/15/93
BROADWAY STORES	CLOTHING	35.00	1,200.00	1/15/93
ALLIED DEPT STORE	HOUSEHOLD EFFECTS, BEDDING, KITCHEN WARE AND CLOTHING	20.00	800.00	1/15-93

5. ATTORNEY FEES
   a. I have paid my attorney for fees and costs: $ -0-   The source of this money was:
   b. I have incurred to date the following fees and costs: N/A
   c. My arrangement for attorney fees and costs is:
   d. ☐ Attorney fees have been requested.
      I confirm this information and fee arrangement.

   ▶ *(signature)*
   (SIGNATURE OF ATTORNEY)
   JANE JUANITA DOE, IN PRO PER
   (TYPE OR PRINT NAME OF ATTORNEY)

Page 3 of 4

Form Adopted by Rule 1285.50b
Judicial Council of California
1285.50b (Rev. January 1, 1993)

EXPENSE INFORMATION
(Family Law)

Civil Code, § 4721

CHILD SUPPORT INFORMATION
Page Four of the Income and Expense Declaration
An example of Page 4 of the Income And Expense Declaration
with the Child Support Information

PETITIONER/PLAINTIFF: JANE J. DOE RESPONDENT/DEFENDANT: JOHN JAMES DOE CHILD SUPPORT INFORMATION OF (name): JANE J. DOE	CASE NUMBER: (SUPPLIED BY COURT)

THIS PAGE MUST BE COMPLETED IF CHILD SUPPORT IS AN ISSUE.

1. Health insurance for my children [X] is [ ] is not available through my employer.
   a. Monthly cost paid by me or on my behalf for the children *only* is: $ 65.00
      Do not include the amount paid or payable by your employer.
   b. Name of carrier: VALLEY HEALTH INSURANCE CO.
   c. Address of carrier: 456 VALEY DRIVE
      VAN NUYS, CA 92000
   d. Policy or group policy number: 1H42A9371

2. Approximate percentage of time each parent has primary physical responsibility for the children:
   Mother 65 % Father 35 %

3. [X] The court is requested to order the following as additional child support:
   a. [X] Child care costs related to employment or to reasonably necessary education or training for employment skills
      (1) Monthly amount presently paid by mother: $ 200.00
      (2) Monthly amount presently paid by father: $ -0-
   b. [ ] Uninsured health care costs for the children *(for each cost state the purpose for which the cost was incurred and the estimated monthly, yearly, or lump sum amount paid by each parent)*:

   c. [ ] Educational or other special needs of the children *(for each cost state the purpose for which the cost was incurred and the estimated monthly, yearly, or lump sum amount paid by each parent)*:

   d. [ ] Travel expense for visitation
      (1) Monthly amount presently paid by mother: $
      (2) Monthly amount presently paid by father: $

4. [ ] The court is requested to allow the deductions identified below, which are justifiable expenses that have caused an extreme financial hardship.

	Amount paid per month	How many months will you need to make these payments
a. [ ] Extraordinary health care expenses *(specify and attach any supporting documents)*:	$ _____	_____
b. [ ] Uninsured catastrophic losses *(specify and attach supporting documents)*:	$ _____	_____
c. [ ] Minimum basic living expenses of dependent minor children from other marriages or relationships who live with you *(specify names and ages of these children)*:	$ _____	_____
d. Total hardship deductions requested *(add lines a–c)*:	$ -0-	

Page 4 of 4

Form Adopted by Rule 1285.50c
Judicial Council of California
1285.50c [New January 1, 1993]

CHILD SUPPORT INFORMATION
(Family Law)

Civil Code, § 4721

STIPULATION TO ESTABLISH OR MODIFY CHILD OR FAMILY SUPPORT
Page One (Front) of the Stipulation
An example of Page 1 of the Stipulation when the parties have agreed upon the child support amount

ATTORNEY OR PARTY WITHOUT ATTORNEY *(Name and Address)*:	TELEPHONE NO.:	FOR COURT USE ONLY
JANE J. DOE 123 ANY STREET LOS ANGELES, CA 92000	213-000-0000	

ATTORNEY FOR *(Name)*: In propria persona

SUPERIOR COURT OF CALIFORNIA, COUNTY OF LOS ANGELES
STREET ADDRESS: 111 N. HILL STREET
MAILING ADDRESS:
CITY AND ZIP CODE: LOS ANGELES, CA 90012
BRANCH NAME:

PETITIONER/PLAINTIFF: JANE JUANITA DOE

RESPONDENT/DEFENDANT: JOHN JAMES DOE

STIPULATION TO ESTABLISH OR MODIFY CHILD SUPPORT AND ORDER	CASE NUMBER: (SUPPLIED BY COURT)

1. a. [X] Mother's net monthly disposable income: $ **1,401.95**
   Father's net monthly disposable income: $ **2,200.00**
   —OR—
   b. [ ] A printout of a computer calculation of the parents' financial circumstances is attached.
2. [X] Percentage of time each parent has primary responsibility for the children: Mother **65** % Father **35** %
3. a. [ ] A hardship is being experienced by the mother for: $ per month because of *(specify)*:

   The hardship will last until *(date)*:
   b. [ ] A hardship is being experienced by the father for: $ per month because of *(specify)*:

   The hardship will last until *(date)*:
4. The amount of child support payable by *(name)*: **JOHN JAMES DOE**, referred to as the "obligor" below, as calculated under the guideline is: $ **508.00** per month.
5. [X] We agree to guideline support.
6. [ ] The guideline amount should be rebutted because of the following:
   a. [ ] We agree to child support in the amount of: $ per month; the agreement is in the best interest of the children; the needs of the children will be adequately met by the agreed amount; and application of the guideline would be unjust or inappropriate in this case.
   b. [ ] Other rebutting factors *(specify)*:
7. Obligor shall pay child support as follows beginning *(date)*: **APRIL 1, 1993**
   a. **BASIC CHILD SUPPORT**

Child's name	Monthly amount	Payable to *(name)*
ROBERT J. DOE	254.00	JANE J. DOE
JUANITA J. DOE	254.00	JANE J. DOE

   Total: $ **508.00** payable [X] on the first of the month [ ] other *(specify)*:
   b. [ ] In addition obligor shall pay the following:
   [ ] $ per month for child care costs to *(name)*:   on *(date)*:
   [ ] $ per month for health care costs not deducted from gross income to *(name)*:   on *(date)*:
   [ ] $ per month for special educational or other needs of the children to *(name)*:   on *(date)*:
   [ ] other *(specify)*:

   c. Total monthly child support payable by obligor shall be: $ **508.00**
   payable [X] on the first of the month [ ] other *(specify)*:

(Continued on reverse)

Form Adopted by Rule 1285.27
Judicial Council of California
1285.27 [Rev. January 1, 1993]

STIPULATION TO ESTABLISH OR MODIFY CHILD SUPPORT AND ORDER
(Family Law — Domestic Violence Prevention — Uniform Parentage)

Civil Code § 4721

STIPULATION TO ESTABLISH OR MODIFY CHILD OR FAMILY SUPPORT
Page Two (Back) of the Stipulation
An example of Page 2 of the Stipulation (Page 1 continued) and Court Order granting the same

PETITIONER/PLAINTIFF: JANE J. DOE
RESPONDENT/DEFENDANT: JOHN JAMES DOE

CASE NUMBER: (SUPPLIED BY COURT)

8. a. Health insurance shall be maintained by *(specify name)*: JANE J. DOE
   b. [X] A health insurance coverage assignment shall issue if available through employment or other group plan or otherwise available at reasonable cost. Both parents are ordered to cooperate in the presentation, collection, and reimbursement of any medical claims.
   c. Any health expenses not paid by insurance shall be shared: Mother   %   Father   100 %

9. a. A Wage and Earnings Assignment Order shall issue.
   b. [ ] We agree that service of the wage assignment be stayed because we have made the following alternative arrangements to ensure payment *(specify)*:

10. [ ] Travel expenses for visitation shall be shared: Mother   %   Father   %

11. [X] We agree that we shall promptly inform each other of any change of residence or employment, including the employer's name, address, and telephone number.

12. [ ] Other *(specify)*:

13. We agree that we are fully informed of our rights under the California child support guidelines.
14. We make this agreement freely without coercion or duress.
15. The right to support
    a. [X] has not been assigned to any county and no application for public assistance is pending.
    b. [ ] has been assigned or an application for public assistance is pending in *(county name)*:
    If you checked b, a district attorney of the county named must sign below, joining in this agreement.
    Date:

    ....
    (TYPE OR PRINT NAME)

    ▶ N/A
    (SIGNATURE OF DISTRICT ATTORNEY)

Notice: If the amount agreed to is less than the guideline amount, no change of circumstances need be shown to obtain a change in the support order to a higher amount.

Date:
3-1-93   JANE JUANITA DOE
         (TYPE OR PRINT NAME)   ▶ *Jane J. Doe*
                                            (SIGNATURE OF PETITIONER)
Date:
3-1-93   JOHN JAMES DOE
         (TYPE OR PRINT NAME)   ▶ *John J. Doe*
                                            (SIGNATURE OF RESPONDENT)
Date:
         (TYPE OR PRINT NAME)   ▶
                                            (SIGNATURE OF ATTORNEY FOR PETITIONER)
Date:
         (TYPE OR PRINT NAME)   ▶
                                            (SIGNATURE OF ATTORNEY FOR RESPONDENT)

THE COURT ORDERS
16. a. [ ] The guideline child support amount in item 4 is rebutted by the factors stated in item 6.
    b. Items 7 through 12 are ordered. All child support payments shall continue until further order of the court, or until the child marries, dies, is emancipated, reaches age 19, or reaches age 18 and is not a full-time high school student, whichever occurs first. Except as modified by this stipulation, all provisions of any previous orders made in this action shall remain in effect.

Date: _____
                                            JUDGE OF THE SUPERIOR COURT

1285.27 (Rev. January 1, 1993)
STIPULATION TO ESTABLISH OR MODIFY CHILD SUPPORT AND ORDER
(Family Law — Domestic Violence Prevention — Uniform Parentage)
Page two

APPLICATION AND ORDER FOR HEALTH INSURANCE COVERAGE
Page One (Front) of the Application
An example of Page 1 of the Application for Health Insurance coverage

---

ATTORNEY OR PARTY WITHOUT ATTORNEY *(Name and Address)*: JANE J. DOE, 123 ANY STREET, LOS ANGELES, CA 92000	TELEPHONE NO. 213-000-0000	FOR COURT USE ONLY

ATTORNEY FOR *(Name)*: In propria persona

SUPERIOR COURT OF CALIFORNIA, COUNTY OF LOS ANGELES
STREET ADDRESS: 111 N. HILL STREET
MAILING ADDRESS:
CITY AND ZIP CODE: LOS ANGELES, CA 90012
BRANCH NAME:

MARRIAGE OF
PETITIONER: JANE JUANITA DOE

RESPONDENT: JOHN JAMES DOE

APPLICATION AND ORDER FOR HEALTH INSURANCE COVERAGE	CASE NUMBER (SUPPLIED BY COURT)

APPLICATION

1. On *(date)*: **APRIL 1, 1993**, this court ordered obligor *(name)*: **JOHN JAMES DOE** to provide health insurance coverage for the children named in the order below.
2. a. [X] On *(date)*: **MARCH 1, 1993** which is at least 15 days before filing this application, I gave written notice to obligor of my intent to seek this order
   [ ] by certified mail   [ ] by personal service.
   OR
   b. [X] Obligor has waived the requirement of written notice.
3. I ask the court to order the employer or other person providing health insurance coverage to enroll or maintain the children in any health insurance coverage available to the obligor.

I declare under penalty of perjury under the laws of the State of California that the foregoing is true and correct.

Date: APRIL 1, 1993

JANE JUANITA DOE   *(signed)* Jane J. Doe
(TYPE OR PRINT NAME)   (SIGNATURE OF APPLICANT)

ORDER FOR HEALTH INSURANCE COVERAGE (ASSIGNMENT)

To employer or other person providing health insurance coverage for obligor *(name)*: **JOHN JAMES DOE**
Social Security Number *(if known)*: 529-00-0000
YOU ARE ORDERED TO

1. Begin or maintain health insurance coverage of:

Name of child	Date of birth	Social Security No.
ROBERT J. DOE	7-25-87	321-00-0000
JUANITA J. DOE	3-01-89	956-00-0000

You may deduct any premium or costs from the wages or earnings of obligor.

2. If the obligor works for you or if you provide health insurance coverage to obligor, give him or her a copy of this order within 10 days after you receive it.
3. If no health insurance coverage is available to the obligor, complete and sign the Declaration of No Health Insurance Coverage on the reverse and mail this form within 20 days to the attorney or person requesting the assignment.

Date: [DATED AND SIGNED BY JUDGE]
                                              (JUDGE OF THE SUPERIOR COURT)
(Continued on reverse)

Form Adopted by Rule 1285.75
Judicial Council of California
1285.75 [Rev. July 1, 1990]

APPLICATION AND ORDER FOR HEALTH INSURANCE COVERAGE
(Family Law)

Civil Code, §§ 4726, 4726.1

APPLICATION AND ORDER FOR HEALTH INSURANCE COVERAGE
Page Two (Back) of the Application
An example of Page 2 of the application with employer's response.

MARRIAGE OF (last name, first name of parties): DOE, JANE AND JOHN	CASE NUMBER: (SUPPLIED BY COURT)

DECLARATION OF NO HEALTH INSURANCE COVERAGE

No health insurance coverage is available to the obligor (name):
because (state reasons):

[NOTE: TO BE COMPLETED BY EMPLOYER OF OBLIGOR]

I declare under penalty of perjury under the laws of the State of California that the foregoing is true and correct.

Date:

....   ▶   _____
(TYPE OR PRINT NAME AND TITLE)   (SIGNATURE OF EMPLOYER OR PERSON PROVIDING HEALTH INSURANCE)

MAIL A COPY OF THIS DECLARATION WITHIN 20 DAYS TO THE ATTORNEY OR PERSON SEEKING THIS ENROLLMENT (SEE INSTRUCTION NO. 5, BELOW).

INSTRUCTIONS FOR EMPLOYER OR OTHER PERSON PROVIDING HEALTH INSURANCE

These instructions apply only to an Order for Health Insurance Coverage issued by a court.

1. If the obligor works for you or is covered by health insurance provided by you, you must give him or her a copy of this order within 10 days after you receive it.
2. Unless you receive a motion to quash the assignment, you must take steps to begin or maintain coverage of the specified children within 10 days after you receive this order. The coverage should begin at the earliest possible time consistent with group plan enrollment rules.
3. The obligor's existing health coverage shall be replaced only if the children are not provided benefits under the existing coverage where they reside.
4. If the obligor is not enrolled in a plan and there is a choice of several plans, you may enroll the children in any plan that will reasonably provide benefits or coverage where they live, unless the court has ordered coverage by a specific plan.
5. If no coverage is available, complete the Declaration of No Health Insurance Coverage at the top of this page and mail the declaration by first class mail to the attorney or person seeking the assignment within 20 days of your receipt of this order. Keep a copy of the form for your records.
6. If coverage is provided, you must supply evidence of coverage to both parents and any person having custody of the child.
7. Upon request of the parents or person having custody of the child, you must provide all forms and other documentation necessary for submitting claims to the insurance carrier to the extent you provide them to other covered individuals.
8. You must notify the applicant of the effective date of the coverage of the children.
9. You will be liable for any amounts incurred for health care services which would otherwise have been covered under the insurance policy if you willfully fail to comply with this order. You can also be held in contempt of court. California law forbids your firing or taking any disciplinary action against any employee because of this order.

EMPLOYEE INFORMATION

1. This order tells your employer or other person providing health insurance coverage to you to enroll or maintain the named children in a health insurance plan available to you and to deduct the appropriate premium or costs, if any, from your wages or other compensation.
2. You have 10 days to contest this order. Civil Code section 4726.1(e) tells you how.
3. Civil Code section 4726.1(k) tells you how and when to petition the court to end this assignment.

1285 75 (Rev. July 1, 1990)   **APPLICATION AND ORDER FOR HEALTH INSURANCE COVERAGE** (Family Law)   Page two

EMPLOYER'S HEALTH INSURANCE RETURN

An example of employer's acknowledgment of health insurance availability

---

PETITIONER/PLAINTIFF: JANE JUANITA DOE	CASE NUMBER:
RESPONDENT/DEFENDANT: JOHN JAMES DOE	SUPPLIED BY COURT)

EMPLOYER'S HEALTH INSURANCE RETURN

1. Name of absent parent employee: [NOTE: TO BE COMPLETED BY RESPONDENT'S EMPLOYER]
   JOHN JAMES DOE

2. Social security number: 529-00-0000

3. Home address of absent parent employee: 321 ANY STREET, SAN DIEGO, CA 92100
   [ ] Not known

4. [ ] The employee has *no* insurance policies for health care, vision care, or dental care through this employment.

5. [ ] The employee has the following insurance policies covering health care, vision care, and dental care:

Company	Type of policy	Policy No.	Persons insured
MESSENGER HEALTH INS. CO. 539 BAY BLVD. LONG BEACH, CA 91200	HOSPITALIZATION AND SURGERY	3SD04783	JOHN J. DOE, ROBERT J. DOE JUANITA J. DOE

Date:

MAC BETH MANUFACTURING CO.
(TYPE OR PRINT NAME OF EMPLOYER)   ▶ (SIGNATURE OF EMPLOYER)

Address: 45600 SCIENCE ROAD
FONTANA, CA 92500

Telephone No.: 805-828-0000

6. Return this completed return to the following district attorney within 30 days *(name and address of district attorney)*:

If any insurance coverage lapses, complete the notice below and return a copy to the same district attorney.

NOTICE OF LAPSE IN HEALTH INSURANCE

7. The health insurance listed on the Employer's Health Insurance Return above has
   [ ] lapsed [ ] terminated FOR *(check one)*:
   a. [ ] all persons insured for the following reason *(specify)*:

   b. [ ] the following person *(name)*:   for the following reason *(specify)*:

Date:

_____   ▶ _____
(TYPE OR PRINT NAME OF EMPLOYER)   (SIGNATURE OF EMPLOYER)

Address:

Telephone No.:

Form Adopted by Rule 1285.76
Judicial Council of California
1285.76 [New January 1, 1992]

EMPLOYER'S HEALTH INSURANCE RETURN
(Family Law — Uniform Parentage)

Civil Code, § 4726.1 (n), (o)

REQUEST TO ENTER DEFAULT
Page One (Front) of the Request

An example of Page 1 of the Request to enter default when with no children, property or debts

---

ATTORNEY OR PARTY WITHOUT ATTORNEY (NAME AND ADDRESS): **JANE J. DOE**, 123 ANY STREET, LOS ANGELES, CA 92000
TELEPHONE NO: 213-000-0000
FOR COURT USE ONLY

ATTORNEY FOR (NAME): In propria persona

SUPERIOR COURT OF CALIFORNIA, COUNTY OF LOS ANGELES
STREET ADDRESS: 111 N. HILL STREET
MAILING ADDRESS:
CITY AND ZIP CODE: LOS ANGELES, CA 90012
BRANCH NAME:

MARRIAGE OF
PETITIONER: JANE JUANITA DOE
RESPONDENT: JOHN JAMES DOE

REQUEST TO ENTER DEFAULT

CASE NUMBER:

---

1. TO THE CLERK: Please enter the default of the respondent who has failed to respond to the petition.
2. A completed ☐ Income and Expense Declaration ☐ Property Declaration is attached.
3. A completed ☒ Income and Expense Declaration ☒ Property Declaration is *not* attached because (check at least one of the following)
   (1) ☒ There have been no changes since the previous filing.
   (2) ☐ The issues subject to disposition by the court in this proceeding are the subject of a written agreement.
   (3) ☒ There are no issues of child custody, child or spousal support, division of community property or attorney fees and costs subject to determination by this court.
   (4) ☒ The petition does not request money, property, costs or attorney fees.

Dated: **MARCH 21, 1993**

JANE JUANITA DOE, In pro per
(Type or print name)   Signature of (Attorney for) Petitioner

3. DECLARATION
   a. ☐ No mailing is required because service was by publication and the address of respondent remains unknown.
   b. ☒ A copy of this Request to Enter Default including any attachments was mailed to the respondent's attorney of record or, if none, to respondent's last known address as follows
      (1) Date of mailing: MARCH 21, 1993 (2) Addressed as follows: JOHN JAMES DOE, 321 ANY STREET, SAN DIEGO CA 91000
   c. I declare under penalty of perjury that the foregoing is true and correct and that this declaration is executed on (date) MARCH 21, 1993 at (place): LOS ANGELES, California.

JANE JUANITA DOE, In pro per
(Type or print name)   (Signature of declarant)

FOR COURT USE ONLY
Default entered as requested on (date):
Default NOT entered. Reason:
Clerk, by:

(See reverse for Memorandum of Costs and Declaration of Nonmilitary Status)

The declaration under penalty of perjury must be signed in California or in a state that authorizes use of a declaration in place of an affidavit; otherwise an affidavit is required. (CCP 2015.5)

Form Adopted by Rule 1286
Judicial Council of California
Revised Effective January 1, 1980

**REQUEST TO ENTER DEFAULT
(FAMILY LAW)**

CCP 585,587

REQUEST TO ENTER DEFAULT
Page One (Front) of the Request

An example of Page 1 of the Request to enter default when Income and Expense, and Property Declarations are attached

---

ATTORNEY OR PARTY WITHOUT ATTORNEY (NAME AND ADDRESS): **JANE JUANITA DOE, 123 ANY STREET, LOS ANGELES, CA 92000** TELEPHONE NO: **213-000-0000**

ATTORNEY FOR (NAME): **In Propria Persona**

SUPERIOR COURT OF CALIFORNIA, COUNTY OF **LOS ANGELES**
STREET ADDRESS: **111 N. HILL STREET**
MAILING ADDRESS:
CITY AND ZIP CODE: **LOS ANGELES, CA 90012**
BRANCH NAME:

MARRIAGE OF
PETITIONER: **JANE JUANITA DOE**
RESPONDENT: **JOHN JAMES DOE**

REQUEST TO ENTER DEFAULT

CASE NUMBER: **(COURT SUPPLIED)**

---

1. TO THE CLERK: Please enter the default of the respondent who has failed to respond to the petition.
2. A completed [X] Income and Expense Declaration [X] Property Declaration is attached.
3. A completed [ ] Income and Expense Declaration [ ] Property Declaration is *not* attached because (check at least one of the following)
   (1) [ ] There have been no changes since the previous filing.
   (2) [ ] The issues subject to disposition by the court in this proceeding are the subject of a written agreement.
   (3) [ ] There are no issues of child custody, child or spousal support, division of community property or attorney fees and costs subject to determination by this court.
   (4) [ ] The petition does not request money, property, costs or attorney fees.

Dated: **MARCH 21, 1993**

JANE JUANITA DOE, IN PRO PER
(Type or print name)   Signature of (Attorney for) Petitioner

3. DECLARATION
   a. [ ] No mailing is required because service was by publication and the address of respondent remains unknown.
   b. [X] A copy of this Request to Enter Default including any attachments was mailed to the respondent's attorney of record or, if none, to respondent's last known address as follows
      (1) Date of mailing: **MARCH 21, 1993** (2) Addressed as follows: **JOHN JAMES DOE, 321 WHY STREET, SAN DIEGO, CA 92000**
   c. I declare under penalty of perjury that the foregoing is true and correct and that this declaration is executed on (date) **MARCH 21, 1993** (place): **LOS ANGELES**, California.

JANE JUANITA DOE, In pro per
(Type or print name)   (Signature of declarant)

FOR COURT USE ONLY
Default entered as requested on (date):   Clerk, by:
Default NOT entered. Reason:

(See reverse for Memorandum of Costs and Declaration of Nonmilitary Status)

The declaration under penalty of perjury must be signed in California or in a state that authorizes use of a declaration in place of an affidavit; otherwise an affidavit is required (CCP 2015.5)

Form Adopted by Rule 1286
Judicial Council of California
Revised Effective January 1, 1980

REQUEST TO ENTER DEFAULT (FAMILY LAW)

CCP 585,587

REQUEST TO ENTER DEFAULT
Page One (Front) of the Request

An example of Page 1 of the Request to enter default when a Marital Settlement Agreement is attached

---

ATTORNEY OR PARTY WITHOUT ATTORNEY (NAME AND ADDRESS):
JANE JAUNITA DOE
123 ANY STREET
LOS ANGELES CA 92000

TELEPHONE NO: 213-000-0000

FOR COURT USE ONLY

ATTORNEY FOR (NAME): In Propria persona

SUPERIOR COURT OF CALIFORNIA, COUNTY OF LOS ANGELES
STREET ADDRESS: 111 N. HILL STREE
MAILING ADDRESS:
CITY AND ZIP CODE: LOS ANGELES, CA 90012
BRANCH NAME:

MARRIAGE OF
PETITIONER: JANE JUANITA DOE
RESPONDENT: JOHN JAMES DOE

REQUEST TO ENTER DEFAULT

CASE NUMBER: (COURT SUPPLIED)

1. TO THE CLERK: Please enter the default of the respondent who has failed to respond to the petition.
2. A completed [ ] Income and Expense Declaration [ ] Property Declaration is attached.
3. A completed [X] Income and Expense Declaration [X] Property Declaration is *not* attached because (check at least one of the following)
   (1) [ ] There have been no changes since the previous filing.
   (2) [X] The issues subject to disposition by the court in this proceeding are the subject of a written agreement.
   (3) [ ] There are no issues of child custody, child or spousal support, division of community property or attorney fees and costs subject to determination by this court.
   (4) [ ] The petition does not request money, property, costs or attorney fees.

Dated: MARCH 21, 1993

JANE JUANITA DOE, In pro per   *Jane J. Doe*
(Type or print name)   Signature of (Attorney for) Petitioner

3. DECLARATION
   a. [ ] No mailing is required because service was by publication and the address of respondent remains unknown.
   b. [X] A copy of this Request to Enter Default including any attachments was mailed to the respondent's attorney of record or, if none, to respondent's last known address as follows
       (1) Date of mailing: MARCH 21, 1993 (2) Addressed as follows: JOHN JAMES DOE
                                                                      321 ANY STREET
                                                                      SAN DIEGO, CA 91000
   c. I declare under penalty of perjury that the foregoing is true and correct and that this declaration is executed on (date) MARCH 21, 1993 at (place): LOS ANGELES .... California

JANE JUANITA DOE, In pro per   *Jane J. Doe*
(Type or print name)   (Signature of declarant)

FOR COURT USE ONLY

Default entered as requested on (date):

Default NOT entered. Reason:

Clerk, by:

(See reverse for Memorandum of Costs and Declaration of Nonmilitary Status)

The declaration under penalty of perjury must be signed in California or in a state that authorizes use of a declaration in place of an affidavit; otherwise an affidavit is required (CCP 2015.5)

Form Adopted by Rule 1286
Judicial Council of California
Revised Effective January 1, 1980

REQUEST TO ENTER DEFAULT (FAMILY LAW)

CCP 585,587

REQUEST TO ENTER DEFAULT
Page Two (Back) of the Request
An example of Page 2 of the Request to enter default when respondent is not in Military Service and no expenses are claimed

4. MEMORANDUM OF COSTS

   a. [X] Costs and disbursements are waived.
   b. Costs and disbursements are listed as follows

   (1) [ ] Clerk's fees . . . . $ . . . .

   (2) [ ] Process server's fees . . . . $ . . . .

   (3) [ ] Other (specify) . . . . $ . . . .

   . . . . $ . . . .

   . . . . $ . . . .

   . . . . $ . . . .

   TOTAL . . . . $ **NOT CLAIMED**

   I am the attorney, agent, or party who claims these costs. To the best of my knowledge and belief the foregoing items of cost are correct and have been necessarily incurred in this cause or proceeding.

   I declare under penalty of perjury that the foregoing is true and correct and that this declaration is executed on (date): **3-21-93** at (place): **LOS ANGELES**, California.

   JANE JUANITA DOE, In pro per   _(signature)_
   (Type or print name)   (Signature of declarant)

5. DECLARATION OF NONMILITARY STATUS

   Respondent is not in the military service or in the military service of the United States as defined in Section 101 of the Soldiers' and Sailors' Relief Act of 1940, as amended, and not entitled to the benefits of such act.

   I declare under penalty of perjury that the foregoing is true and correct and that this declaration is executed on (date): **3-21-93** at (place): **LOS ANGELES**, California.

   JANE JUANITA DOE, In pro per   _(signature)_
   (Type or print name)   (Signature of declarant)

REQUEST TO ENTER DEFAULT
Page Two (Back) of the Request
An example of Page 2 of the Request to enter default when respondent is in Military Service and expenses are claimed

4. MEMORANDUM OF COSTS

   a. ☐ Costs and disbursements are waived.
   b. Costs and disbursements are listed as follows

   (1) ☐ Clerk's fees .... $ 182.00
   (2) ☐ Process server's fees .... $ 40.00
   (3) ☐ Other (specify) .... $
   .... $
   .... $
   .... $
   TOTAL .... $ 222.00

   I am the attorney, agent, or party who claims these costs. To the best of my knowledge and belief the foregoing items of cost are correct and have been necessarily incurred in this cause or proceeding.

   I declare under penalty of perjury that the foregoing is true and correct and that this declaration is executed on (date): 3-21-93   at (place): LOS ANGELES, California.

   JANE JUANITA DOE, In pro per   _____(Jane J. Doe)_____
   (Type or print name)   (Signature of declarant)

5. DECLARATION OF NONMILITARY STATUS

   Respondent is not in the military service or in the military service of the United States as defined in Section 101 of the Soldiers' and Sailors' Relief Act of 1940, as amended, and not entitled to the benefits of such act.

   I declare under penalty of perjury that the foregoing is true and correct and that this declaration is executed on (date): .... at (place): ...., California.

   [LEAVE BLANK IF RESPONDENT IS IN MILITARY]

   _____   _____
   (Type or print name)   (Signature of declarant)

DECLARATION FOR DEFAULT
Page One (Front) of the Declaration
An example of Page 1 of the Declaration when with child support, spousal support, property and debts

ATTORNEY OR PARTY WITHOUT ATTORNEY (Name and Address):	TELEPHONE NO.	FOR COURT USE ONLY
JANE J. DOE 123 ANY STREET LOS ANGELES, CA 92000	213-000-0000	
ATTORNEY FOR (Name): In propria persona		

SUPERIOR COURT OF CALIFORNIA, COUNTY OF LOS ANGELES
STREET ADDRESS 111 N. HILL STREET
MAILING ADDRESS
CITY AND ZIP CODE LOS ANGELES, CA 90012
BRANCH NAME

MARRIAGE OF
PETITIONER: JANE JUANITA DOE

RESPONDENT: JOHN JAMES DOE

DECLARATION FOR DEFAULT OR UNCONTESTED [X] DISSOLUTION or [ ] LEGAL SEPARATION	CASE NUMBER: (SUPPLIED BY COURT)

(NOTE: Items 1 through 12 apply to both dissolution and legal separation proceedings.)

1. I declare that if I appeared in court and were sworn, I would testify to the truth of the facts in this declaration.

2. I stipulate that proof will be by this declaration and that I will not appear before the court unless I am ordered by the court to do so.

3. All the information in the [X] Petition [ ] Response is true and correct.

4. *(Check a or b)*
   a. [X] The default of the respondent was entered or is being requested, and I am not seeking any relief not requested in the petition.
   OR
   b. [ ] The parties have stipulated that the matter may proceed as an uncontested matter without notice, and the stipulation is attached or it is incorporated in the attached property agreement.

5. PROPERTY AGREEMENT *(Check a or b)*
   a. [ ] The parties have entered into an AGREEMENT regarding their property and marital rights, the original or a true copy of which is or has been submitted, I request the court to approve the agreement.
   OR
   b. [X] There is NO AGREEMENT, and the following statements are true *(check at least one)*:
      (1) [ ] There are no community or quasi-community assets to be disposed of by the court.
      (2) [ ] There are no community debts to be disposed of by the court.
      (3) [X] The community and quasi-community assets and debts are listed on the attached **completed** Property Declaration. The division in the proposed Judgment (Family Law) is a fair and equal division of the property and debts.

6. SUPPORT *If a support order or attorney fees are requested, submit a completed Judicial Council form 1285.50, Income and Expense Declaration, unless a current form is on file. Include your best estimate of the other party's income and expenses*

   a. Spousal support *(check at least one)*
      (1) [ ] I knowingly give up forever any right to receive spousal support.
      (2) [ ] I ask the court to reserve jurisdiction to award spousal support in the future to *(name)*:
      (3) [X] Spousal support should be ordered as set forth in the proposed Judgment (Family Law).

   b. [X] Child support should be ordered as set forth in the proposed Judgment (Family Law).

   c. [ ] Family support should be ordered as set forth in the proposed Judgment (Family Law).

   d. [ ] Attorney fees should be ordered as set forth in the proposed Judgment (Family Law).

(Continued on reverse)

Form Adopted by Rule 1286.50
Judicial Council of California
1286.50 (Rev. July 1, 1990)

**DECLARATION FOR DEFAULT
OR UNCONTESTED DISSOLUTION OR LEGAL SEPARATION
(Family Law)**

Civil Code § 4511
Cal Rules of Court, rule 1241

DECLARATION FOR DEFAULT
Page One (Front) of the Declaration
An example of Page 1 of the Declaration when respondent signed the Appearance Form and a Marital Settlement Agreement is filed

---

ATTORNEY OR PARTY WITHOUT ATTORNEY (Name and Address):   TELEPHONE NO.: 213-000-0000   FOR COURT USE ONLY

JANE J. DOE
123 ANY STREET
LOS ANGELES, CA 92000

ATTORNEY FOR (Name): **In propria persona**

SUPERIOR COURT OF CALIFORNIA, COUNTY OF LOS ANGELES
STREET ADDRESS: 111 N. HILL STREET
MAILING ADDRESS:
CITY AND ZIP CODE: LOS ANGELES, CA 90012
BRANCH NAME:

MARRIAGE OF
PETITIONER: JANE JUANITA DOE

RESPONDENT: JOHN JAMES DOE

DECLARATION FOR DEFAULT OR UNCONTESTED
[X] DISSOLUTION or [ ] LEGAL SEPARATION

CASE NUMBER: (SUPPLIED BY COURT)

(NOTE: Items 1 through 12 apply to both dissolution and legal separation proceedings.)

1. I declare that if I appeared in court and were sworn, I would testify to the truth of the facts in this declaration.

2. I stipulate that proof will be by this declaration and that I will not appear before the court unless I am ordered by the court to do so.

3. All the information in the [ ] Petition [ ] Response is true and correct.

4. (Check a or b)
   a. [ ] The default of the respondent was entered or is being requested, and I am not seeking any relief not requested in the petition.
   OR
   b. [X] The parties have stipulated that the matter may proceed as an uncontested matter without notice, and the stipulation is attached or it is incorporated in the attached property agreement.

5. PROPERTY AGREEMENT (Check a or b)
   a. [X] The parties have entered into an AGREEMENT regarding their property and marital rights, the original or a true copy of which is or has been submitted, I request the court to approve the agreement.
   OR
   b. [ ] There is NO AGREEMENT, and the following statements are true (check at least one):
      (1) [ ] There are no community or quasi-community assets to be disposed of by the court.
      (2) [ ] There are no community debts to be disposed of by the court.
      (3) [ ] The community and quasi-community assets and debts are listed on the attached **completed** Property Declaration. The division in the proposed Judgment (Family Law) is a fair and equal division of the property and debts.

6. SUPPORT   If a support order or attorney fees are requested, submit a completed Judicial Council form 1285.50, Income and Expense Declaration, unless a current form is on file. Include your best estimate of the other party's income and expenses.

   a. Spousal support (check at least one)
      (1) [ ] I knowingly give up forever any right to receive spousal support.
      (2) [ ] I ask the court to reserve jurisdiction to award spousal support in the future to (name):
      (3) [ ] Spousal support should be ordered as set forth in the proposed Judgment (Family Law).

   b. [ ] Child support should be ordered as set forth in the proposed Judgment (Family Law).

   c. [ ] Family support should be ordered as set forth in the proposed Judgment (Family Law).

   d. [ ] Attorney fees should be ordered as set forth in the proposed Judgment (Family Law).

   (Continued on reverse)

Form Adopted by Rule 1286.50
Judicial Council of California
1286.50 [Rev July 1, 1990]

**DECLARATION FOR DEFAULT
OR UNCONTESTED DISSOLUTION OR LEGAL SEPARATION
(Family Law)**

Civil Code, § 4511
Cal Rules of Court, rule 1241

DECLARATION FOR DEFAULT
Page Two (Back) of the Declaration
An example of Page 2 of the Declaration when with children and a reason for non-appearance stated

MARRIAGE OF (last name, first name of parties): DOE, JANE AND JOHN	CASE NUMBER: (SUPPLIED BY COURT)

7. a. I [ ] am receiving [X] am not receiving [ ] intend to apply for public assistance for the child or children listed in the proposed order.
   b. To the best of my knowledge the other party [ ] is [X] is not receiving public assistance.

8. [ ] Petitioner [ ] Respondent is presently receiving public assistance and all support should be made payable to (specify name and address):

9. [X] CHILD CUSTODY should be ordered as set forth in the proposed Judgment (Family Law).

10. [X] CHILD VISITATION should be ordered as set forth in the proposed Judgment (Family Law).

11. This declaration may be reviewed by a commissioner sitting as a temporary judge who may determine whether to grant this request or require my appearance under section 4511 of the Civil Code.

12. There are irreconcilable differences that have led to the irremediable breakdown of the marriage and there is no possibility of saving the marriage through counseling or other means.

[ ] STATEMENTS IN THIS BOX APPLY ONLY TO DISSOLUTIONS—items 13 through 16

13. Either the petitioner or the respondent has been a resident of this county for at least three months and of the State of California for at least six months continuously and immediately preceding the date of the filing of the petition.

14. I ask that the court grant the request for a Judgment for Dissolution of Marriage based upon irreconcilable differences and that the court make the orders set forth in the proposed Judgment (Family Law) submitted with this declaration.

15. [ ] This declaration is for the termination of **marital status only**. I ask the court to reserve jurisdiction over all issues whose determination is not requested in this declaration.

16. [ ] Wife requests restoration of her former name as set forth in the proposed Judgment (Family Law).

[ ] THIS STATEMENT APPLIES ONLY TO LEGAL SEPARATIONS

17. I ask that the court grant the request for a judgment for legal separation based upon irreconcilable differences and that the court make the orders set forth in the proposed Judgment (Family Law) submitted with this declaration.
    I UNDERSTAND THAT A JUDGMENT OF LEGAL SEPARATION DOES NOT TERMINATE A MARRIAGE AND I AM STILL MARRIED.

---

18. [X] Other (specify):

   [IF APPLICABLE: IF IT WILL BE INCONVENIENT FOR YOU TO ATTEND A HEARING, STATE YOUR REASON HERE, FOR EXAMPLE, MY CURRENT JOB ASSIGNMENT WOULD REQUIRE ME TO MISS A DAYS WORK AND TRAVEL 100 MILES ROUND TRIP, ETC.]

I declare under penalty of perjury under the laws of the State of California that the foregoing is true and correct.

Date:

JANE JUANITA DOE, IN PRO PER
(TYPE OR PRINT NAME)

▶ *Jane J. Doe*
(SIGNATURE OF DECLARANT)

1286 50 (Rev July 1, 1990)

**DECLARATION FOR DEFAULT
OR UNCONTESTED DISSOLUTION OR LEGAL SEPARATION**
(Family Law)

Page two

JUDGMENT
Page 1 of a one page Judgment

An example of a one page Judgment when Judgment granted by Declaration; respondent appeared; wife restored former name; and no children, property or debts

---

ATTORNEY OR PARTY WITHOUT ATTORNEY (Name and Address):	TELEPHONE NO.:	FOR COURT USE ONLY
JANE J. DOE 123 ANY STREET LOS ANGELES, CA 92000	213-000-0000	

ATTORNEY FOR (Name): **In propria persona**

SUPERIOR COURT OF CALIFORNIA, COUNTY OF LOS ANGELES
STREET ADDRESS: 111 N. HILL STREET
MAILING ADDRESS:
CITY AND ZIP CODE: LOS ANGELES, CA 90012
BRANCH NAME:

MARRIAGE OF
PETITIONER: JANE JUANITA DOE
RESPONDENT: JOHN JAMES DOE

JUDGMENT
[X] Dissolution [ ] Legal separation [ ] Nullity
[ ] Status only
[ ] Reserving jurisdiction over termination of marital status
Date marital status ends: **SEPTEMBER 2, 1993**

CASE NUMBER: **(SUPPLIED BY COURT)**

1. This proceeding was heard as follows: [ ] default or uncontested [X] by declaration under Civil Code, § 4511 [ ] contested
   a. Date: Dept.:   Rm.:
   b. Judge (name):   [ ] Temporary judge
   c. [ ] Petitioner present in court   [ ] Attorney present in court (name):
   d. [ ] Respondent present in court   [ ] Attorney present in court (name):
   e. [ ] Claimant present in court (name):   [ ] Attorney present in court (name):
2. The court acquired jurisdiction of the respondent on (date): **MARCH 1, 1993**   **(DATE RESPONDENT SIGNED APPEARANCE FORM)**
   [ ] Respondent was served with process   [X] Respondent appeared
3. THE COURT ORDERS, GOOD CAUSE APPEARING:
   a. [X] Judgment of dissolution be entered. Marital status is terminated and the parties are restored to the status of unmarried persons
      (1) [X] on the following date (specify): **SEPTEMBER 2, 1993**
      (2) [ ] on a date to be determined on noticed motion of either party or on stipulation.
   b. [ ] Judgment of legal separation be entered.
   c. [ ] Judgment of nullity be entered. The parties are declared to be unmarried persons on the ground of (specify):
   d. [X] Wife's former name be restored (specify): **JANE JUANITA DOE**
   e. [ ] This judgment shall be entered nunc pro tunc as of (date):
   f. [ ] Jurisdiction is reserved over all other issues and all present orders remain in effect except as provided below.
   g. [X] Other (specify):
      a. THE COURT'S JURISDICTION TO AWARD SPOUSAL SUPPORT TO EITHER PARTY IS HEREBY TERMINATED.
      b. EACH PARTY SHALL WAIVE ALL RIGHTS TO THE OTHER PARTY'S ACCURED RETIREMENTS BENEFITS.
   h. Jurisdiction is reserved to make other orders necessary to carry out this judgment.

Date:
_____
JUDGE OF THE SUPERIOR COURT

4. Number of additional pages attached: [ ] Signature follows last attachment   Page 1 of **1**

NOTICE

Please review your will, insurance policies, retirement benefit plans, credit cards, other credit accounts and credit reports, and other matters you may want to change in view of the dissolution or annulment of your marriage, or your legal separation.
A debt or obligation may be assigned to one party as part of the division of property and debts, but if that party does not pay the debt or obligation, the creditor may be able to collect from the other party.
An earnings assignment will automatically be issued if child support, family support, or spousal support is ordered.

Form Adopted by Rule 1287
Judicial Council of California
1287 [Rev. January 1, 1993]

JUDGMENT
(Family Law)

Civil Code, § 4514

JUDGMENT
Page 1 of a one page Judgment

An example of a one page Judgment when Judgment granted by Declaration; respondent made an appearance; and a Marital Settlement Agreement was filed

---

ATTORNEY OR PARTY WITHOUT ATTORNEY (Name and Address):   TELEPHONE NO.:   FOR COURT USE ONLY

JANE J. DOE   213-000-0000
123 ANY STREET
LOS ANGELES, CA 92000

ATTORNEY FOR (Name):   In propria persona

SUPERIOR COURT OF CALIFORNIA, COUNTY OF   LOS ANGELES
STREET ADDRESS: 111 N. HILL STREET
MAILING ADDRESS:
CITY AND ZIP CODE: LOS ANGELES, CA 90012
BRANCH NAME:

MARRIAGE OF
PETITIONER: JANE JUANITA DOE

RESPONDENT: JOHN JAMES DOE

JUDGMENT
[X] Dissolution   [ ] Legal separation   [ ] Nullity
     [ ] Status only
     [ ] Reserving jurisdiction over termination of marital status
Date marital status ends: SEPTEMBER 2, 1993

CASE NUMBER:

(SUPPLIED BY COURT)

1. This proceeding was heard as follows: [ ] default or uncontested [X] by declaration under Civil Code, § 4511 [ ] contested
   a. Date: Dept.:   Rm.:
   b. Judge (name):   [ ] Temporary judge
   c. [ ] Petitioner present in court   [ ] Attorney present in court (name):
   d. [ ] Respondent present in court   [ ] Attorney present in court (name):
   e. [ ] Claimant present in court (name):   [ ] Attorney present in court (name):
2. The court acquired jurisdiction of the respondent on (date): MARCH 1, 1993   (DATE RESPONDENT SIGNED APPEARANCE FORM)
   [ ] Respondent was served with process   [X] Respondent appeared
3. THE COURT ORDERS, GOOD CAUSE APPEARING:
   a. [X] Judgment of dissolution be entered. Marital status is terminated and the parties are restored to the status of unmarried persons
      (1) [X] on the following date (specify): SEPTEMBER 2, 1993
      (2) [ ] on a date to be determined on noticed motion of either party or on stipulation.
   b. [ ] Judgment of legal separation be entered.
   c. [ ] Judgment of nullity be entered. The parties are declared to be unmarried persons on the ground of (specify):
   d. [ ] Wife's former name be restored (specify):
   e. [ ] This judgment shall be entered nunc pro tunc as of (date):
   f. [ ] Jurisdiction is reserved over all other issues and all present orders remain in effect except as provided below.
   g. [X] Other (specify):
      IT IS FURTHER ORDERED THAT THE MARITAL SETTLEMENT AGREEMENT OF THE PARTIES DATED MARCH 15, 1993, IS APPROVED, ATTACHED HERETO AND INCORPORATED BY REFERENCE, AND EACH OF THE PARTIES IS ORDERED TO COMPLY WITH ALL OF THE TERMS AND CONDITIONS STATED THEREIN.
   h. Jurisdiction is reserved to make other orders necessary to carry out this judgment.

Date:

JUDGE OF THE SUPERIOR COURT

4. Number of additional pages attached: [ ] Signature follows last attachment   Page 1 of 1

NOTICE

Please review your will, insurance policies, retirement benefit plans, credit, cards, other credit accounts and credit reports, and other matters you may want to change in view of the dissolution or annulment of your marriage, or your legal separation.

A debt or obligation may be assigned to one party as part of the division of property and debts, but if that party does not pay the debt or obligation, the creditor may be able to collect from the other party.

An earnings assignment will automatically be issued if child support, family support, or spousal support is ordered.

Form Adopted by Rule 1287
Judicial Council of California
1287 (Rev. January 1, 1993)

JUDGMENT
(Family Law)

Civil Code, § 4514

JUDGMENT
Page 1 of a four page Judgment

An example of Page 1 of a 4 page Judgment when granted by Default; respondent served with process; 3 continuation pages attached for children, property and debts

---

ATTORNEY OR PARTY WITHOUT ATTORNEY *(Name and Address)*: TELEPHONE NO.: 213-000-0000 FOR COURT USE ONLY

JANE J. DOE
123 ANY STREET
LOS ANGELES, CA 92000

ATTORNEY FOR *(Name)*: In propria persona

SUPERIOR COURT OF CALIFORNIA, COUNTY OF LOS ANGELES
STREET ADDRESS: 111 N. HILL STREET
MAILING ADDRESS:
CITY AND ZIP CODE: LOS ANGELES, CA 90012
BRANCH NAME:

MARRIAGE OF
PETITIONER: JANE JUANITA DOE
RESPONDENT: JOHN JAMES DOE

JUDGMENT
[X] Dissolution [ ] Legal separation [ ] Nullity
[ ] Status only
[ ] Reserving jurisdiction over termination of marital status
Date marital status ends: **AUGUST 16, 1993**

CASE NUMBER:

---

1. This proceeding was heard as follows: [X] default or uncontested [ ] by declaration under Civil Code, § 4511 [ ] contested
   a. Date: **APRIL 1, 1993** Dept.: **B** Rm.:
   b. Judge *(name)*: [ ] Temporary judge
   c. [X] Petitioner present in court [ ] Attorney present in court *(name)*:
   d. [ ] Respondent present in court [ ] Attorney present in court *(name)*:
   e. [ ] Claimant present in court *(name)*: [ ] Attorney present in court *(name)*:
2. The court acquired jurisdiction of the respondent on *(date)*: **FEBRUARY 15, 1993**   DATE RESPONDENT WAS
   [X] Respondent was served with process [ ] Respondent appeared   SERVED PROCESS
3. THE COURT ORDERS, GOOD CAUSE APPEARING:
   a. [X] Judgment of dissolution be entered. Marital status is terminated and the parties are restored to the status of unmarried persons
      (1) [X] on the following date *(specify)*: **AUGUST 16, 1993**
      (2) [ ] on a date to be determined on noticed motion of either party or on stipulation.
   b. [ ] Judgment of legal separation be entered.
   c. [ ] Judgment of nullity be entered. The parties are declared to be unmarried persons on the ground of *(specify)*:
   d. [ ] Wife's former name be restored *(specify)*:
   e. [ ] This judgment shall be entered nunc pro tunc as of *(date)*:
   f. [ ] Jurisdiction is reserved over all other issues and all present orders remain in effect except as provided below.
   g. [ ] Other *(specify)*:

   h. Jurisdiction is reserved to make other orders necessary to carry out this judgment.

Date: **(DATE SIGNED BY THE JUDGE)**
_____
JUDGE OF THE SUPERIOR COURT

4. Number of additional pages attached: **3**   [X] Signature follows last attachment   Page 1 of **4**

NOTICE

Please review your will, insurance policies, retirement benefit plans, credit, cards, other credit accounts and credit reports, and other matters you may want to change in view of the dissolution or annulment of your marriage, or your legal separation.
A debt or obligation may be assigned to one party as part of the division of property and debts, but if that party does not pay the debt or obligation, the creditor may be able to collect from the other party.
An earnings assignment will automatically be issued if child support, family support, or spousal support is ordered.

Form Adopted by Rule 1287
Judicial Council of California
1287 (Rev. January 1, 1993)

JUDGMENT
(Family Law)

Civil Code, § 4514

CONTINUATION OF JUDGMENT
Page 2 of the 4 page Judgment
An example of Page 2 of the 4 page Judgment with provisions for child custody, support, visitation, health insurance, life insurance, etc.

SHORT TITLE: DOE, JANE JUANITA AND JOHN JAMES	CASE NUMBER: (SUPPLIED BY COURT)

CONTINUATION OF JUDGMENT

THE COURT FURTHER ORDERS:

1. That the primary physical responsibility of the minor children of the parties, to wit:

   | Robert J. Doe | Born 7-25-87 | (age) 5 yrs. 7 mos. |
   | Juanita J Doe | Born 3-01-89 | (age) 3 yrs. 11 mos. |

   shall be with petitioner, with reasonable visitation rights granted to respondent as follows:
   a. respondent shall have primary physical responsibility of the minor children every other Saturday and Sunday, commencing the week of April 1, 1993;
   b. respondent shall have primary physical responsibility of the minor children every other national holiday, commencing with the new years holiday; and
   c. respondent shall have primary physical responsibility of the minor children during the summer months of July and August, each year.

2. That respondent shall pay child support to petitioner in the amount of $508.00, per month, commencing April 1, 1993, and continuing each month thereafter until each child either marries, dies, is emancipated, reaches age 19, or reaches age 18 and is not a full time high school student residing with petitioner, whichever occurs first.

3. That the child support amount has been calculated by using the California Civil Code Section 4721, as amended 1992, with the higher net earners physical responsibility of the minor children calculated at 35% of the time annually.

4. That respondent shall maintain in force a policy of insurance providing medical, dental and vision coverage for each child

5. That child support shall be paid by an assignment of respondent's wages, whose employer is MAC BETH MANUFACTURING CO, 45600 Science Road Fontana, CA 92500.

6. That respondent shall maintain in force a policy of life insurance in the minimun amount of $150,000, naming petitioner and the minor children as irrevocable beneficiaries, and respondent shall not borrow, assign or otherwise encumber the policy in any way.

7. That each parent shall inform the other as to any changes in the health, educational or well being of each minor child.

(CONTINUED)

Page 2 of 4

Form Approved by the Judicial Council of California MC-020 (New January 1, 1987)

ADDITIONAL PAGE
Attach to Judicial Council Form or Other Court Paper

CRC 201, 501

CONTINUATION OF JUDGMENT
Page 3 of the 4 page Judgment
An example of Page 3 of the 4 page Judgment with provisions for spousal support, confirmation of separate property, community property, etc.

SHORT TITLE: DOE, JANE JUANITA AND JOHN JAMES

CASE NUMBER: (SUPPLIED BY COURT)

CONTINUATION OF JUDGMENT

THE COURT FURTHER ORDERS:

8. That neither parent shall remove the children from the State of California for more than 5 days without the written consent of the other parent.

9. That respondent shall have the right to claim the children as dependent deductions on his Federal and State Income Tax Return, unless further ordered by the Court.

10. That respondent John James Doe shall pay supousal support to the petitioner Jane Juanita Doe in the amount of $350.00 per month, commencing April 1, 1993, and continuing each month thereafter until either March 1, 1997, the death of either party, the remarriage of petitioner or when petitioner complete her studies as a Registered Nurse and receives a Bachelor of Science Degree in Nursing;

11. That said Spousal Support shall be paid by an assignment of the wages of respondent, whose employer is MAC BETH MANUFACTURING CO, 45600 Science Road Fontana, CA 92500;

12. That the termination date, conditions and amount payable as spousal support are absolute and no court shall have jurisdiction to modify or amend either the terms, amount, conditions or duration of said spousal support;

13. That the Court confirms the following property to be the separate property of respondent, and that petitioner shall waive all right, claim or interest in the same, to wit:

   a. 1985 Ford Bronco, VIN 4BVO396407.
   b. Richards Motor Boat with Evinrude Motor and accessories.

14. That the Court confirms the following property to be the separate property of petitioner, and that respondent shall waive all rights, claim or interest in the same, to wit:
   a. 1984 Chevrolet Blazer, VIN AF73802943.
   b. Yamaha Dirt Bike, Serial No. 456654FC.

15. That the Court awards the respondent, the following community or quasi-community property, to wit:

   a. Personal clothing and effects in possession.
   b. Winchester 12 gauge shot gun.
   c. Emerson 19 inch television.

(CONTINUED)

Page 3 of 4

Form Approved by the Judicial Council of California MC-020 (New January 1, 1987)

ADDITIONAL PAGE
Attach to Judicial Council Form or Other Court Paper

CRC 201, 501

CONTINUATION OF JUDGMENT
Page 4 of the 4 page Judgment
An example of Page 4 of the 4 page Judgment providing for the division of debts; income tax refunds or obligations; execution of instruments, etc.

SHORT TITLE: DOE, JANE JUANITA AND JOHN JAMES	CASE NUMBER: (SUPPLIED BY COURT)

CONTINUATION OF JUDGMENT

THE COURT FURTHER ORDERS:

16. That the Court awards the petitioner the following community or quasi-community property, to wit:
    a. 3 Bedroom home, described as lot 1020, Valley Subdivision, Los Angeles County, California.
    b. Personal clothing and effects in possession.
    c. Household furnishings, including: 7 piece living room, 5 piece dining set, 5 piece bedroom set, RCA 25 inch TV

17. That the respondent shall pay the following debts, which were incurred during the term of the marriage, and shall indemnify and hold petitioner harmless against any and all claims, demands or actions regarding said debts, to wit:

    a. Royal Finance Company, Acct. No. 14567D $2,700.00
    b. Bank of America Acct. No. 4567689129   4,500.00
    c. Citi-Bank Visa Card, Acct. No. 574378932102   2,200.00

18. That the petitioner shall pay ther following debts, which were incurred during the term of the marriage, and shall indemnify and hold respondent harmless against any and all claims, demands or actions regarding said debts, to wit:

    a. Sears Charge Card, Time pay account No. 43872 $1,500.00
    b. Broadway Stores Charge Card No. 83712679   1,200.00
    c. Allied Department Store, Acct. No. 78321   800.00

19. That neither party shall make or incur any debt or obligation for which the other party may be held liable. And in the event, any such claim is brought, each shall hold the other harmless and defend such claim.

20. That each party shall execute and deliver unto the other party, any documents, instruments, or papers, and to perform all acts necessary to carry out the transfer or conveyance of property.

(WILL BE DATED AND SIGNED BY THE JUDGE)

Date: _____   _____
                                  JUDGE OF THE SUPERIOR COURT

I consent to the above Judgment and approve it as to form and content.

Dated: 3-20-93   *Jane J. Doe*
                   Petitioner

Dated: 3-20-93   *John J. Doe*
                   Respondent

Form Approved by the Judicial Council of California
MC-020 (New January 1, 1987)

ADDITIONAL PAGE
Attach to Judicial Council Form or Other Court Paper

CRC 201, 501

WAGE AND EARNINGS ASSIGNMENT ORDER
Page 1 (Front) of the Wage Assignment Order
An example of Page 1 of the Wage and Earnings Assignment Order for Child Support

ATTORNEY OR PARTY WITHOUT ATTORNEY *(Name and Address)*:   TELEPHONE NO.: 213-000-0000   FOR COURT USE ONLY

JANE J. DOE
123 ANY STREET
LOS ANGELES, CA 92000

ATTORNEY FOR *(Name)*: In propria persona

SUPERIOR COURT OF CALIFORNIA, COUNTY OF LOS ANGELES
STREET ADDRESS: 111 N. HILL STREET
MAILING ADDRESS:
CITY AND ZIP CODE: LOS ANGELES, CA 90012
BRANCH NAME:

PETITIONER/PLAINTIFF: JANE JUANITA DOE

RESPONDENT/DEFENDANT: JOHN JAMES DOE

WAGE AND EARNINGS ASSIGNMENT ORDER
[ ] Modification   [X] Child Support   [ ] Spousal or Family Support

CASE NUMBER: (SUPPLED BY COURT)

TO THE PAYOR: This is a court order. You must withhold a portion of the earnings of *(obligor's name and Social Security number)*:
JOHN JAMES DOE; 529-00-0000
and pay as directed below. *(An explanation of this order is printed on the reverse.)*

THE COURT ORDERS YOU TO

1. Pay part of the earnings of the employee or other person ordered to pay support as follows:
   a. [X] $ 508.00 per month current **child support**.   d. [ ] $ per month **child support arrearages**.
   b. [ ] $ per month current **spousal support**.   e. [ ] $ per month **spousal support arrearages**.
   c. [ ] $ per month current **family support**.   f. [ ] $ per month **family support arrearages**.

   g. [ ] $ per month **attorney fees**, until the total of: $ has been paid.

2. [X] The payments ordered under items 1a, 1b, and 1c shall be paid to *(name, address)*: JANE JUANITA DOE
   123 ANY STREET, LOS ANGELES, CA 92000

3. [ ] The payments ordered under item 1d, 1e, and 1f shall be paid to *(name, address)*:

4. [ ] The payments ordered under item 1g shall be paid to *(name, address)*:

5. The payments ordered under item 1 shall continue until further written notice from payee or the court.

6. [ ] This order modifies an existing order. **The amount you must withhold may have changed.** The existing order continues in effect until this modification is effective.

7. This order affects all earnings payable beginning as soon as possible but not later than 10 days after you receive it.

8. Give the obligor a copy of this order within 10 days.

9. [ ] Other *(specify)*:

THE COURT FINDS the total arrearage to be as follows:
           Amount   As of *(date)*
10. a. [ ] Child support:
     b. [ ] Spousal support:
     c. [ ] Family support:

Date: [SIGNED AND DATED BY THE JUDGE] _____
                                                  JUDGE OF THE SUPERIOR COURT

(See reverse for information and instructions)

Form Adopted by Rule 1285.70
Judicial Council of California
1285.70 [Rev. July 1, 1991]

WAGE AND EARNINGS ASSIGNMENT ORDER
(Family Law — Domestic Violence Prevention — Uniform Parentage)

Civil Code, § 4390
Code of Civil Procedure, § 706.031
15 U.S.C. §§ 1672-1673

WAGE AND EARNINGS ASSIGNMENT ORDER
Page 2 (Back) of the Wage Assignment Order
Information about the Wage and Earnings Assignment Order

INFORMATION ABOUT THE WAGE AND EARNINGS ASSIGNMENT ORDER

1. **DEFINITIONS OF IMPORTANT WORDS IN THIS INFORMATION:**

   A. **Obligor:** any person ordered by a court to pay child support, spousal support, or family support. Named before item one on the reverse.

   B. **Obligee:** the person to whom the support is to be paid, including the district attorney or other government agency in some cases. Named in item 2 on the reverse.

   C. **Payor:** the person or entity, including an employer, that pays earnings to an obligor.

   D. **Earnings:**
      a. wages, salary, bonuses, vacation pay, retirement pay, commissions, paid by an employer;
      b. payments for services of independent contractors;
      c. dividends, rents, royalties, and residuals;
      d. patent rights, mineral or other natural resource rights;
      e. any payments due as a result of written or oral contracts for services or sales, regardless of their title; and
      f. any other payments or credits that result from an enforceable obligation.

   E. **Wage and Earnings Assignment Order:** A court order issued in every court case where one person is ordered to pay for the support of another person. The support may be child, spousal, or family support. This order has top priority over any other orders such as garnishments or earnings withholding orders. Earnings should not be withheld for any other order until the amounts necessary to satisfy this order have been withheld in full.

   When this order is for child support, it has top priority over a similar order for spousal support. The front of this form tells which types of support this order is for.

2. **INFORMATION FOR ALL PAYORS:** Withhold money from the earnings payable to the obligor as soon as possible but not later than 10 days after you receive this order. Send it to the obligee within 10 days of the pay date. You may deduct $1.00 from the obligor's earnings for each periodic payment you make.

   When sending the withheld earnings to the payee, state the date of the check from which the earnings were withheld. If you are unable to pay the withheld amounts for six months or more because the person named in item 2 on the reverse has not notified you of a change of address, make no further payments under this order and return all undeliverable payments to the obligor. You will be liable for any amount you fail to withhold and can be cited for contempt of court.

3. *Special computation instructions for payors who are employers:*

   A. State and Federal laws limit the amount of earnings that you should withhold and pay as directed by this order. This limitation applies only to earnings described in item 1Da. The limitation is stated as a specified percentage of the employee's disposable earnings.

   Disposable earnings are different from gross pay or take-home pay. Disposable earnings are the earnings left after subtracting the money that state or federal law requires an employer to withhold. Generally these required deductions are (1) federal income tax, (2) social security, (3) state income tax, (4) state disability insurance, and (5) payments to public employees' retirement systems.

   After the employee's disposable earnings are known, withhold the amount required by the order, BUT NEVER WITHHOLD MORE THAN 50 PERCENT OF THE DISPOSABLE EARNINGS UNLESS THE COURT ORDER SPECIFIED A HIGHER PERCENTAGE. Federal law prohibits withholding more than 65 percent of disposable earnings of an employee in any case.

   B. If the employee is paid by a different time period from that specified in the order, prorate the amount ordered to be withheld so part of it is withheld from each of the employee's paychecks.

   C. If the employee stops working for you, notify the obligee, not later than the date of the next payment, by first class mail, giving the name and address of any new employer if you know them.

   D. California law prohibits you from firing, refusing to hire, or taking any disciplinary action against any employee because of a Wage and Earnings Assignment Order. Such action can lead to a $500 civil penalty per employee.

4. **INFORMATION FOR ALL OBLIGORS:** Civil Code section 4390.9 describes the procedures available for you to ask the court to quash this order. You may file a motion to quash this order but you must act within ten days after you receive a copy of the order from the payor. See the procedure set forth in Civil Code section 4390.11.

   Civil Code section 4390.14 describes the procedure by which an obligor may request the court to terminate the assignment order.

   These laws may be found in any law library. Each California county has a law library.

5. *Special information for the obligor who is an employee:* Civil Code section 4390.7 requires you to notify the obligee (item 2 on the reverse) if you change your employment. You must provide the name and address of your new employer.

1285.70 (Rev. July 1, 1991)

WAGE AND EARNINGS ASSIGNMENT ORDER
(Family Law—Domestic Violence Prevention—Uniform Parentage)

Page two

NOTICE OF ENTRY OF JUDGMENT

An example when judgment was entered for the dissolution of marriage

---

ATTORNEY OR PARTY WITHOUT ATTORNEY (Name and Address):	TELEPHONE NO.:	FOR COURT USE ONLY
JANE J. DOE 123 ANY STREET LOS ANGELES, CA 92000	213-000-0000	
ATTORNEY FOR (Name): In propria persona		

SUPERIOR COURT OF CALIFORNIA, COUNTY OF LOS ANGELES
STREET ADDRESS: 111 N. HILL STREET
MAILING ADDRESS:
CITY AND ZIP CODE: LOS ANGELES, CA 90012
BRANCH NAME:

MARRIAGE OF
PETITIONER: JANE JUANITA DOE
RESPONDENT: JOHN JAMES DOE

NOTICE OF ENTRY OF JUDGMENT

CASE NUMBER: (SUPPLIED BY COURT)

You are notified that the following judgment was entered on (date): APRIL 15, 1993

1. [X] Dissolution of Marriage
2. [ ] Dissolution of Marriage – Status Only
3. [ ] Dissolution of Marriage – Reserving Jurisdiction over Termination of Marital Status
4. [ ] Legal Separation
5. [ ] Nullity
6. [ ] Other (specify):

Date: _____ Clerk, by _____, Deputy

— NOTICE TO ATTORNEY OF RECORD OR PARTY WITHOUT ATTORNEY —
Pursuant to the provisions of Code of Civil Procedure section 1952, if no appeal is filed the court may order the exhibits destroyed or otherwise disposed of after 60 days from the expiration of the appeal time.

Effective date of termination of marital status (specify): AUGUST 11, 1993
WARNING: NEITHER PARTY MAY REMARRY UNTIL THE EFFECTIVE DATE OF THE TERMINATION OF MARITAL STATUS AS SHOWN IN THIS BOX.

CLERK'S CERTIFICATE OF MAILING

I certify that I am not a party to this cause and that a true copy of the Notice of Entry of Judgment was mailed first class, postage fully prepaid, in a sealed envelope addressed as shown below, and that the notice was mailed at (place): _____, California,
on (date): _____
Date: _____ Clerk, by _____, Deputy

JANE JUANITA DOE
123 ANY STREET
LOS ANGELES, CA 92000

JOHN JAMES DOE
321 ANY STREET
SAN DIEGO, CA 91000

Form Adopted by Rule 1290
Judicial Council of California
1290 (Rev. July 1, 1985)

NOTICE OF ENTRY OF JUDGMENT
(Family Law)

APPLICATION FOR WAIVER OF COURT FEES AND COSTS

Page 1 (Front) of the Application and Order

An example of Page 1 of the Application For Waiver of Court Fees and Cost

---

— THIS FORM MUST BE KEPT CONFIDENTIAL —

ATTORNEY OR PARTY WITHOUT ATTORNEY (Name and Address):	TELEPHONE NO	FOR COURT USE ONLY
JANE J. DOE 123 ANY STREET LOS ANGELES, CA 92000	213-000-0000	

ATTORNEY FOR (Name): In propria persona

NAME OF COURT: SUPERIOR COURT OF LOS ANGELES COUNTY
STREET ADDRESS: 111 N. HILL STREET
MAILING ADDRESS:
CITY AND ZIP CODE: LOS ANGELES, CA 90012
BRANCH NAME:

PLAINTIFF or PETITIONER: JANE JUANITA DOE

DEFENDANT or RESPONDENT: JOHN JAMES DOE

APPLICATION FOR WAIVER OF COURT FEES AND COSTS	CASE NUMBER: (SUPPLIED BY COURT)

I request a court order so that I do not have to pay court fees and costs.

1. My address and date of birth are (specify):

   123 ANY STREET
   LOS ANGELES, CA 92000
   DOB: 3-7-62

2. [ ] I am receiving financial assistance under one or more of the following programs:
   a. [ ] **SSI and SSP:** The Supplemental Security Income and State Supplemental Payments Programs
   b. [ ] **AFDC:** The Aid to Families with Dependent Children Program
   c. [ ] **Food Stamps:** The Food Stamps Program
   d. [ ] County Relief, General Relief (G.R.) or General Assistance (G.A.)

[If you checked box 2 above, sign at the bottom of this side and DO NOT fill out the rest of the form.]

3. [ ] My gross monthly income is less than the amount shown on the Information Sheet on Waiver of Court Fees and Costs available from the clerk's office.

[If you checked box 3 above, skip 4, complete 5 and 6 on the back of this form, and sign at the bottom of this side.]

4. [X] My income is not enough to pay for the common necessaries of life for me and the people in my family I support and also pay court fees and costs. *[If you checked this box you must complete the back of this form.]*

WARNING: You must immediately tell the court if you become able to pay court fees or costs during this action. For the next three (3) years you may be ordered to appear in court and answer questions about your ability to pay court fees or costs.

I declare under penalty of perjury under the laws of the State of California that the foregoing is true and correct.

Date: FEBRUARY 1, 1993

JANE JUANITA DOE, In pro per   *Jane J. Doe*
(TYPE OR PRINT NAME)   (SIGNATURE)

Form Adopted by the
Judicial Council of California
982(a)(17) (Rev. January 1, 1985)

APPLICATION FOR WAIVER OF COURT FEES AND COSTS
(In Forma Pauperis)

Gov Code
§ 68511.3

APPLICATION FOR WAIVER OF COURT FEES AND COSTS
Page 2 (Back) of the Application and Order
An example of the required financial information

PLAINTIFF	JANE JUANITA DOE	CASE NUMBER
DEFENDANT	JOHN JAMES DOE	(SUPPLIED BY COURT)

FINANCIAL INFORMATION

5. [ ] My pay changes considerably from month to month. *[If you check this box, each of the amounts reported in 6 should be your average for the past 12 months.]*

6. My monthly income:
   a. My gross monthly pay is: .... $ 1,700.00
   b. My payroll deductions are *(specify purpose and amount)*:
      (1) STATE TAX $ 28.00
      (2) FEDERAL TAX $ 140.00
      (3) FICA $ 130.05
      (4) _____ $ _____
      My TOTAL payroll deduction amount is: $ 298.05
   c. My monthly take-home pay is
      (a. minus b.): .... $ 1,401.95

   d. Other money I get each month is *(specify source and amount)*:
      (1) _____ $ _____
      (2) _____ $ _____
      The TOTAL amount of other money is: $ _____
   e. MY TOTAL MONTHLY INCOME IS
      (c. plus d.): .... $ 1,401.95
   f. The number of people in my family, including me, supported by this money is: 3

7. a. [ ] I am *not* able to pay any of the court fees and costs.
   b. [ ] I am able to pay *only* the following court fees and costs *(specify)*:

8. My monthly expenses are:
   a. Rent or house payment & maintenance $ 300.00
   b. Food and household supplies ...... $ 200.00
   c. Utilities and telephone .... $ 100.00
   d. Clothing .... $ 25.00
   e. Laundry and cleaning .... $ 25.00
   f. Medical and dental payments ...... $ 50.00
   g. Insurance (life, health, accident, etc.) $ 0.00
   h. School, child care .... $ 200.00
   i. Child, spousal support (prior marriage) $ 0.00
   j. Transportation and auto expenses
      (insurance, gas, repair) .... $ 100.00
   k. Installment payments *(specify purpose and amount)*:
      (1) CHARGE ACCT. $ 50.00
      (2) FURNITURE $ 175.00
      (3) _____ $ _____
      The TOTAL amount of monthly
      installment payments is: .... $ 225.00

   l. Amounts deducted due to wage assignments and earnings withholding orders $ _____
   m. Other expenses *(specify)*
      (1) INSURANCE $ 25.00
      (2) CABLE TV $ 25.00
      (3) CHURCH TITHE $ 25.00
      (4) _____ $ _____
      (5) _____ $ _____
      (6) _____ $ _____
      The TOTAL amount of other monthly
      expenses is: .... $ 75.00
   n. MY TOTAL MONTHLY EXPENSES ARE
      (add a. through m.): .... $ 1,300.00

9. I own the following property:
   a. Cash .... $ 0.00
   b. Checking, savings and credit union accounts *(list banks)*:
      (1) _____ $ _____
      (2) _____ $ _____
      (3) _____ $ _____
   c. Cars, other vehicles and boat equity *(list make, year of each)*:
      (1) CHEVROLET 1984 $ 2,000.00
      (2) _____ $ _____
      (3) _____ $ _____
   d. Real estate equity .... $ 0.00

   e. Other personal property — jewelry, furniture, furs, stocks, bonds, etc. *(list separately)*:
      HOUSEHOLD FURNISHING   500.00
      PERSONAL EFFECTS   250.00

      $ 750.00

10. Other facts which support this application are *(describe unusual medical needs, expenses for recent family emergencies, or other unusual expenses to help the judge understand your budget)*. If more space is needed, attach page labeled attachment 10.

WARNING: You must immediately tell the court if you become able to pay court fees or costs during this action. For the next three (3) years you may be ordered to appear in court and answer questions about your ability to pay court fees or costs.

982(a)(17) (Rev January 1, 1985)   **APPLICATION FOR WAIVER OF COURT FEES AND COSTS**   Page two
(In Forma Pauperis)

ATTORNEY OR PARTY WITHOUT ATTORNEY (NAME AND ADDRESS):	TELEPHONE NO.:	FOR COURT USE ONLY
ATTORNEY FOR (NAME):		

SUPERIOR COURT OF CALIFORNIA, COUNTY OF
STREET ADDRESS
MAILING ADDRESS
CITY AND ZIP CODE
BRANCH NAME

MARRIAGE OF
PETITIONER

RESPONDENT

☐ PETITIONER'S ☐ RESPONDENT'S   (ATTACHMENT 4)   CASE NUMBER:
☐ COMMUNITY & QUASI-COMMUNITY PROPERTY DECLARATION
☒ SEPARATE PROPERTY DECLARATION

INSTRUCTIONS

When this form is attached to Petition or Response, values and your proposal regarding division need not be completed. Do not list community, including quasi-community, property with separate property on the same form. Quasi-community property must be so identified. For additional space, use the form "Continuation of Property Declaration."

ITEM NO	BRIEF DESCRIPTION	GROSS FAIR MARKET VALUE	AMOUNT OF DEBT	NET FAIR MARKET VALUE	PROPOSAL FOR DIVISION AWARD TO PETITIONER	RESPONDENT
		$	$	$	$	$
1.	REAL ESTATE					
2.	HOUSEHOLD FURNITURE, FURNISHINGS, APPLIANCES					
3.	JEWELRY, ANTIQUES, ART, COIN COLLECTIONS, etc.					
4.	VEHICLES, BOATS, TRAILERS					
5.	SAVINGS, CHECKING, CREDIT UNION, CASH					

(Continued on reverse)

The declaration under penalty of perjury must be signed in California or in a state that authorizes use of a declaration in place of an affidavit; otherwise an affidavit is required.

Form Adopted by Rule 1285.55
Judicial Council of California
Effective January 1, 1980

**PROPERTY DECLARATION
(FAMILY LAW)**

ITEM NO	BRIEF DESCRIPTION	GROSS FAIR MARKET VALUE	AMOUNT OF DEBT	NET FAIR MARKET VALUE	PROPOSAL FOR DIVISION AWARD TO PETITIONER	RESPONDENT
6.	LIFE INSURANCE (CASH VALUE)					
7.	EQUIPMENT, MACHINERY, LIVESTOCK					
8.	STOCKS, BONDS, SECURED NOTES					
9.	RETIREMENT, PENSION, PROFIT-SHARING, ANNUITIES					
10.	ACCOUNTS RECEIVABLE, UNSECURED NOTES, TAX REFUNDS					
11.	PARTNERSHIPS, OTHER BUSINESS INTERESTS					
12.	OTHER ASSETS AND DEBTS					
13.	TOTAL FROM CONTINUATION SHEET					
14.	TOTALS	$	$	$	$	$

15. ☐ A Continuation of Property Declaration is attached and incorporated by reference.

_____ _____
(Type or print name of attorney)   (Signature of attorney)

I declare under penalty of perjury that, to the best of my knowledge, the foregoing is a true and correct listing of assets and obligations and that the amounts shown are correct; and that this declaration was executed on (date): .... at (place): .... , California.

_____ _____
(Type or print name)   (Signature)

ATTORNEY OR PARTY WITHOUT ATTORNEY (NAME AND ADDRESS):	TELEPHONE NO.:	FOR COURT USE ONLY
ATTORNEY FOR (NAME):		

SUPERIOR COURT OF CALIFORNIA, COUNTY OF
STREET ADDRESS
MAILING ADDRESS
CITY AND ZIP CODE
BRANCH NAME

MARRIAGE OF
PETITIONER

RESPONDENT

☐ PETITIONER'S ☐ RESPONDENT'S (ATTACHMENT 4)	CASE NUMBER:
☐ COMMUNITY & QUASI-COMMUNITY PROPERTY DECLARATION	
☒ SEPARATE PROPERTY DECLARATION	

INSTRUCTIONS

When this form is attached to Petition or Response, values and your proposal regarding division need not be completed. Do not list community, including quasi-community, property with separate property on the same form. Quasi-community property must be so identified. For additional space, use the form "Continuation of Property Declaration."

ITEM NO.	BRIEF DESCRIPTION	GROSS FAIR MARKET VALUE	AMOUNT OF DEBT	NET FAIR MARKET VALUE	PROPOSAL FOR DIVISION AWARD TO PETITIONER	RESPONDENT
		$	$	$	$	$
1.	REAL ESTATE					
2.	HOUSEHOLD FURNITURE, FURNISHINGS, APPLIANCES					
3.	JEWELRY, ANTIQUES, ART, COIN COLLECTIONS, etc.					
4.	VEHICLES, BOATS, TRAILERS					
5.	SAVINGS, CHECKING, CREDIT UNION, CASH					

(Continued on reverse)

The declaration under penalty of perjury must be signed in California or in a state that authorizes use of a declaration in place of an affidavit; otherwise an affidavit is required.

Form Adopted by Rule 1285.55
Judicial Council of California
Effective January 1, 1980

**PROPERTY DECLARATION
(FAMILY LAW)**

ITEM NO	BRIEF DESCRIPTION	GROSS FAIR MARKET VALUE	AMOUNT OF DEBT	NET FAIR MARKET VALUE	PROPOSAL FOR DIVISION AWARD TO
		$	$	$	PETITIONER $ / RESPONDENT $
6.	LIFE INSURANCE (CASH VALUE)				
7.	EQUIPMENT, MACHINERY, LIVESTOCK				
8.	STOCKS, BONDS, SECURED NOTES				
9.	RETIREMENT, PENSION, PROFIT-SHARING, ANNUITIES				
10.	ACCOUNTS RECEIVABLE, UNSECURED NOTES, TAX REFUNDS				
11.	PARTNERSHIPS, OTHER BUSINESS INTERESTS				
12.	OTHER ASSETS AND DEBTS				
13.	TOTAL FROM CONTINUATION SHEET				
14.	TOTALS				

15. ☐ A Continuation of Property Declaration is attached and incorporated by reference.

....   _____
(Type or print name of attorney)   (Signature of attorney)

I declare under penalty of perjury that, to the best of my knowledge, the foregoing is a true and correct listing of assets and obligations and that the amounts shown are correct; and that this declaration was executed on .... (date): at (place): ...., California.

....   _____
(Type or print name)   (Signature)

ATTORNEY OR PARTY WITHOUT ATTORNEY (NAME AND ADDRESS)	TELEPHONE NO.	FOR COURT USE ONLY
ATTORNEY FOR (NAME)		

SUPERIOR COURT OF CALIFORNIA, COUNTY OF
STREET ADDRESS
MAILING ADDRESS
CITY AND ZIP CODE
BRANCH NAME

MARRIAGE OF
PETITIONER

RESPONDENT

☐ PETITIONER'S ☐ RESPONDENT'S (ATTACHMENT 5)
☒ COMMUNITY & QUASI-COMMUNITY PROPERTY DECLARATION
☐ SEPARATE PROPERTY DECLARATION

CASE NUMBER

INSTRUCTIONS

When this form is attached to Petition or Response, values and your proposal regarding division need not be completed. Do not list community, including quasi-community, property with separate property on the same form. Quasi-community property must be so identified. For additional space, use the form "Continuation of Property Declaration."

ITEM NO	BRIEF DESCRIPTION	GROSS FAIR MARKET VALUE	AMOUNT OF DEBT	NET FAIR MARKET VALUE	PROPOSAL FOR DIVISION AWARD TO PETITIONER	RESPONDENT
		$	$	$	$	$
1.	REAL ESTATE					
2.	HOUSEHOLD FURNITURE, FURNISHINGS, APPLIANCES					
3.	JEWELRY, ANTIQUES, ART, COIN COLLECTIONS, etc.					
4.	VEHICLES, BOATS, TRAILERS					
5.	SAVINGS, CHECKING, CREDIT UNION, CASH					

(Continued on reverse)

The declaration under penalty of perjury must be signed in California or in a state that authorizes use of a declaration in place of an affidavit, otherwise an affidavit is required

Form Adopted by Rule 1285.55
Judicial Council of California
Effective January 1, 1980

**PROPERTY DECLARATION
(FAMILY LAW)**

ITEM NO	BRIEF DESCRIPTION	GROSS FAIR MARKET VALUE	AMOUNT OF DEBT	NET FAIR MARKET VALUE	PROPOSAL FOR DIVISION AWARD TO PETITIONER	RESPONDENT
6.	LIFE INSURANCE (CASH VALUE)					
7.	EQUIPMENT, MACHINERY, LIVESTOCK					
8.	STOCKS, BONDS, SECURED NOTES					
9.	RETIREMENT, PENSION, PROFIT-SHARING, ANNUITIES					
10.	ACCOUNTS RECEIVABLE, UNSECURED NOTES, TAX REFUNDS					
11.	PARTNERSHIPS, OTHER BUSINESS INTERESTS					
12.	OTHER ASSETS AND DEBTS					
13.	TOTAL FROM CONTINUATION SHEET					
14.	TOTALS	$	$	$	$	$

15. ☐ A Continuation of Property Declaration is attached and incorporated by reference.

_____
(Type or print name of attorney)

_____
(Signature of attorney)

I declare under penalty of perjury that, to the best of my knowledge, the foregoing is a true and correct listing of assets and obligations and that the amounts shown are correct; and that this declaration was executed on .... (date): .... at (place): ...., California.

_____   _____
(Type or print name)   (Signature)

ATTORNEY OR PARTY WITHOUT ATTORNEY (NAME AND ADDRESS):	TELEPHONE NO.:	FOR COURT USE ONLY
ATTORNEY FOR (NAME):		

SUPERIOR COURT OF CALIFORNIA, COUNTY OF
STREET ADDRESS
MAILING ADDRESS
CITY AND ZIP CODE
BRANCH NAME

MARRIAGE OF
PETITIONER

RESPONDENT

☐ PETITIONER'S ☐ RESPONDENT'S   (ATTACHMENT 5)
☒ COMMUNITY & QUASI-COMMUNITY PROPERTY DECLARATION
☐ SEPARATE PROPERTY DECLARATION

CASE NUMBER:

INSTRUCTIONS

When this form is attached to Petition or Response, values and your proposal regarding division need not be completed. Do not list community, including quasi-community, property with separate property on the same form. Quasi-community property must be so identified. For additional space, use the form "Continuation of Property Declaration."

ITEM NO	BRIEF DESCRIPTION	GROSS FAIR MARKET VALUE	AMOUNT OF DEBT	NET FAIR MARKET VALUE	PROPOSAL FOR DIVISION AWARD TO PETITIONER	RESPONDENT
1.	REAL ESTATE	$	$	$	$	$
2.	HOUSEHOLD FURNITURE, FURNISHINGS, APPLIANCES					
3.	JEWELRY, ANTIQUES, ART, COIN COLLECTIONS, etc.					
4.	VEHICLES, BOATS, TRAILERS					
5.	SAVINGS, CHECKING, CREDIT UNION, CASH					

(Continued on reverse)

The declaration under penalty of perjury must be signed in California or in a state that authorizes use of a declaration in place of an affidavit, otherwise an affidavit is required.

Form Adopted by Rule 1285.55
Judicial Council of California
Effective January 1, 1980

**PROPERTY DECLARATION
(FAMILY LAW)**

ITEM NO	BRIEF DESCRIPTION	GROSS FAIR MARKET VALUE	AMOUNT OF DEBT	NET FAIR MARKET VALUE	PROPOSAL FOR DIVISION AWARD TO PETITIONER	RESPONDENT
6.	LIFE INSURANCE (CASH VALUE)					
7.	EQUIPMENT, MACHINERY, LIVESTOCK					
8.	STOCKS, BONDS, SECURED NOTES					
9.	RETIREMENT, PENSION, PROFIT-SHARING, ANNUITIES					
10.	ACCOUNTS RECEIVABLE, UNSECURED NOTES, TAX REFUNDS					
11.	PARTNERSHIPS, OTHER BUSINESS INTERESTS					
12.	OTHER ASSETS AND DEBTS					
13.	TOTAL FROM CONTINUATION SHEET					
14.	TOTALS	$	$	$	$	$

15. ☐ A Continuation of Property Declaration is attached and incorporated by reference.

(Type or print name of attorney) ....

_____
(Signature of attorney)

I declare under penalty of perjury that, to the best of my knowledge, the foregoing is a true and correct listing of assets and obligations and that the amounts shown are correct; and that this declaration was executed on (date): ...., at (place): ...., California.

(Type or print name) ....

_____
(Signature)

ATTORNEY OR PARTY WITHOUT ATTORNEY (Name and Address):	TELEPHONE NO.:	FOR COURT USE ONLY
ATTORNEY FOR (Name):		

SUPERIOR COURT OF CALIFORNIA, COUNTY OF
STREET ADDRESS:
MAILING ADDRESS:
CITY AND ZIP CODE:
BRANCH NAME:
CASE NAME:

DECLARATION UNDER UNIFORM CHILD CUSTODY JURISDICTION ACT (UCCJA)	CASE NUMBER:

1. **I am a party** to this proceeding to determine custody of a child.
2. *(Number)*:   minor children are subject to this proceeding as follows:
   (Insert the information requested below. The residence information must be given for the last FIVE years.)

a. Child's name		Place of birth	Date of birth	Sex
Period of residence	Address	Person child lived with *(name and present adress)*		Relationship
to present				
to				
to				
to				

b. Child's name		Place of birth	Date of birth	Sex
☐ Residence information is the same as given above for child a. *(If NOT the same, provide the information below.)*				
Period of residence	Address	Person child lived with *(name and present address)*		Relationship
to present				
to				
to				
to				

c. ☐ Additional children are listed on Attachment 2c. *(Provide requested information for additional children on an attachment.)*

(Continued on reverse)

Form Approved by the
Judicial Council of California
MC-150 [Rev. January 1, 1987] [Cor. 1/2/87]

**DECLARATION UNDER
UNIFORM CHILD CUSTODY JURISDICTION ACT (UCCJA)**

Civil Code, § 5158
Probate Code, §§ 1510(f), 1512

SHORT TITLE:	CASE NUMBER:

3. Have you participated as a party or a witness or in some other capacity in another litigation or custody proceeding, in California or elsewhere, concerning custody of a child subject to this proceeding?
☐ No ☐ Yes *(If yes, provide the following information:)*

   a. Name of each child:

   b. Capacity of declarant: ☐ party ☐ witness ☐ other *(specify):*

   c. Court *(specify name, state, location):*

   d. Court order or judgment *(date):*

4. Do you have information about a custody proceeding pending in a California court or any other court concerning a child subject to this proceeding, other than that stated in item 3?
☐ No ☐ Yes *(If yes, provide the following information:)*

   a. Name of each child:

   b. Nature of proceeding: ☐ dissolution or divorce ☐ guardianship ☐ adoption ☐ other *(specify):*

   c. Court *(specify name, state, location):*

   d. Status of proceeding:

5. Do you know of any person who is not a party to this proceeding who has physical custody or claims to have custody of or visitation rights with any child subject to this proceeding?
☐ No ☐ Yes *(If yes, provide the following information:)*

a. Name and address of person	b. Name and address of person	c. Name and address of person
☐ Has physical custody ☐ Claims custody rights ☐ Claims visitation rights	☐ Has physical custody ☐ Claims custody rights ☐ Claims visitation rights	☐ Has physical custody ☐ Claims custody rights ☐ Claims visitation rights
Name of each child	Name of each child	Name of each child

I declare under penalty of perjury under the laws of the State of California that the foregoing is true and correct.
Date:

.... ▶ ....
(TYPE OR PRINT NAME) (SIGNATURE OF DECLARANT)

6. ☐ Number of pages attached after this page:

NOTICE TO DECLARANT: You have a continuing duty to inform this court if you obtain any information about a custody proceeding in a California court or any other court concerning a child subject to this proceeding.

DECLARATION UNDER
UNIFORM CHILD CUSTODY JURISDICTION ACT (UCCJA)

ATTORNEY OR PARTY WITHOUT ATTORNEY *(Name and Address)*:	TELEPHONE NO.:	FOR COURT USE ONLY

SUPERIOR COURT OF CALIFORNIA, COUNTY OF
STREET ADDRESS:
MAILING ADDRESS:
CITY AND ZIP CODE:
BRANCH NAME:

PETITIONER/PLAINTIFF:

RESPONDENT/DEFENDANT:

APPLICATION FOR EXPEDITED CHILD SUPPORT ORDER [Civil Code, § 4357.5]	CASE NUMBER:

Notice to applicant: This form must be served before it is filed with the court.

To *(name)*:

1. I am requesting the court to order you to pay child support in the sum of: $_____ per month until trial of this action. (See item 2 of the proposed EXPEDITED CHILD SUPPORT ORDER attached to this form.) Attached is a completed Income and Expense Declaration for each parent and a worksheet showing the basis for the support.

2. I ☐ am receiving ☐ am not receiving ☐ intend to apply for public assistance for the child or children listed in the proposed order.

I declare under penalty of perjury under the laws of the State of California that the foregoing is true and correct.

Date:

.... ▶ ....
(TYPE OR PRINT NAME)   (SIGNATURE)

IF YOU DO NOT WANT TO PAY THE AMOUNT OF CHILD SUPPORT ASKED FOR, YOU MUST FILE A WRITTEN RESPONSE WITHIN 30 DAYS AND ASK FOR A COURT HEARING. The necessary forms (three blank copies of the Response to Application for Expedited Child Support Order and Notice of Hearing, and three blank copies of the Income and Expense Declaration) are attached. You do not have to pay any fee for filing the Response.

Contact the clerk's office by telephone or in person and ask for a date for a hearing. The hearing date must be at least 20 days and not more than 30 days after you file the Response to Application for Expedited Child Support Order. Complete and file the Response after serving a copy on the other parent. You must have someone over 18 years old, other than you, serve the forms. Have that person mail the papers to the address of the other parent or attorney for the other parent as shown on the top of the Application, or have that person personally give the papers to the other parent or attorney for the other parent. See the back of the Response for details. Have the person serving the Response complete and sign the Proof of Service on the back of the Response.

If you have this matter set for hearing, you must bring a copy of your most recent state income tax return (whether individual or joint) to the hearing. You may examine the other parent's tax return and ask questions about it. The other parent may examine your tax return and ask questions about it. If you cannot find a copy of your tax return you must ask for a copy from the State Franchise Tax Board, Data Storage, c/o R.I.D. Unit, Sacramento, CA 95867.

Tell them your name, the year of the return, your social security number, and the address to which they should mail the return. Sign the letter in the same way as you signed your tax return. Make a copy of the letter before you mail the original and bring it to the hearing.

If you have not filed a tax return for the last three years, you do not need to bring any return.

- IMPORTANT WARNING -
Unless you file a written response **within 30 calendar days** from the date this form is served on you, and ask the court for a hearing, you will be ordered to pay child support in the amount shown.

(Proof of service on reverse)

Form Adopted by Rule 1297
Judicial Council of California
1297 (New January 1, 1986)

**APPLICATION FOR EXPEDITED
CHILD SUPPORT ORDER
[Civil Code, § 4357.5]**
(Family Law)

PETITIONER/PLAINTIFF:	CASE NUMBER:
RESPONDENT/DEFENDANT:	

PROOF OF SERVICE — APPLICATION FOR EXPEDITED CHILD SUPPORT ORDER

1. I served the
   a. Application for Expedited Child Support Order, proposed Expedited Child Support Order, a completed Income and Expense Declaration for both parents, a worksheet setting forth the basis of the amount of support requested, three blank copies of the Income and Expense Declaration, and three blank copies of the Response to Application for Expedited Child Support Order and Notice of Hearing.

   b. on ☐ petitioner/plaintiff ☐ respondent/defendant

   c. by serving ☐ petitioner/plaintiff ☐ respondent/defendant
      ☐ other (name and title or relationship to person served):

   d. ☐ by delivery ☐ at home ☐ at business
      (1) date:
      (2) time:
      (3) address:

   e. ☐ by mailing
      (1) date:
      (2) place:

2. Manner of service (check proper box):
   a. ☐ Personal service. By personally delivering copies. (CCP 415.10)
   b. ☐ Substituted service on natural person. By leaving copies at the dwelling house, usual place of abode, or usual place of business of the person served in the presence of a competent member of the household or a person apparently in charge of the office or place of business, at least 18 years of age, who was informed of the general nature of the papers, and thereafter mailing (by first-class mail, postage prepaid) copies to the person served at the place where the copies were left. (CCP 415.20(b)) (Attach separate declaration or affidavit stating acts relied on to establish reasonable diligence in first attempting personal service.)
   c. ☐ Mail and acknowledgment service. By mailing (by first-class mail or airmail, postage prepaid) copies to the person served, together with two copies of the form of notice and acknowledgment and a return envelope, postage prepaid, addressed to the sender. (CCP 415.30) (Attach completed acknowledgment of receipt.)
   d. ☐ Certified or registered mail service. By mailing to an address outside California (by first-class mail, postage prepaid, requiring a return receipt) copies to the person served. (CCP 415.40) (Attach signed return receipt or other evidence of actual delivery to the person served.)

3. At the time of service I was at least 18 years of age and not a party to this action.
4. Fee for service: $
5. Person serving:
   a. ☐ California sheriff, marshal, or constable.
   b. ☐ Registered California process server.
   c. ☐ Employee or independent contractor of a registered California process server.
   d. ☐ Not a registered California process server.
   e. ☐ Exempt from registration under Bus. & Prof. Code 22350(b).
   f. Name, address, and telephone number and, if applicable, county of registration and number:

I declare under penalty of perjury under the laws of the State of California that the foregoing is true and correct.

(For California sheriff, marshal, or constable use only)
I certify that the foregoing is true and correct.

Date:

Date:

▶ _____ (SIGNATURE)

▶ _____ (SIGNATURE)

1297 [New January 1, 1986]

APPLICATION FOR EXPEDITED CHILD SUPPORT ORDER
[Civil Code, § 4357.5]
(Family Law)

Page two

ATTORNEY OR PARTY WITHOUT ATTORNEY (Name and Address)	TELEPHONE NO	FOR COURT USE ONLY
ATTORNEY FOR (Name)		

SUPERIOR COURT OF CALIFORNIA, COUNTY OF
STREET ADDRESS
MAILING ADDRESS
CITY AND ZIP CODE
BRANCH NAME

PETITIONER/PLAINTIFF:

RESPONDENT/DEFENDANT:

RESPONSE TO APPLICATION FOR EXPEDITED CHILD SUPPORT ORDER AND NOTICE OF HEARING [Civil Code, § 4357.5]	CASE NUMBER

To (name):

1. I object to the proposed expedited child support order for the following reasons (check one or more):
   a. ☐ I am not the parent of the child or children involved in this action.
   b. ☐ My income is incorrectly stated in the application.
   c. ☐ The other parent's income is incorrectly stated in the application.
   d. ☐ I am entitled to hardship deductions as shown in the attached Income and Expense Declaration.
   e. ☐ The other parent is not entitled to hardship deductions claimed in the application.
   f. ☐ The amount of support is incorrectly computed.
   g. ☐ other (specify):

2. I have attached a completed copy of my Income and Expense Declaration.

3. At my request, the court has set a hearing on the application as follows:

   a. date: time: in ☐ dept.:   ☐ rm.:

   b. The address of court ☐ is shown above ☐ is:

I declare under penalty of perjury under the laws of the State of California that the foregoing is true and correct.
Date:

▶

_____   _____
(TYPE OR PRINT NAME)   (SIGNATURE)

You must bring a copy of your most recent state income tax return (whether individual or joint) to the hearing or declare at the hearing that it doesn't exist or that you don't have it and have requested it from the Franchise Tax Board. Otherwise the court may grant the other party's request.

(Proof of service on reverse)

Form Adopted by Rule 1297.10
Judicial Council of California
1297.10 [New January 1, 1986]

RESPONSE TO APPLICATION FOR EXPEDITED CHILD SUPPORT ORDER AND NOTICE OF HEARING
[Civil Code, § 4357.5]
(Family Law)

PLAINTIFF/PETITIONER (name):	CASE NUMBER:
DEFENDANT/RESPONDENT (name):	

PROOF OF SERVICE BY ☐ **PERSONAL SERVICE** ☐ **MAIL**

> Service of the response on the other party may be made by anyone at least 18 years of age EXCEPT you. Service is made in one of the following ways:
> (1) Personally delivering it to the attorney for the other party or, if no attorney, to the other party.
> OR
> (2) Mailing it, postage prepaid, to the last known address of the attorney for the other party or, if no attorney, to the other party.
> Anyone at least 18 years of age EXCEPT ANY PARTY may personally serve or mail the response. Be sure whoever served the response fills out and signs this proof of service. File this proof of service with the court as soon as the response is served.

1. At the time of service I was at least 18 years of age and not a party to this legal action.

2. I served a copy of the Response to Application for Expedited Child Support Order and Notice of Hearing as follows (check either a or b below):

   a. ☐ **Personal service.** I personally delivered the response as follows:
      (1) Name of person served:
      (2) Address where served:
      (3) Date served:
      (4) Time served:

   b. ☐ **Mail.** I deposited the response in the United States mail, in a sealed envelope with postage fully prepaid. The envelope was addressed as follows:
      (1) Name of person served:
      (2) Address:
      (3) Date of mailing:
      (4) Place of mailing (city and state):
      (5) I am a resident of or employed in the county where the response was mailed.

   c. My residence or business address is (specify):

   d. My phone number is (specify):

I declare under penalty of perjury under the laws of the State of California that the foregoing is true and correct.

Date:

▶

....
(TYPE OR PRINT NAME OF PERSON WHO SERVED THE RESPONSE) (SIGNATURE OF PERSON WHO SERVED THE RESPONSE)

**RESPONSE TO APPLICATION FOR EXPEDITED CHILD SUPPORT
ORDER AND NOTICE OF HEARING**
[Civil Code, § 4357.5]
(Family Law)

1297.10 [New January 1, 1986]

ATTORNEY OR PARTY WITHOUT ATTORNEY (Name and Address):	TELEPHONE NO.:	FOR COURT USE ONLY
ATTORNEY FOR (Name):		

SUPERIOR COURT OF CALIFORNIA, COUNTY OF

PETITIONER/PLAINTIFF:

RESPONDENT/DEFENDANT:

EXPEDITED CHILD SUPPORT ORDER
[Civil Code, § 4357.5]
☐ Proposed

CASE NUMBER:

THE COURT FINDS No Response to Application for Expedited Child Support Order has been filed and 30 days have elapsed since service of the application on the other parent on *(date)*:

THE COURT ORDERS Pending trial or until further order of this court

1. Existing orders shall continue in effect, except as modified by this order.

2. Support of the minor children of the parties is fixed as follows beginning on *(date)*:

   Child's name   Monthly amount   Payable by   Payable to   Payable on (dates)

3. ☐ The monthly deductions allowed for extreme financial hardship total: $

4. ☐ The hardship deduction is allowed for the period beginning *(date)*:   and ending *(date)*:

5. ☐ The payments for monthly child support shall change as follows beginning on *(date)*:

   Child's name   Monthly amount   Payable by   Payable to   Payable on (dates)

6. Child support payments shall continue until further order of the court, or until the child marries, dies, is emancipated, reaches age 19, or reaches age 18 and is not a full-time high school student residing with a parent, whichever occurs first.

Date: _____

JUDGE OF THE SUPERIOR COURT

— NOTICE —

AN ASSIGNMENT OF YOUR WAGES WILL BE OBTAINED WITHOUT FURTHER NOTICE TO YOU IF YOU FAIL TO PAY ANY COURT-ORDERED CHILD SUPPORT OR IF REQUESTED BY THE DISTRICT ATTORNEY.

THIS ORDER IS ENFORCEABLE AS SOON AS IT HAS BEEN SIGNED BY A JUDGE.

Form Adopted by Rule 1297.20
Judicial Council of California
1297.20 [New January 1, 1986]

EXPEDITED CHILD SUPPORT ORDER
[Civil Code, § 4357.5]
(Family Law)

ATTORNEY OR PARTY WITHOUT ATTORNEY *(Name and Address)*:	TELEPHONE NO.:	**FOR COURT USE ONLY**
ATTORNEY FOR *(Name)*:		

SUPERIOR COURT OF CALIFORNIA, COUNTY OF
STREET ADDRESS:
MAILING ADDRESS:
CITY AND ZIP CODE:
BRANCH NAME:

PETITIONER/PLAINTIFF:

RESPONDENT/DEFENDANT:

INCOME AND EXPENSE DECLARATION	CASE NUMBER:

Step 1
Attachments to this summary

I have completed ☐ Income ☐ Expense ☐ Child Support Information forms.
(If child support is not an issue, do not complete the Child Suport Information Form. If your only income is AFDC, do not complete the Income Information Form.)

Step 2
Answer all questions that apply to you

1. Are you receiving or have you applied for or do you intend to apply for welfare or AFDC?
   ☐ Receiving ☐ Applied for ☐ Intend to apply for ☐ No
2. What is your date of birth *(month/day/year)*? ....
3. What is your occupation? _____
4. Highest year of education completed: _____
5. Are you presently employed? ☐ Yes ☐ No
   a. If yes: (1) Where do you work? *(name and address)*: _____
   (2) When did you start work there *(month/year)*? ....
   b. If no: (1) When did you last work *(month/year)*? ....
   (2) What were your gross monthly earnings? ....
6. What is your social security number: _____
7. What is the total number of minor children you are legally obligated to support? ....

Step 3
Monthly income information

8. Net monthly disposable income *(from line 16a of Income Information)*: .... $
9. Current net monthly disposable income *(if different from line 8, explain below or on Attachment 9)*: $

Step 4
Expense information

10. Total monthly expenses from line 2e of Expense Information: .... $
11. Total monthly expenses from line 3m of Expense Information *(if completed)*: .... $
12. Amount of these expenses paid by others: .... $

Step 5 Other party's income

13. My estimate of the other party's gross monthly income is: .... $

Step 6
Date and sign this form

I declare under penalty of perjury under the laws of the State of California that the foregoing and the attached information forms are true and correct.

Date:

_____
(TYPE OR PRINT NAME OF DECLARANT)

▶

_____
(SIGNATURE OF DECLARANT)
☐ Petitioner ☐ Respondent

Page one of _____

Form Adopted by Rule 1285.50
Judicial Council of California
1285.50 [Rev. January 1, 1993]

INCOME AND EXPENSE DECLARATION
(Family Law)

Civil Code, § 4721

ATTORNEY OR PARTY WITHOUT ATTORNEY (Name and Address):	TELEPHONE NO.:	FOR COURT USE ONLY
ATTORNEY FOR (Name):		

SUPERIOR COURT OF CALIFORNIA, COUNTY OF
STREET ADDRESS:
MAILING ADDRESS:
CITY AND ZIP CODE:
BRANCH NAME:

PETITIONER/PLAINTIFF:

RESPONDENT/DEFENDANT:

INCOME AND EXPENSE DECLARATION	CASE NUMBER:

Step 1
Attachments to this summary

I have completed [ ] Income [ ] Expense [ ] Child Support Information forms.
(If child support is not an issue, do not complete the Child Support Information Form. If your only income is AFDC, do not complete the Income Information Form.)

Step 2
Answer all questions that apply to you

1. Are you receiving or have you applied for or do you intend to apply for welfare or AFDC?
   [ ] Receiving [ ] Applied for [ ] Intend to apply for [ ] No
2. What is your date of birth *(month/day/year)*? .... _____
3. What is your occupation? _____
4. Highest year of education completed: _____
5. Are you presently employed? [ ] Yes [ ] No
   a. If yes: (1) Where do you work? *(name and address)*: _____
   (2) When did you start work there *(month/year)*? .... _____
   b. If no: (1) When did you last work *(month/year)*? .... _____
   (2) What were your gross monthly earnings? .... _____
6. What is your social security number: _____
7. What is the total number of minor children you are legally obligated to support? .... _____

Step 3
Monthly income information

8. Net monthly disposable income *(from line 16a of Income Information)*: .... $ _____
9. Current net monthly disposable income *(if different from line 8, explain below or on Attachment 9)*: $ _____

Step 4
Expense information

10. Total monthly expenses from line 2e of Expense Information: .... $ _____
11. Total monthly expenses from line 3m of Expense Information *(if completed)*: .... $ _____
12. Amount of these expenses paid by others: .... $ _____

Step 5 Other party's income

13. My estimate of the other party's gross monthly income is: .... $ _____

Step 6
Date and sign this form

I declare under penalty of perjury under the laws of the State of California that the foregoing and the attached information forms are true and correct.

Date:

....
(TYPE OR PRINT NAME OF DECLARANT)

▶

....
(SIGNATURE OF DECLARANT)

[ ] Petitioner [ ] Respondent

Page one of _____

Form Adopted by Rule 1285.50
Judicial Council of California
1285.50 [Rev. January 1, 1993]

INCOME AND EXPENSE DECLARATION
(Family Law)

Civil Code, § 4721

PETITIONER/PLAINTIFF:	CASE NUMBER:
RESPONDENT/DEFENDANT:	
INCOME INFORMATION OF (name):	

1. Total gross salary or wages, including commissions, bonuses, and overtime paid during the last 12 months: 1. $ _____
2. All other money received during the last 12 months **except welfare, AFDC, SSI, spousal support from this marriage, or any child support.** *Specify sources below:*
   Include pensions, social security, disability, unemployment, military basic allowance for quarters (BAQ), spousal support from a different marriage, dividends, interest or royalty, trust income, and annuities. Include income from a business, rental properties, and reimbursement of job-related expenses.
   ▶ *Prepare and attach a schedule showing gross receipts less cash expenses for each business or rental property.*

   2a. $ _____
   2b. $ _____
   2c. $ _____
   2d. $ _____

3. Add lines 1 through 2d .... 3. $ _____
   Divide line 3 by 12 and place result on line 4a.

	Average last 12 months:	Last month:
4. Gross income	4a. $ _____	4b. $ _____
5. State income tax	5a. $ _____	5b. $ _____
6. Federal income tax	6a. $ _____	6b. $ _____
7. Social Security and Hospital Tax ("FICA" and "MEDI") or self-employment tax, or the amount used to secure retirement or disability benefits	7a. $ _____	7b. $ _____
8. Health insurance for you and any children you are required to support ...	8a. $ _____	8b. $ _____
9. State disability insurance	9a. $ _____	9b. $ _____
10. Mandatory union dues	10a. $ _____	10b. $ _____
11. Mandatory retirement and pension fund contributions .... *Do not include any deduction claimed in item 7.*	11a. $ _____	11b. $ _____
12. Court-ordered child support, court-ordered spousal support, and voluntarily paid child support in an amount not more than the guideline amount, **actually being paid for a relationship *other* than that involved in this proceeding:**	12a. $ _____	12b. $ _____
13. Necessary job-related expenses *(attach explanation)*	13a. $ _____	13b. $ _____
14. Hardship deduction (Line 4d on Child Support Information Form)	14a. $ _____	14b. $ _____
15. Add lines 5 through 14. .... **Total monthly deductions:**	15a. $	15b. $
16. Subtract line 15 from line 4. .... **Net monthly disposable income:**	16a. $	16b. $

17. AFDC, welfare, spousal support from this marriage, and child support from other relationships received each month: .... 17. $ _____
18. Cash and checking accounts: .... 18. $ _____
19. Savings, credit union, certificates of deposit, and money market accounts: .... 19. $ _____
20. Stocks, bonds, and other liquid assets: .... 20. $ _____
21. All other property, real or personal *(specify below)*: .... 21. $ _____

▶ **Attach a copy of your three most recent pay stubs.**

Page _____ of _____

Form Adopted by Rule 1285.50a
Judicial Council of California
1285.50a [Rev. January 1, 1993]

INCOME INFORMATION
(Family Law)

Civil Code, § 4721

PETITIONER/PLAINTIFF:	CASE NUMBER:
RESPONDENT/DEFENDANT:	
INCOME INFORMATION OF (name):	

1. Total gross salary or wages, including commissions, bonuses, and overtime paid during the last 12 months: 1. $ _____
2. All other money received during the last 12 months **except welfare, AFDC, SSI, spousal support from this marriage, or any child support.** *Specify sources below:*
      2a. $ _____
   Include pensions, social security, disability, unemployment, military basic allowance for quarters (BAQ), spousal support from a different marriage, dividends, interest or royalty, trust income, and annuities.
      2b. $ _____
   Include income from a business, rental properties, and reimbursement of job-related expenses.
      2c. $ _____
   ▶ Prepare and attach a schedule showing gross receipts less cash expenses for each business or rental property.
      2d. $ _____
3. Add lines 1 through 2d . . . . 3. $ _____
   Divide line 3 by 12 and place result on line 4a.

	Average last 12 months:	Last month:
4. Gross income	4a. $ _____	4b. $ _____
5. State income tax	5a. $ _____	5b. $ _____
6. Federal income tax	6a. $ _____	6b. $ _____
7. Social Security and Hospital Tax ("FICA" and "MEDI") or self-employment tax, or the amount used to secure retirement or disability benefits	7a. $ _____	7b. $ _____
8. Health insurance for you and any children you are required to support . . .	8a. $ _____	8b. $ _____
9. State disability insurance	9a. $ _____	9b. $ _____
10. Mandatory union dues	10a. $ _____	10b. $ _____
11. Mandatory retirement and pension fund contributions . . . . *Do not include any deduction claimed in item 7.*	11a. $ _____	11b. $ _____
12. Court-ordered child support, court-ordered spousal support, and voluntarily paid child support in an amount not more than the guideline amount, **actually being paid for a relationship** *other* **than that involved in this proceeding:**	12a. $ _____	12b. $ _____
13. Necessary job-related expenses *(attach explanation)*	13a. $ _____	13b. $ _____
14. Hardship deduction (Line 4d on Child Support Information Form)	14a. $ _____	14b. $ _____
15. Add lines 5 through 14. . . . . **Total monthly deductions:**	15a. $	15b. $
16. Subtract line 15 from line 4. . . . . **Net monthly disposable income:**	16a. $	16b. $

17. AFDC, welfare, spousal support from this marriage, and child support from other relationships received each month: . . . . 17. $ _____
18. Cash and checking accounts: . . . . 18. $ _____
19. Savings, credit union, certificates of deposit, and money market accounts: . . . . 19. $ _____
20. Stocks, bonds, and other liquid assets: . . . . 20. $ _____
21. All other property, real or personal *(specify below)*: . . . . 21. $ _____

▶ **Attach a copy of your three most recent pay stubs.**

Form Adopted by Rule 1285.50a
Judicial Council of California
1285.50a [Rev. January 1, 1993]

INCOME INFORMATION
(Family Law)

Civil Code, § 4721

PETITIONER/PLAINTIFF:	CASE NUMBER:
RESPONDENT/DEFENDANT:	
EXPENSE INFORMATION OF (name):	

1. a. List all persons living in your home **whose expenses are included below** and their income:
    ☐ Continued on Attachment 1a.

	name	age	relationship	gross monthly income
1.				
2.				
3.				
4.				

    b. List all other persons living in your home and their income:
    ☐ Continued on Attachment 1b.

1.				
2.				
3.				

MONTHLY EXPENSES

2. *Required to be listed in all cases*
    a. Residence payments
        (1) ☐ Rent or ☐ mortgage ...... $_____
        (2) Taxes .... $_____
        (3) Insurance .... $_____
        (4) Maintenance .... $_____
    b. Unreimbursed medical and dental expenses .... $_____
    c. Child care .... $_____
    d. Children's education .... $_____
    e. TOTAL ITEM 2 EXPENSES .... $_____

3. *Required for spousal support or special needs*
    a. Food at home and household supplies .... $_____
    b. Food eating out .... $_____
    c. Utilities .... $_____
    d. Telephone .... $_____
    e. Laundry and cleaning .... $_____
    f. Clothing .... $_____
    g. Insurance *(life, accident, etc. Do not include auto, home, or health insurance)* ...... $_____
    h. Education *(specify)*: ...... $_____
    i. Entertainment .... $_____
    j. Transportation and auto expenses (insurance, gas, oil, repair) .... $_____
    k. Installment payments *(insert total and itemize below in item 4)* .... $_____
    l. Other *(specify)*: .... $_____
    m. TOTAL ITEM 3 EXPENSES .... $_____

4. ITEMIZATION OF INSTALLMENT PAYMENTS OR OTHER DEBTS ☐ Continued on Attachment 4.

CREDITOR'S NAME	PAYMENT FOR	MONTHLY PAYMENT	BALANCE	DATE LAST PAYMENT MADE

5. ATTORNEY FEES
    a. I have paid my attorney for fees and costs: $_____ The source of this money was:
    b. I have incurred to date the following fees and costs:

    c. My arrangement for attorney fees and costs is:
    d. ☐ Attorney fees have been requested.
        I confirm this information and fee arrangement.

    ▶ _____
    (SIGNATURE OF ATTORNEY)

    ....
    (TYPE OR PRINT NAME OF ATTORNEY)

    Page _____ of _____

Form Adopted by Rule 1285.50b
Judicial Council of California
1285.50b [Rev. January 1, 1993]

EXPENSE INFORMATION
(Family Law)

Civil Code, § 4721

PETITIONER/PLAINTIFF:	CASE NUMBER:
RESPONDENT/DEFENDANT:	
EXPENSE INFORMATION OF (name):	

1. a. List all persons living in your home **whose expenses are included below** and their income:
    ☐ Continued on Attachment 1a.

	name	age	relationship	gross monthly income
1.				
2.				
3.				
4.				

   b. List all other persons living in your home and their income:
    ☐ Continued on Attachment 1b.

1.				
2.				
3.				

MONTHLY EXPENSES

2. *Required to be listed in all cases*
   a. Residence payments
   (1) ☐ Rent or ☐ mortgage .... $_____
   (2) Taxes .... $_____
   (3) Insurance .... $_____
   (4) Maintenance .... $_____

3. *Required for spousal support or special needs*
   a. Food at home and household supplies ... $_____
   b. Food eating out .... $_____
   c. Utilities .... $_____
   d. Telephone .... $_____
   e. Laundry and cleaning .... $_____
   f. Clothing .... $_____
   g. Insurance (life, accident, etc. Do not include auto, home, or health insurance) ...... $_____

   b. Unreimbursed medical and dental expenses .... $_____
   c. Child care .... $_____
   d. Children's education .... $_____
   e. TOTAL ITEM 2 EXPENSES .... $_____

   h. Education (specify): .... $_____
   i. Entertainment .... $_____
   j. Transportation and auto expenses (insurance, gas, oil, repair) .... $_____
   k. Installment payments (insert total and itemize below in item 4) .... $_____
   l. Other (specify): .... $_____
   m. TOTAL ITEM 3 EXPENSES .... $_____

4. ITEMIZATION OF INSTALLMENT PAYMENTS OR OTHER DEBTS ☐ Continued on Attachment 4.

CREDITOR'S NAME	PAYMENT FOR	MONTHLY PAYMENT	BALANCE	DATE LAST PAYMENT MADE

5. ATTORNEY FEES
   a. I have paid my attorney for fees and costs: $ _____   The source of this money was:
   b. I have incurred to date the following fees and costs:

   c. My arrangement for attorney fees and costs is:
   d. ☐ Attorney fees have been requested.
       I confirm this information and fee arrangement.

   ▶ _____
   (SIGNATURE OF ATTORNEY)

   ....
   (TYPE OR PRINT NAME OF ATTORNEY)

   Page _____ of _____

Form Adopted by Rule 1285.50b
Judicial Council of California
1285.50b [Rev. January 1, 1993]

EXPENSE INFORMATION
(Family Law)

Civil Code, § 4721

PETITIONER/PLAINTIFF:	CASE NUMBER:
RESPONDENT/DEFENDANT:	
CHILD SUPPORT INFORMATION OF *(name)*:	

THIS PAGE MUST BE COMPLETED IF CHILD SUPPORT IS AN ISSUE.

1. Health insurance for my children ☐ is ☐ is not available through my employer.
   a. Monthly cost paid by me or on my behalf for the children *only* is: $_____
      Do not include the amount paid or payable by your employer.
   b. Name of carrier:
   c. Address of carrier:

   d. Policy or group policy number:

2. Approximate percentage of time each parent has primary physical responsibility for the children:
   Mother _____ %   Father _____ %

3. ☐ The court is requested to order the following as additional child support:
   a. ☐ Child care costs related to employment or to reasonably necessary education or training for employment skills
      (1) Monthly amount presently paid by mother: $
      (2) Monthly amount presently paid by father: $
   b. ☐ Uninsured health care costs for the children *(for each cost state the purpose for which the cost was incurred and the estimated monthly, yearly, or lump sum amount paid by each parent)*:

   c. ☐ Educational or other special needs of the children *(for each cost state the purpose for which the cost was incurred and the estimated monthly, yearly, or lump sum amount paid by each parent)*:

   d. ☐ Travel expense for visitation
      (1) Monthly amount presently paid by mother: $
      (2) Monthly amount presently paid by father: $

4. ☐ The court is requested to allow the deductions identified below, which are justifiable expenses that have caused an extreme financial hardship.

	Amount paid per month	How many months will you need to make these payments
a. ☐ Extraordinary health care expenses *(specify and attach any supporting documents)*:	$ _____	_____
b. ☐ Uninsured catastrophic losses *(specify and attach supporting documents)*:	$ _____	_____
c. ☐ Minimum basic living expenses of dependent minor children from other marriages or relationships who live with you *(specify names and ages of these children)*:	$ _____	_____

   d. Total hardship deductions requested *(add lines a–c)*: $ _____

Page _____ of _____

Form Adopted by Rule 1285.50c
Judicial Council of California
1285.50c [New January 1, 1993]

CHILD SUPPORT INFORMATION
(Family Law)

Civil Code, § 4721

PETITIONER/PLAINTIFF: RESPONDENT/DEFENDANT: CHILD SUPPORT INFORMATION OF *(name)*:	CASE NUMBER:

THIS PAGE MUST BE COMPLETED IF CHILD SUPPORT IS AN ISSUE.

1. Health insurance for my children ☐ is ☐ is not available through my employer.
   a. Monthly cost paid by me or on my behalf for the children *only* is: $_____
      Do not include the amount paid or payable by your employer.
   b. Name of carrier:
   c. Address of carrier:

   d. Policy or group policy number:

2. Approximate percentage of time each parent has primary physical responsibility for the children:
   Mother   %   Father   %

3. ☐ The court is requested to order the following as additional child support:
   a. ☐ Child care costs related to employment or to reasonably necessary education or training for employment skills
      (1) Monthly amount presently paid by mother: $
      (2) Monthly amount presently paid by father: $
   b. ☐ Uninsured health care costs for the children *(for each cost state the purpose for which the cost was incurred and the estimated monthly, yearly, or lump sum amount paid by each parent)*:

   c. ☐ Educational or other special needs of the children *(for each cost state the purpose for which the cost was incurred and the estimated monthly, yearly, or lump sum amount paid by each parent)*:

   d. ☐ Travel expense for visitation
      (1) Monthly amount presently paid by mother: $
      (2) Monthly amount presently paid by father: $

4. ☐ The court is requested to allow the deductions identified below, which are justifiable expenses that have caused an extreme financial hardship.

	Amount paid per month	How many months will you need to make these payments
a. ☐ Extraordinary health care expenses *(specify and attach any supporting documents)*:	$_____	_____
b. ☐ Uninsured catastrophic losses *(specify and attach supporting documents)*:	$_____	_____
c. ☐ Minimum basic living expenses of dependent minor children from other marriages or relationships who live with you *(specify names and ages of these children)*:	$_____	_____

   d. Total hardship deductions requested *(add lines a–c)*: $_____

Form Adopted by Rule 1285.50c
Judicial Council of California
1285.50c [New January 1, 1993]

CHILD SUPPORT INFORMATION
(Family Law)

Civil Code, § 4721

ATTORNEY OR PARTY WITHOUT ATTORNEY (Name and Address):	TELEPHONE NO.:	FOR COURT USE ONLY
ATTORNEY FOR (Name):		

SUPERIOR COURT OF CALIFORNIA, COUNTY OF
STREET ADDRESS:
MAILING ADDRESS:
CITY AND ZIP CODE:
BRANCH NAME:

PETITIONER/PLAINTIFF:

RESPONDENT/DEFENDANT:

STIPULATION TO ESTABLISH OR MODIFY CHILD SUPPORT AND ORDER

CASE NUMBER:

1. a. ☐ Mother's net monthly disposable income: $
      Father's net monthly disposable income: $
      —OR—
   b. ☐ A printout of a computer calculation of the parents' financial circumstances is attached.
2. ☐ Percentage of time each parent has primary responsibility for the children: Mother   % Father   %
3. a. ☐ A hardship is being experienced by the mother for: $ per month because of (specify):

      The hardship will last until (date):
   b. ☐ A hardship is being experienced by the father for: $ per month because of (specify):

      The hardship will last until (date):
4. The amount of child support payable by (name):   , referred to as the "obligor" below, as calculated under the guideline is: $ per month.
5. ☐ We agree to guideline support.
6. ☐ The guideline amount should be rebutted because of the following:
   a. ☐ We agree to child support in the amount of: $ per month; the agreement is in the best interest of the children; the needs of the children will be adequately met by the agreed amount; and application of the guideline would be unjust or inappropriate in this case.
   b. ☐ Other rebutting factors (specify):
7. Obligor shall pay child support as follows beginning (date):
   a. **BASIC CHILD SUPPORT**

Child's name	Monthly amount	Payable to (name)

   Total: $ payable ☐ on the first of the month ☐ other (specify):
   b. ☐ In addition obligor shall pay the following:
      ☐ $ per month for child care costs to (name):   on (date):
      ☐ $ per month for health care costs not deducted from gross income
                     to (name):   on (date):
      ☐ $ per month for special educational or other needs of the children
                     to (name):   on (date):
      ☐ other (specify):
   c. **Total monthly child support** payable by obligor shall be: $
      payable ☐ on the first of the month ☐ other (specify):

(Continued on reverse)

Form Adopted by Rule 1285.27
Judicial Council of California
1285.27 [Rev. January 1, 1993]

STIPULATION TO ESTABLISH OR MODIFY CHILD SUPPORT AND ORDER
(Family Law — Domestic Violence Prevention — Uniform Parentage)

Civil Code, § 4721

1285.27 (Rev. January 1, 1993)   **STIPULATION TO ESTABLISH OR MODIFY CHILD SUPPORT AND ORDER**   Page two
(Family Law — Domestic Violence Prevention — Uniform Parentage)

PETITIONER/PLAINTIFF:	CASE NUMBER:
RESPONDENT/DEFENDANT:	

8. a. Health insurance shall be maintained by (specify name):
   b. ☐ A health insurance coverage assignment shall issue if available through employment or other group plan or otherwise available at reasonable cost. Both parents are ordered to cooperate in the presentation, collection, and reimbursement of any medical claims.
   c. Any health expenses not paid by insurance shall be shared: Mother _____% Father _____%

9. a. A Wage and Earnings Assignment Order shall issue.
   b. ☐ We agree that service of the wage assignment be stayed because we have made the following alternative arrangements to ensure payment (specify):

10. ☐ Travel expenses for visitation shall be shared: Mother _____% Father _____%

11. ☐ We agree that we shall promptly inform each other of any change of residence or employment, including the employer's name, address, and telephone number.

12. ☐ Other (specify):

13. We agree that we are fully informed of our rights under the California child support guidelines.
14. We make this agreement freely without coercion or duress.
15. The right to support
   a. ☐ has not been assigned to any county and no application for public assistance is pending.
   b. ☐ has been assigned or an application for public assistance is pending in (county name):

If you checked b, a district attorney of the county named must sign below, joining in this agreement.

Date: ....
(TYPE OR PRINT NAME)
▶ _____
(SIGNATURE OF DISTRICT ATTORNEY)

Notice: If the amount agreed to is less than the guideline amount, no change of circumstances need be shown to obtain a change in the support order to a higher amount.

Date: ....
(TYPE OR PRINT NAME)
▶ _____
(SIGNATURE OF PETITIONER)

Date: .... (TYPE OR PRINT NAME)   ▶ _____ (SIGNATURE OF RESPONDENT)

Date: .... (TYPE OR PRINT NAME)   ▶ _____ (SIGNATURE OF ATTORNEY FOR PETITIONER)

.... (TYPE OR PRINT NAME)   ▶ _____ (SIGNATURE OF ATTORNEY FOR RESPONDENT)

THE COURT ORDERS
16. a. ☐ The guideline child support amount in item 4 is rebutted by the factors stated in item 6.
   b. Items 7 through 12 are ordered. All child support payments shall continue until further order of the court, or until the child marries, dies, is emancipated, reaches age 19, or reaches age 18 and is not a full-time high school student, whichever occurs first. Except as modified by this stipulation, all provisions of any previous orders made in this action shall remain in effect.

Date: _____
                JUDGE OF THE SUPERIOR COURT

ATTORNEY OR PARTY WITHOUT ATTORNEY (Name and Address):	TELEPHONE NO.:	FOR COURT USE ONLY
ATTORNEY FOR (Name):		

SUPERIOR COURT OF CALIFORNIA, COUNTY OF
STREET ADDRESS:
MAILING ADDRESS:
CITY AND ZIP CODE:
BRANCH NAME:

MARRIAGE OF
PETITIONER:

RESPONDENT:

APPLICATION AND ORDER FOR HEALTH INSURANCE COVERAGE	CASE NUMBER:

APPLICATION

1. On *(date)*: _____ , this court ordered obligor *(name)*:
   to provide health insurance coverage for the children named in the order below.

2. a. ☐ On *(date)*: _____ which is at least 15 days before filing this application,
      I gave written notice to obligor of my intent to seek this order
      ☐ by certified mail ☐ by personal service.
   OR
   b. ☐ Obligor has waived the requirement of written notice.

3. I ask the court to order the employer or other person providing health insurance coverage to enroll or maintain the children in any health insurance coverage available to the obligor.

I declare under penalty of perjury under the laws of the State of California that the foregoing is true and correct.
Date:

....   ▶   ....
(TYPE OR PRINT NAME)   (SIGNATURE OF APPLICANT)

ORDER FOR HEALTH INSURANCE COVERAGE (ASSIGNMENT)

To employer or other person providing health insurance coverage for obligor *(name)*:
Social Security Number *(if known)*:
YOU ARE ORDERED TO

1. Begin or maintain health insurance coverage of:

Name of child	Date of birth	Social Security No.

You may deduct any premium or costs from the wages or earnings of obligor.

2. If the obligor works for you or if you provide health insurance coverage to obligor, give him or her a copy of this order within 10 days after you receive it.

3. If no health insurance coverage is available to the obligor, complete and sign the Declaration of No Health Insurance Coverage on the reverse and mail this form within 20 days to the attorney or person requesting the assignment.

Date: _____   _____
                                                          (JUDGE OF THE SUPERIOR COURT)
(Continued on reverse)

Form Adopted by Rule 1285.75
Judicial Council of California
1285.75 [Rev. July 1, 1990]

APPLICATION AND ORDER FOR HEALTH INSURANCE COVERAGE
(Family Law)

Civil Code, §§ 4726, 4726.1

1285.75 (Rev. July 1, 1990)

APPLICATION AND ORDER FOR
HEALTH INSURANCE COVERAGE
(Family Law)

Page two

MARRIAGE OF *(last name, first name of parties):* | CASE NUMBER:

DECLARATION OF NO HEALTH INSURANCE COVERAGE

No health insurance coverage is available to the obligor *(name):*

because *(state reasons):*

I declare under penalty of perjury under the laws of the State of California that the foregoing is true and correct.

Date:

.... ▲ ....
(TYPE OR PRINT NAME AND TITLE)   (SIGNATURE OF EMPLOYER OR PERSON PROVIDING HEALTH INSURANCE)

MAIL A COPY OF THIS DECLARATION WITHIN 20 DAYS TO THE ATTORNEY OR PERSON SEEKING THIS ENROLLMENT
(SEE INSTRUCTION NO. 5, BELOW).

**INSTRUCTIONS
FOR EMPLOYER OR OTHER PERSON
PROVIDING HEALTH INSURANCE**

These instructions apply only to an Order for Health Insurance Coverage issued by a court.

1. If the obligor works for you or is covered by health insurance provided by you, you must give him or her a copy of this order within 10 days after you receive it.
2. Unless you receive a motion to quash the assignment, you must take steps to begin or maintain coverage of the specified children within 10 days after you receive this order. The coverage should begin at the earliest possible time consistent with group plan enrollment rules.
3. The obligor's existing health coverage shall be replaced only if the children are not provided benefits under the existing coverage where they reside.
4. If the obligor is not enrolled in a plan and there is a choice of several plans, you may enroll the children in any plan that will reasonably provide benefits or coverage where they live, unless the court has ordered coverage by a specific plan.
5. If no coverage is available, complete the Declaration of No Health Insurance Coverage at the top of this page and mail the declaration by first class mail to the attorney or person seeking the assignment within 20 days of your receipt of this order. Keep a copy of the form for your records.
6. If coverage is provided, you must supply evidence of coverage to both parents and any person having custody of the child.
7. Upon request of the parents or person having custody of the child, you must provide all forms and other documentation necessary for submitting claims to the insurance carrier to the extent you provide them to other covered individuals.
8. You must notify the applicant of the effective date of the coverage of the children.
9. You will be liable for any amounts incurred for health care services which would otherwise have been covered under the insurance policy if you willfully fail to comply with this order. You can also be held in contempt of court. California law forbids your firing or taking any disciplinary action against any employee because of this order.

EMPLOYEE INFORMATION

1. This order tells your employer or other person providing health insurance coverage to you to enroll or maintain the named children in a health insurance plan available to you and to deduct the appropriate premium or costs, if any, from your wages or other compensation.
2. You have 10 days to contest this order. Civil Code section 4726.1(e) tells you how.
3. Civil Code section 4726.1(k) tells you how and when to petition the court to end this assignment.

PETITIONER/PLAINTIFF:	CASE NUMBER:
RESPONDENT/DEFENDANT:	

EMPLOYER'S HEALTH INSURANCE RETURN

1. Name of absent parent employee:

2. Social security number:

3. Home address of absent parent employee:
   ☐ Not known

4. ☐ The employee has *no* insurance policies for health care, vision care, or dental care through this employment.

5. ☐ The employee has the following insurance policies covering health care, vision care, and dental care:

Company	Type of policy	Policy No.	Persons insured

Date:

....
(TYPE OR PRINT NAME OF EMPLOYER)

▶ ....
(SIGNATURE OF EMPLOYER)

Address:

Telephone No.:

6. Return this completed return to the following district attorney within 30 days *(name and address of district attorney)*:

If any insurance coverage lapses, complete the notice below and return a copy to the same district attorney.

NOTICE OF LAPSE IN HEALTH INSURANCE

7. The health insurance listed on the Employer's Health Insurance Return above has
   ☐ lapsed ☐ terminated FOR *(check one)*:
   a. ☐ all persons insured for the following reason *(specify)*:

   b. ☐ the following person *(name)*:   for the following reason *(specify)*:

Date:

....
(TYPE OR PRINT NAME OF EMPLOYER)

▶ ....
(SIGNATURE OF EMPLOYER)

Address:

Telephone No.:

Form Adopted by Rule 1285.76
Judicial Council of California
1285.76 [New January 1, 1992]

EMPLOYER'S HEALTH INSURANCE RETURN
(Family Law — Uniform Parentage)

Civil Code, § 4726.1 (n), (o)

ATTORNEY OR PARTY WITHOUT ATTORNEY *(Name and Address)*:	TELEPHONE NO.:	*FOR COURT USE ONLY*
ATTORNEY FOR *(Name)*:		

SUPERIOR COURT OF CALIFORNIA, COUNTY OF
STREET ADDRESS:
MAILING ADDRESS:
CITY AND ZIP CODE:
BRANCH NAME:

MARRIAGE OF
PETITIONER:

RESPONDENT:

JUDGMENT	CASE NUMBER:
☐ Dissolution ☐ Legal separation ☐ Nullity	
☐ Status only	
☐ Reserving jurisdiction over termination of marital status	
Date marital status ends:	

1. This proceeding was heard as follows: ☐ default or uncontested ☐ by declaration under Civil Code, § 4511 ☐ contested
   a. Date: Dept.: Rm.:
   b. Judge *(name)*: ☐ Temporary judge
   c. ☐ Petitioner present in court ☐ Attorney present in court *(name)*:
   d. ☐ Respondent present in court ☐ Attorney present in court *(name)*:
   e. ☐ Claimant present in court *(name)*: ☐ Attorney present in court *(name)*:

2. The court acquired jurisdiction of the respondent on *(date)*:
   ☐ Respondent was served with process ☐ Respondent appeared

3. THE COURT ORDERS, GOOD CAUSE APPEARING:
   a. ☐ Judgment of dissolution be entered. Marital status is terminated and the parties are restored to the status of unmarried persons
      (1) ☐ on the following date *(specify)*:
      (2) ☐ on a date to be determined on noticed motion of either party or on stipulation.
   b. ☐ Judgment of legal separation be entered.
   c. ☐ Judgment of nullity be entered. The parties are declared to be unmarried persons on the ground of *(specify)*:
   d. ☐ Wife's former name be restored *(specify)*:
   e. ☐ This judgment shall be entered nunc pro tunc as of *(date)*:
   f. ☐ Jurisdiction is reserved over all other issues and all present orders remain in effect except as provided below.
   g. ☐ Other *(specify)*:

   h. Jurisdiction is reserved to make other orders necessary to carry out this judgment.

Date:

_____
JUDGE OF THE SUPERIOR COURT

4. Number of additional pages attached: ☐ Signature follows last attachment Page 1 of ____

NOTICE

Please review your will, insurance policies, retirement benefit plans, credit, cards, other credit accounts and credit reports, and other matters you may want to change in view of the dissolution or annulment of your marriage, or your legal separation.
A debt or obligation may be assigned to one party as part of the division of property and debts, but if that party does not pay the debt or obligation, the creditor may be able to collect from the other party.
An earnings assignment will automatically be issued if child support, family support, or spousal support is ordered.

Form Adopted by Rule 1287
Judicial Council of California
1287 [Rev. January 1, 1993]

JUDGMENT
(Family Law)

Civil Code, § 4514

SHORT TITLE:	CASE NUMBER:

CONTINUATION OF JUDGMENT

THE COURT FURTHER ORDERS:

(CONTINUED)

Page ____ of ____

Form Approved by the Judicial Council of California
MC-020 [New January 1, 1987]

ADDITIONAL PAGE
Attach to Judicial Council Form or Other Court Paper

CRC 201, 501

SHORT TITLE:	CASE NUMBER:

CONTINUATION OF JUDGMENT

THE COURT FURTHER ORDERS:

(CONTINUED)

Page ____ of ____

Form Approved by the
Judicial Council of California
MC-020 [New January 1, 1987]

ADDITIONAL PAGE
Attach to Judicial Council Form or Other Court Paper

CRC 201, 501

SHORT TITLE:	CASE NUMBER:

CONTINUATION OF JUDGMENT

THE COURT FURTHER ORDERS:

Date: _____   _____
JUDGE OF THE SUPERIOR COURT

I consent to the above Judgment and approve it as to form and content.

Dated: _____ _____
Petitioner

Dated: _____ _____
Respondent

Page ____ of ____

Form Approved by the Judicial Council of California
MC-020 [New January 1, 1987]

ADDITIONAL PAGE
Attach to Judicial Council Form or Other Court Paper

CRC 201, 501

SHORT TITLE:	CASE NUMBER:

CONTINUATION OF JUDGMENT

THE COURT FURTHER ORDERS:

Date: _____

_____
JUDGE OF THE SUPERIOR COURT

I consent to the above Judgment and approve it as to form and content.

Dated: _____ _____
                                    Petitioner

Dated: _____ _____
                                    Respondent

Page _____ of _____

Form Approved by the
Judicial Council of California
MC-020 [New January 1, 1987]

ADDITIONAL PAGE
Attach to Judicial Council Form or Other Court Paper

CRC 201, 501

ATTORNEY OR PARTY WITHOUT ATTORNEY *(Name and Address)*:	TELEPHONE NO.:	**FOR COURT USE ONLY**
ATTORNEY FOR *(Name)*:		

SUPERIOR COURT OF CALIFORNIA, COUNTY OF
STREET ADDRESS:
MAILING ADDRESS:
CITY AND ZIP CODE:
BRANCH NAME:

PETITIONER/PLAINTIFF:

RESPONDENT/DEFENDANT:

WAGE AND EARNINGS ASSIGNMENT ORDER ☐ Modification ☐ Child Support ☐ Spousal or Family Support	CASE NUMBER:

TO THE PAYOR: This is a court order. You must withhold a portion of the earnings of *(obligor's name and Social Security number)*:

and pay as directed below. *(An explanation of this order is printed on the reverse.)*

THE COURT ORDERS YOU TO
1. Pay part of the earnings of the employee or other person ordered to pay support as follows:
   a. ☐ $ _____ per month current **child support**.   d. ☐ $ _____ per month **child support arrearages**.
   b. ☐ $ _____ per month current **spousal support**. e. ☐ $ _____ per month **spousal support arrearages**.
   c. ☐ $ _____ per month current **family support**.   f. ☐ $ _____ per month **family support arrearages**.

   g. ☐ $ _____ per month **attorney fees,** until the total of: $ _____ has been paid.

2. ☐ The payments ordered under items 1a, 1b, and 1c shall be paid to *(name, address)*:

3. ☐ The payments ordered under item 1d, 1e, and 1f shall be paid to *(name, address)*:

4. ☐ The payments ordered under item 1g shall be paid to *(name, address)*:

5. The payments ordered under item 1 shall continue until further written notice from payee or the court.

6. ☐ This order modifies an existing order. **The amount you must withhold may have changed.** The existing order continues in effect until this modification is effective.

7. This order affects all earnings payable beginning as soon as possible but not later than 10 days after you receive it.

8. **Give the obligor a copy of this order within 10 days.**

9. ☐ Other *(specify)*:

THE COURT FINDS the total arrearage to be as follows:
                            Amount   As of *(date)*
10. a. ☐ Child support:
    b. ☐ Spousal support:
    c. ☐ Family support:

Date: _____

_____
JUDGE OF THE SUPERIOR COURT

(See reverse for information and instructions)

Form Adopted by Rule 1285.70
Judicial Council of California
1285.70 [Rev. July 1, 1991]

WAGE AND EARNINGS ASSIGNMENT ORDER
(Family Law—Domestic Violence Prevention—Uniform Parentage)

Civil Code, § 4390
Code of Civil Procedure, § 706.031
15 U.S.C. §§ 1672–1673

1285.70 (Rev. July 1, 1991)

WAGE AND EARNINGS ASSIGNMENT ORDER
(Family Law—Domestic Violence Prevention—Uniform Parentage)

Page two

INFORMATION ABOUT THE WAGE AND EARNINGS ASSIGNMENT ORDER

1. **DEFINITIONS OF IMPORTANT WORDS IN THIS INFORMATION:**

   A. **Obligor:** any person ordered by a court to pay child support, spousal support, or family support. Named before item one on the reverse.

   B. **Obligee:** the person to whom the support is to be paid, including the district attorney or other government agency in some cases. Named in item 2 on the reverse.

   C. **Payor:** the person or entity, including an employer, that pays earnings to an obligor.

   D. **Earnings:**

   a. wages, salary, bonuses, vacation pay, retirement pay, commissions, paid by an employer;

   b. payments for services of independent contractors;

   c. dividends, rents, royalties, and residuals;

   d. patent rights, mineral or other natural resource rights;

   e. any payments due as a result of written or oral contracts for services or sales, regardless of their title; and

   f. any other payments or credits that result from an enforceable obligation.

   E. **Wage and Earnings Assignment Order:** A court order issued in every court case where one person is ordered to pay for the support of another person. The support may be child, spousal, or family support. This order has top priority over any other orders such as garnishments or earnings withholding orders. Earnings should not be withheld for any other order until the amounts necessary to satisfy this order have been withheld in full.

   When this order is for child support, it has top priority over a similar order for spousal support. The front of this form tells which types of support this order is for.

2. **INFORMATION FOR ALL PAYORS:** Withhold money from the earnings payable to the obligor as soon as possible but not later than 10 days after you receive this order. Send it to the obligee within 10 days of the pay date. You may deduct $1.00 from the obligor's earnings for each periodic payment you make.

   When sending the withheld earnings to the payee, state the date of the check from which the earnings were withheld. If you are unable to pay the withheld amounts for six months or more because the person named in item 2 on the reverse has not notified you of a change of address, make no further payments under this order and return all undeliverable payments to the obligee. You will be liable for any amount you fail to withhold and can be cited for contempt of court.

3. **Special computation instructions for payors who are employers:**

   A. State and Federal laws limit the amount of earnings that you should withhold and pay as directed by this order. This limitation applies only to earnings described in item 1Da. The limitation is stated as a specified percentage of the employee's disposable earnings.

   Disposable earnings are different from gross pay or take-home pay. Disposable earnings are the earnings left after subtracting the money that federal law requires an employer to withhold. Generally these required deductions are (1) federal income tax, (2) social security, (3) state income tax, (4) state disability insurance, and (5) payments to public employees' retirement systems. After the employee's disposable earnings are known, withhold the amount required by the order, BUT NEVER WITHHOLD MORE THAN 50 PERCENT OF THE DISPOSABLE EARNINGS UNLESS THE COURT ORDER SPECIFIED A HIGHER PERCENTAGE. Federal law prohibits withholding more than 65 percent of disposable earnings of an employee in any case.

   B. If the employee is paid by a different time period from that specified in the order, prorate the amount ordered to be withheld so part of it is withheld from each of the employee's paychecks.

   C. If the employee stops working for you, notify the obligee, not later than the date of the next payment, by first class mail, giving the name and address of any new employer if you know them.

   D. California law prohibits you from firing, refusing to hire, or taking any disciplinary action against any employee because of a Wage and Earnings Assignment Order. Such action can lead to a $500 civil penalty per employee.

4. **INFORMATION FOR ALL OBLIGORS:** Civil Code section 4390.9 describes the procedures available for you to ask the court to quash this order. You may file a motion to quash this order but you must act within ten days after you receive a copy of the order from the payor. See the procedure set forth in Civil Code section 4390.11.

   Civil Code section 4390.14 describes the procedure by which an obligor may request the court to terminate the assignment order.

   These laws may be found in any law library. Each California county has a law library.

5. **Special information for the obligor who is an employee:** Civil Code section 4390.7 requires you to notify the obligee (item 2 on the reverse) if you change your employment. You must provide the name and address of your new employer.

ATTORNEY OR PARTY WITHOUT ATTORNEY *(Name and Address)*:	TELEPHONE NO.:	*FOR COURT USE ONLY*
ATTORNEY FOR *(Name)*:		

SUPERIOR COURT OF CALIFORNIA, COUNTY OF
STREET ADDRESS:
MAILING ADDRESS:
CITY AND ZIP CODE:
BRANCH NAME:

PETITIONER/PLAINTIFF:

RESPONDENT/DEFENDANT:

WAGE AND EARNINGS ASSIGNMENT ORDER ☐ Modification ☐ Child Support ☐ Spousal or Family Support	CASE NUMBER:

TO THE PAYOR: This is a court order. You must withhold a portion of the earnings of *(obligor's name and Social Security number)*:

and pay as directed below. *(An explanation of this order is printed on the reverse.)*

THE COURT ORDERS YOU TO
1. Pay part of the earnings of the employee or other person ordered to pay support as follows:
   a. ☐ $ _____ per month current **child support.**   d. ☐ $ _____ per month **child support arrearages.**
   b. ☐ $ _____ per month current **spousal support.**   e. ☐ $ _____ per month **spousal support arrearages.**
   c. ☐ $ _____ per month current **family support.**   f. ☐ $ _____ per month **family support arrearages.**

   g. ☐ $ _____ per month **attorney fees,** until the total of: $ _____ has been paid.

2. ☐ The payments ordered under items 1a, 1b, and 1c shall be paid to *(name, address)*:

3. ☐ The payments ordered under item 1d, 1e, and 1f shall be paid to *(name, address)*:

4. ☐ The payments ordered under item 1g shall be paid to *(name, address)*:

5. The payments ordered under item 1 shall continue until further written notice from payee or the court.

6. ☐ This order modifies an existing order. **The amount you must withhold may have changed.** The existing order continues in effect until this modification is effective.

7. This order affects all earnings payable beginning as soon as possible but not later than 10 days after you receive it.

8. **Give the obligor a copy of this order within 10 days.**

9. ☐ Other *(specify)*:

THE COURT FINDS the total arrearage to be as follows:
                        Amount   As of *(date)*
10. a. ☐ Child support:
    b. ☐ Spousal support:
    c. ☐ Family support:

Date: _____
                                                    JUDGE OF THE SUPERIOR COURT

(See reverse for information and instructions)

Form Adopted by Rule 1285.70
Judicial Council of California
1285.70 [Rev. July 1, 1991]

WAGE AND EARNINGS ASSIGNMENT ORDER
(Family Law — Domestic Violence Prevention — Uniform Parentage)

Civil Code, § 4390
Code of Civil Procedure, § 706.031
15 U.S.C. §§ 1672–1673

1285.70 (Rev. July 1, 1991)

WAGE AND EARNINGS ASSIGNMENT ORDER
(Family Law—Domestic Violence Prevention—Uniform Parentage)

Page two

INFORMATION ABOUT THE WAGE AND EARNINGS ASSIGNMENT ORDER

1. **DEFINITIONS OF IMPORTANT WORDS IN THIS INFORMATION:**

   A. **Obligor:** any person ordered by a court to pay child support, spousal support, or family support. Named before item one on the reverse.

   B. **Obligee:** the person to whom the support is to be paid, including the district attorney or other government agency in some cases. Named in item 2 on the reverse.

   C. **Payor:** the person or entity, including an employer, that pays earnings to an obligor.

   D. **Earnings:**

   a. wages, salary, bonuses, vacation pay, retirement pay, commissions, paid by an employer;

   b. payments for services of independent contractors;

   c. dividends, rents, royalties, and residuals;

   d. patent rights, mineral or other natural resource rights;

   e. any payments due as a result of written or oral contracts for services or sales, regardless of their title; and

   f. any other payments or credits that result from an enforceable obligation.

   E. **Wage and Earnings Assignment Order:** A court order issued in every court case where one person is ordered to pay for the support of another person. The support may be child, spousal, or family support. This order has top priority over any other orders such as garnishments or earnings withholding orders. Earnings should not be withheld for any other order until the amounts necessary to satisfy this order have been withheld in full.

   When this order is for child support, it has top priority over a similar order for spousal support. The front of this form tells which types of support this order is for.

2. **INFORMATION FOR ALL PAYORS:** Withhold money from the earnings payable to the obligor as soon as possible but not later than 10 days after you receive this order. Send it to the obligee within 10 days of the pay date. You may deduct $1.00 from the obligor's earnings for each periodic payment you make.

   When sending the withheld earnings to the payee, state the date of the check from which the earnings were withheld. If you are unable to pay the withheld amounts for six months or more because the person named in item 2 on the reverse has not notified you of a change of address, make no further payments under this order and return all undeliverable payments to the obligor. You will be liable for any amount you fail to withhold and can be cited for contempt of court.

3. **Special computation instructions for payors who are employers:**

   A. State and Federal laws limit the amount of earnings that you should withhold and pay as directed by this order. This limitation applies only to earnings described in item 1Da. The limitation is stated as a specified percentage of the employee's disposable earnings.

   Disposable earnings are different from gross pay or take-home pay. Disposable earnings are the earnings left after subtracting the money that federal law requires an employer to withhold. Generally these required deductions are (1) federal income tax, (2) social security, (3) state income tax, (4) state disability insurance, and (5) payments to public employees' retirement systems. After the employee's disposable earnings are known, withhold the amount required by the order, BUT NEVER WITHHOLD MORE THAN 50 PERCENT OF THE DISPOSABLE EARNINGS UNLESS THE COURT ORDER SPECIFIED A HIGHER PERCENTAGE. Federal law prohibits withholding more than 65 percent of disposable earnings of an employee in any case.

   B. If the employee is paid by a different time period from that specified in the order, prorate the amount ordered to be withheld so part of it is withheld from each of the employee's paychecks.

   C. If the employee stops working for you, notify the obligee, not later than the date of the next payment, by first class mail, giving the name and address of any new employer if you know them.

   D. California law prohibits you from firing, refusing to hire, or taking any disciplinary action against any employee because of a Wage and Earnings Assignment Order. Such action can lead to a $500 civil penalty per employee.

4. **INFORMATION FOR ALL OBLIGORS:** Civil Code section 4390.9 describes the procedures available for you to ask the court to quash this order. You may file a motion to quash this order but you must act within ten days after you receive a copy of the order from the payor. See the procedure set forth in Civil Code section 4390.11.

   Civil Code section 4390.14 describes the procedure by which an obligor may request the court to terminate the assignment order.

   These laws may be found in any law library. Each California county has a law library.

5. **Special information for the obligor who is an employee:** Civil Code section 4390.7 requires you to notify the obligee (item 2 on the reverse) if you change your employment. You must provide the name and address of your new employer.

INFORMATION SHEET ON WAIVER OF COURT FEES AND COSTS

(California Rules of Court, Rule 985)

If you have been sued or if you wish to sue somebody, and if you cannot afford to pay court fees and costs, you may not have to pay if:

1. You are receiving **financial assistance** under one or more of the following programs:

   - SSI and SSP (The Supplemental Security Income and State Supplemental Payments Programs)
   - AFDC (The Aid to Families with Dependent Children Program)
   - The Food Stamps Program
   - County Relief, General Relief (G.R.) or General Assistance (G.A.)

   —OR—

2. Your gross **monthly income** is less than the following amounts:

NUMBER IN FAMILY	FAMILY INCOME
1	$ 709.38
2	957.30
3	1,205.21
4	1,453.13
5	1,701.05
6	1,948.96
7	2,196.88
8	2,444.80
Each additional	247.92

   —OR—

3. Your income is not enough to pay for the common **necessaries** of life for yourself and the people you support and also to pay court fees and costs.

To apply, fill out the Application for Waiver of Court Fees and Costs available from the clerk's office.

If you have any questions and cannot afford an attorney, you may wish to consult the legal aid office, legal services office, or lawyer referral service in your county (listed in the yellow pages under "Attorneys").

If you are asking for review of the decision of an administrative body under Code of Civil Procedure section 1094.5 (administrative mandate), you may ask for a transcript of the administrative proceedings at the expense of the administrative body.

— THIS FORM MUST BE KEPT CONFIDENTIAL —

ATTORNEY OR PARTY WITHOUT ATTORNEY (Name and Address):	TELEPHONE NO.	FOR COURT USE ONLY
ATTORNEY FOR (Name):		
NAME OF COURT:		
STREET ADDRESS:		
MAILING ADDRESS:		
CITY AND ZIP CODE:		
BRANCH NAME:		

PLAINTIFF or PETITIONER:

DEFENDANT or RESPONDENT:

APPLICATION FOR WAIVER OF COURT FEES AND COSTS	CASE NUMBER:

I request a court order so that I do not have to pay court fees and costs.

1. My address and date of birth are (specify):

2. ☐ I am receiving financial assistance under one or more of the following programs:
   a. ☐ **SSI and SSP**: The Supplemental Security Income and State Supplemental Payments Programs
   b. ☐ **AFDC**: The Aid to Families with Dependent Children Program
   c. ☐ **Food Stamps**: The Food Stamps Program
   d. ☐ **County Relief, General Relief (G.R.) or General Assistance (G.A.)**

[If you checked box 2 above, sign at the bottom of this side and DO NOT fill out the rest of the form.]

3. ☐ My gross monthly income is less than the amount shown on the Information Sheet on Waiver of Court Fees and Costs available from the clerk's office.

[If you checked box 3 above, skip 4, complete 5 and 6 on the back of this form, and sign at the bottom of this side.]

4. ☐ My income is not enough to pay for the common necessaries of life for me and the people in my family I support and also pay court fees and costs. [If you checked this box you must complete the back of this form.]

WARNING: You must immediately tell the court if you become able to pay court fees or costs during this action. For the next three (3) years you may be ordered to appear in court and answer questions about your ability to pay court fees or costs.

I declare under penalty of perjury under the laws of the State of California that the foregoing is true and correct.

Date:

_____   _____
(TYPE OR PRINT NAME)   (SIGNATURE)

Form Adopted by the Judicial Council of California
982(a)(17) [Rev. January 1, 1985]

APPLICATION FOR WAIVER OF COURT FEES AND COSTS
(In Forma Pauperis)

Gov. Code,
§ 68511.3

982(a)(17) [Rev. January 1, 1985] **APPLICATION FOR WAIVER OF COURT FEES AND COSTS** Page two
(In Forma Pauperis)

PLAINTIFF	CASE NUMBER
DEFENDANT	

FINANCIAL INFORMATION

5. ☐ My pay changes considerably from month to month. [If you check this box, each of the amounts reported in 6 should be your average for the past 12 months.]

6. My monthly income:
   a. My gross monthly pay is: $ _____
   b. My payroll deductions are (specify purpose and amount):
      (1) $ _____
      (2) $ _____
      (3) $ _____
      (4) $ _____
      My TOTAL payroll deduction amount is: $ _____
   c. My monthly take-home pay is (a. minus b.): $ _____
   d. Other money I get each month is (specify source and amount):
      (1) $ _____
      (2) $ _____
      The TOTAL amount of other money is: $ _____
   e. **MY TOTAL MONTHLY INCOME IS** (c. plus d.): $ _____
   f. The number of people in my family, including me, supported by this money is: _____

7. a. ☐ I am **not** able to pay any of the court fees and costs.
   b. ☐ I am able to pay **only** the following court fees and costs (specify):

8. My monthly expenses are:
   a. Rent or house payment & maintenance $ _____
   b. Food and household supplies $ _____
   c. Utilities and telephone $ _____
   d. Clothing $ _____
   e. Laundry and cleaning $ _____
   f. Medical and dental payments $ _____
   g. Insurance (life, health, accident, etc.) $ _____
   h. School, child care $ _____
   i. Child, spousal support (prior marriage) $ _____
   j. Transportation and auto expenses (insurance, gas, repair) $ _____
   k. Installment payments (specify purpose and amount):
      (1) $ _____
      (2) $ _____
      (3) $ _____
      The TOTAL amount of monthly installment payments is: $ _____
   l. Amounts deducted due to wage assignments and earnings withholding orders $ _____
   m. Other expenses (specify)
      (1) $ _____
      (2) $ _____
      (3) $ _____
      (4) $ _____
      (5) $ _____
      (6) $ _____
      The TOTAL amount of other monthly expenses is: $ _____
   n. **MY TOTAL MONTHLY EXPENSES ARE** (add a. through m.): $ _____

9. I own the following property:
   a. Cash $ _____
   b. Checking, savings and credit union accounts (list banks):
      (1) $ _____
      (2) $ _____
      (3) $ _____
   c. Cars, other vehicles and boat equity (list make, year of each):
      (1) $ _____
      (2) $ _____
      (3) $ _____
   d. Real estate equity $ _____
   e. Other personal property — jewelry, furniture, furs, stocks, bonds, etc. (list separately):

10. Other facts which support this application are (describe unusual medical needs, expenses for recent family emergencies, or other unusual expenses to help the judge understand your budget). If more space is needed, attach page labeled attachment 10.

WARNING: You must immediately tell the court if you become able to pay court fees or costs during this action. For the next three (3) years you may be ordered to appear in court and answer questions about your ability to pay court fees or costs.

ATTORNEY OR PARTY WITHOUT ATTORNEY (Name and Address):	TELEPHONE NO.:	FOR COURT USE ONLY
ATTORNEY FOR (Name):		

NAME OF COURT, JUDICIAL DISTRICT OR BRANCH COURT, IF ANY:

PLAINTIFF:

DEFENDANT:

ORDER ON APPLICATION FOR WAIVER OF COURT FEES AND COSTS

CASE NUMBER:

1. The application was filed
   a. on (date):
   b. by (name):
2. ☐ **IT IS ORDERED THAT the application is granted and the applicant is permitted to proceed in this action as follows:**
   a. ☐ without payment of any court fees or costs listed in rule 985(i), California Rules of Court.
   b. ☐ without payment of any court fees or costs listed in rule 985(i), California Rules of Court, except the following:
   c. ☐ without payment of the following court fees or costs (specify):

   d. The reasons for denial of any requested waiver are (specify):

   e. ☐ The clerk of the court is directed to mail a copy of this order to the applicant's attorney, if any, or to the applicant if unrepresented.
   f. ☐ All unpaid fees and costs shall be deemed to be taxable costs if applicant is entitled to costs and shall be a lien on any judgment recovered by the applicant and shall be paid to the clerk upon such recovery.
3. ☐ **IT IS ORDERED THAT the application is denied for the following reasons** (specify):

   a. **The applicant must pay any fees and costs due in this action within ten days from the date of service of this order or any paper filed by the applicant with the clerk will be of no effect.**
   b. The clerk of the court is directed to mail a copy of this order to all parties who have appeared in this action.
4. ☐ **IT IS ORDERED THAT a hearing be held.**
   a. The substantial evidentiary conflict to be resolved by the hearing is (specify):

   b. Applicant should be present at the hearing to be held:

   hearing date: time: in ☐ Dept.:   ☐ Div.:   ☐ Rm.:
   address of court:

   c. The clerk of the court is directed to mail a copy of this order to the applicant only.

Dated: _____

(Clerk's certification on page 2)   (Signature of Judge)

Form Adopted by Rule 982
Judicial Council of California
Revised effective July 1, 1981
[982(a)(18)]

ORDER ON APPLICATION FOR WAIVER OF COURT FEES AND COSTS (IN FORMA PAUPERIS)

Govt. Code § 68511.3

ORDER ON APPLICATION FOR WAIVER OF COURT FEES AND COSTS

PLAINTIFF (Name):	CASE NUMBER
DEFENDANT (Name):	

CLERK'S CERTIFICATE OF MAILING

I certify that I am not a party to this cause and that a copy of the foregoing was mailed first class, postage prepaid, in a sealed envelope addressed as shown below, and that the mailing of the foregoing and execution of this certificate occurred at (place): ...., California,

on (date): .... Clerk, by .... (Deputy)

CLERK'S CERTIFICATION

(SEAL)

I certify that the foregoing is a true copy of the original on file in my office.

Dated: .... Clerk, by .... (Deputy)

Page 2

ATTORNEY OR PARTY WITHOUT ATTORNEY (Name and Address):	TELEPHONE NO.:	FOR COURT USE ONLY
ATTORNEY FOR (Name):		

NAME OF COURT, JUDICIAL DISTRICT OR BRANCH COURT, IF ANY

PLAINTIFF

DEFENDANT

NOTICE OF WAIVER OF COURT FEES AND COSTS

CASE NUMBER

---

1. The application for waiver of court fees and costs was filed

    a. on (date):

    b. by (name):

2. The application was granted by operation of law.

3. The applicant may proceed in this action without payment of
    a. ☐ court fees and costs listed in rule 985(i) California Rules of Court.
    b. ☐ the following court fees and costs (specify):

Dated: . . . . Clerk, by . . . .
(Deputy)

CLERK'S CERTIFICATION

(SEAL)

I certify that the foregoing is a true copy of the original on file in my office.

Dated: . . . . Clerk, by . . . .
(Deputy)

Form Adopted by Rule 982
Judicial Council of California
Revised effective July 1, 1981

[982(a)(19)]

**NOTICE OF WAIVER OF COURT FEES AND COSTS
(IN FORMA PAUPERIS)**

Govt. Code
§ 68511.3
CRC Rule 985(e)

SHORT TITLE:	CASE NUMBER:

26 *(Required for verified pleading)* The items on this page stated on information and belief are *(specify item numbers, **not** line numbers)*:

27 This page may be used with any Judicial Council form or any other paper filed with the court.

Page _____

Form Approved by the
Judicial Council of California
MC-020 (New January 1, 1987)

ADDITIONAL PAGE
Attach to Judicial Council Form or Other Court Paper

CRC 201, 501

MARRIAGE OF (Last name—first names of parties)			CASE NUMBER		

☐ **PETITIONER'S** ☐ **RESPONDENT'S**
   ☐ **COMMUNITY & QUASI-COMMUNITY PROPERTY DECLARATION**
   ☐ **SEPARATE PROPERTY DECLARATION**

ITEM NO.	BRIEF DESCRIPTION	GROSS FAIR MARKET VALUE	AMOUNT OF DEBT	NET FAIR MARKET VALUE	PROPOSAL FOR DIVISION AWARD TO PETITIONER	RESPONDENT
		$	$	$	$	$

(Continued on reverse)

Form Adopted by Rule 1285.56
Judicial Council of California
Effective January 1, 1980

**CONTINUATION OF PROPERTY DECLARATION
(FAMILY LAW)**

ITEM NO.	BRIEF DESCRIPTION	GROSS FAIR MARKET VALUE	AMOUNT OF DEBT	NET FAIR MARKET VALUE	PROPOSAL FOR DIVISION AWARD TO PETITIONER	RESPONDENT
		$	$	$	$	$

MARRIAGE OF (Last name—first names of parties)			CASE NUMBER		

☐ PETITIONER'S ☐ RESPONDENT'S
　☐ COMMUNITY & QUASI-COMMUNITY PROPERTY DECLARATION
　☐ SEPARATE PROPERTY DECLARATION

ITEM NO.	BRIEF DESCRIPTION	GROSS FAIR MARKET VALUE	AMOUNT OF DEBT	NET FAIR MARKET VALUE	PROPOSAL FOR DIVISION AWARD TO PETITIONER	RESPONDENT
		$	$	$	$	$

(Continued on reverse)

Form Adopted by Rule 1285.56
Judicial Council of California
Effective January 1, 1980

**CONTINUATION OF PROPERTY DECLARATION
(FAMILY LAW)**

ITEM NO.	BRIEF DESCRIPTION	GROSS FAIR MARKET VALUE	AMOUNT OF DEBT	NET FAIR MARKET VALUE	PROPOSAL FOR DIVISION AWARD TO PETITIONER	RESPONDENT
		$	$ (on reverse)	$	$	$